THE DECADE
OF
ENERGY POLICY

THE DECADE
OF
ENERGY POLICY

Policy Analysis in
Oil-Importing Countries

Paul Kemezis
Ernest J. Wilson III

PRAEGER

PRAEGER SPECIAL STUDIES • PRAEGER SCIENTIFIC

New York • Philadelphia • Eastbourne, UK
Toronto • Hong Kong • Tokyo • Sydney

Library of Congress Cataloging in Publication Data

Kemezis, Paul.
    The decade of energy policy.

    Bibliography: p.
    Includes index.
    1. Energy policy. I. Wilson, Ernest J. II. Title.
III. Title: Oil-importing countries.
HD9502.A2K45   1984   333.79   84-15936
ISBN 0-03-062783-4 (alk. paper)

Published in 1984 by Praeger Publishers
CBS Educational and Professional Publishing
a Division of CBS Inc.
521 Fifth Avenue, New York, NY 10175 USA
©1984 by Praeger Publishers

56789 052 98765432

Printed in the United States of America
on acid-free paper

INTRODUCTION

WHY A BOOK ON OIL IMPORTING COUNTRIES?

This book provides a unique policy-by-policy approach to
energy decision making by oil importer countries throughout
the world. Whether large or small, rich or poor, socialist or
capitalist, importers have resorted to a finite number of supply-
and-demand policies over the last ten years in their effort to
adjust to the international energy shocks of the 1970s and 1980s.

We try to account for the similarities, as well as the differences, in public policy toward the major fuels—oil, gas, coal,
nuclear, renewables—and toward conservation. We also try to
give the reader a sense of the individual countries' peculiar
energy-relevant institutional, political, and economic features.
But we have deliberately avoided fuel-by-fuel or country-by-
country analysis, believing a policy-centered approach to be
the most instructive.

We center our attention on the major importers, including
key industrialized countries—the United States, Japan, Germany,
the United Kingdom, France, and Canada, as well as developing
countries, such as Brazil, India, Kenya, and Korea. We use
country-specific information to clarify policy categories through
national examples, but do not attempt to describe the detailed
energy policy of any single country. The narrative is organized
in each section to deal separately with the United States, then
the other industrialized nations, and thirdly with the developing
countries. This arbitrary division of these groups of nations
will be convenient for readers with specific country or regional
interests.

The Decade of Energy Policy focuses on the alternatively
halting and hurried course of energy policy making between
1973 and 1983. We show how government officials in the major
importing nations were forced to adjust their national policies
both to the ups and downs of the volatile international oil market,
and to its changed industrial structure.

Now, in hindsight, it is clear that no other problem burst
forth so suddenly to confront private citizens and public officials
during the last ten years. No other issue wrought such massive
changes in our capital markets, inflation rates, and unemployment statistics. The sums involved were staggering, with

billions of dollars drained away annually from consumer country economies. Governments struggled to adjust to these tumultuous changes, with some more successful than others, yet even now, a decade after the first oil shock, this process is only imperfectly understood.

Worse than being improperly understood, the problems of oil-importing countries are still insufficiently examined. There are dozens of book-length treatments on OPEC or the Seven Sister oil companies; but there are very few that describe and evaluate what happened to the largest group of actors: the buyers of oil, the consumers, the importing countries. They confronted a sudden and unprecedented revolution and learned, each in their own way, to adapt their domestic policies and institutions to massive international disruptions.

This book grew from two concerns, one practical and the other more academic, and is aimed at two audiences. In our work in the practical world of government and business we were struck by how little American policymakers in Washington, and the informed public in general, knew about the energy problems of our allies and trading partners overseas. In Washington we were especially surprised by the woeful lack of information on the energy imperatives of important countries like Japan, France, Korea, or Brazil. Yet energy was a fundamental issue of moment that affected our domestic economy and our international commercial, political, and strategic relations.

Yet if Americans were guilty of ignorance of the international energy questions, the same was true on the other side of the Atlantic. Precisely because the U.S. system is so unique, it was very hard for non-Americans to fathom. In our discussions with energy officials in Europe, Africa, and Latin America we confronted misunderstandings, misapprehensions, and frustration at the American way of handling energy time and again. Why wouldn't the American president keep his word on energy? Why don't Americans stop using oil so profligately in overlarge cars and homes kept too cool in summer and too hot in winter? These were questions frequently put to us in the course of our research. We found the differences of perception, values, and information led to tremendous friction among industrialized countries and between the United States and the third world. Thus this book is partially addressed to government and corporate actors in importing countries.

There was also an academic, analytic purpose. When we tried to find scholarly materials written on the importing countries, there was little available. Information was scattered, analysis extremely fragmented, reflecting the division of past energy studies by fuel, or by country. There were some very good comparative nuclear studies (Nelkin and Pollack 1981) or comparative oil studies (Mendershausen 1976), but no book-length, multi-fuel, cross-national study of national energy policies in importing countries. This lack of analysis presented a real challenge when Wilson began designing comparative energy policy courses at the University of Pennsylvania. Kemezis, one of the few who had written consistently in this area, was invited to lecture. We both saw the need for a comparative energy text on policies in the consuming countries that could be useful to practitioners and students in Washington, Paris, or Seoul.

Thus it was out of our twin practical and scholarly concerns that we agreed to write this book. We met with top officials in Saudi Arabia, Algeria, Nigeria, the Soviet Union, Mexico, and Britain on the exporting side, and in Brazil, Austria, Germany, France, Italy, Ivory Coast, Kenya, and Senegal on the importing side. We also interviewed countless public officials and company managers in the United States. They were universally generous with their time and consideration. We were also fortunate enough to meet with senior officials in the Organization of Petroleum Exporting Countries in Vienna, and in the International Energy Agency in Paris. In the private sector we met with top oil company managers, and with small contractors and drillers. These visits proved invaluable by providing not only up-to-date information, but, more importantly, revealing to us the very different interpretations and evaluations of the "facts". For example, the definition and evaluation of government-to-government oil deals depended very much on the country in which we asked the question. We have taken pains to convey faithfully but critically such differences in this study, for they were crucially important for energy policy over the course of the decade.

WHAT IS THIS BOOK ABOUT?

This book is about national adaptation to the radical changes in the international oil market between 1973 and 1983. The book focuses mainly on the past ten years, but also looks toward the coming ten. Boiled down to essentials, there are three lessons from our research applicable to the conduct of future energy policy:

First is the abiding importance of cycles and fluctuations in the world oil market. It was not just high prices that caused

so much distress over the decade, nor low prices, but the rapid
and volatile vaulting between the two. It was this volatility
that unnerved and paralyzed governments that had to plan,
businesses that needed to invest, and consumers who had to
buy on the domestic market. We trace these fluctuations over
the course of the decade, which show up as an M-shaped line
of rising and falling price movements in the international market.

The second lesson is the critical role of politics. Whether
in the form of new movements like the Greens in Germany,
governmental institutions, or national political-economic traditions, the political factor had great power to retard or promote
domestic adjustment to international transformations, raising it
far beyond the business-as-usual mode of the previous period.

The third factor, borne of the first two, is the vast out-
pouring of new energy regulations, laws, government buy-outs
and take-overs, and other interventions, all consumer government responses to the international energy market changes.
We term this the Energy Policy Explosion. This explosion of
government intervention has been marked by several factors—
much more continuous and high level surveillance of energy
issues by senior government officials, more activist policies by
government officials at all levels as they are pushed to become
more directly involved with domestic and international energy
markets, policies aimed for the first time at the intricate linkages
between fuels, and in some ways the most radical—the regular
involvement of government officials in demand management as
well as traditional supply side policies.

The development of these new goals by governments in
turn forced public officials to develop a wider and more sophisticated array of policy tools. These included everything from
national oil companies in Britain and Korea, to new demand
management units in France like the Agence pour les Économies
d'Energie. These new efforts in turn compelled governments
to commit unparalleled amounts of increasingly scarce financial
and human resources to new energy problems. The World Bank
estimates that the less developed countries (LDCs) alone will
need to invest on the order of $130 billion each year for the rest
of the decade simply to build up their domestic energy capacities.

HOW IS THIS BOOK ORGANIZED?

Chapters 1 and 2 set out the basic parameters of the problem addressed in this book—how did governments in oil-importing
countries adapt their domestic energy policies and institutions

to the radical changes that beset the world oil market between 1973 and 1983? These first chapters introduce the major themes we see as fundamental to the decade—the M-shaped market, the role of politics, the Energy Policy Explosion.

Chapter 3 stresses the central role that oil imports play in the process of adaptation. This chapter also connects our overview of macro-issues with the detailed policy-specific chapters that follow. The middle chapters, 4, 5, and 6, zero in on the substantive issues that formed the core of the decade's "Energy Policy Explosion," the nuts and bolts of demand and supply policies. Chapters 4 and 5 explore governments' efforts to exercise greater control over both international supplies (Chapter 4), and domestic energy supplies (Chapter 5). Chapter 6 lays out the most important demand management policies pursued by importing country officials over the decade.

Finally, Chapter 7 analyzes the contentious politics and administration of energy policy between 1973 and 1983, bringing us back to our initial focus on politics, market volatility and public policy.

ACKNOWLEDGMENTS

We would both like to acknowledge the cooperation, understanding, and, in some instances, financial support provided
by many individuals and organizations as we prepared this
study.

Resources for the Future provided as rich and stimulating
an environment as one could hope to find in a project like this
during Ernest Wilson's stay there as one of the first Gilbert
White Fellowship winners. Colleagues were extremely supportive
yet helpfully critical of a political scientist in a den of economists.
Milton Russell, then director of the Center for Energy Policy
Research, and Emery Castle, president of RFF, were very
generous with their time and their own personal energy. In
addition, Joel Darmstadter, Lincoln Gordon, Joy Dunkerly,
and later, Harry Broadman, all read parts of the manuscript
and offered helpful comments. Friends and colleagues at
Harvard University's Kennedy School of Government were similarly supportive and collegial during Wilson's stay as a fellow
there. He wishes to thank Dean Graham Allison; Paul Doty,
director of the Center for Science and International Studies;
Bill Hogan and Henry Lee of the Energy and Environmental
Policy Center; and David Deese and Joseph Nye of the Energy
and Security project for their support. The latter was also
good enough to read part of the manuscript.

On Capitol Hill we would like to thank Gina Despres, Elizabeth Moller and James Bruce as well as several other congressional staff members on both the House and the Senate side who
helped with suggestions and criticisms.

Others most helpful outside of the United States included
Faisal al-Bashir, deputy planning minister of Saudi Arabia;
Dr. Aureliano Chaves, vice president of Brazil; Clive Jones,
deputy minister of the British Ministry of Energy; John Guess;
Jorge de Noronha; Ramon and Roberto Labarthe. The following
were also generous with their time in reading parts of the manuscript: Melvin Conant (who was generous throughout with his
comments and encouragements), Michael Lynch, Tom Neff, and
Walter Rosenbaum, and Robert Sahr. Ronald Inglehart was
good enough to share with us some of his own research on
energy attitudes.

The Rockefeller Family and Associates, the Ford Foundation, Resources for the Future, the John F. Kennedy School at Harvard, and the Horace Rackham Graduate School at the University of Michigan provided financial support for this study. The Energy Management and Policy Program at the University of Pennsylvania offered valuable institutional support, as did the Institute for Public Policy Studies and the Political Science department at Michigan. The entire secretarial staff of the Political Science department helped in all aspects of manuscript preparation; their cooperation and good cheer were invaluable.

The usual caveats about guilt and absolution apply; advice generously tendered could not always be accepted, often because of the press of time and the limits on space. We alone are responsible for any errors of fact or interpretation that may appear here.

This book is affectionately dedicated to our families, Kathy and Katie Walker Kemezis, and Francille and Malik Wilson.

CONTENTS

LIST OF ACRONYMS
AND ABBREVIATIONS

AEE	Agence pour les Économies d'Énergie.
b/d	Barrels per day.
BNOC	British National Oil Corporation—North Sea.
BP	British Petroleum.
BTU	British thermal units.
CFP	Compagnie Française des Pétroles.
DONG	Danish Oil and Natural Gas A/S—Oil Importer.
DUP	Déclaration d'Utilité Publique.
EDF	Electricité de France.
EEC	European Economic Community.
ENI	Ente Nazionale Idrocarburi, of Italy.
ERDA	Energy Research and Development Agency.
GDP	Gross domestic product.
GNP	Gross national product.
IAFA	International Atomic Energy Agency.
IEA	International Energy Agency.
IMF	International Monetary Fund.
JNOC	Japan National Oil Corporation.
LDC	Less developed countries.
MNC	Multinational corporation.
MTOE	Millions of tons of oil equivalent.
NEP	National energy policy.
NICs	Newly industrialized countries.
NOCs	National oil company.
OAPEC	Organization of Arab Petroleum Exporting Countries.
OECD	Organization for Economic Co-operation and Development.
OLADE	Organization Latinoamericana de Energia.
OPEC	Organization of Petroleum Exporting Countries
STATOIL	Den Norske Stats Olijeselskap As. The Norwegian State Oil Company.
UN	United Nations.
UNCTAD	United Nations Conference on Trade and Development.

THE DECADE
OF
ENERGY POLICY

1

ENERGY POLICY
IN AN UNCERTAIN WORLD

INTRODUCTION

The decade of the 1970s was a roller coaster ride for the governments of oil-importing countries. Prices soared over 500 percent by late 1973, then leveled off between 1975 and 1978 only to skyrocket again as the decade closed. Just as importantly, the longstanding, set patterns of oil supply were radically distorted. As these commercial supply and price conditions changed, the world's 110-plus consumer governments were forced to adjust their international, and eventually their domestic energy policies. This book is about their adaptations, successful and otherwise.

Some consumer governments quickly recognized the long-term direction in which world energy markets were heading, despite the temporary lulls. Public policy helped domestic markets adjust effectively, thereby minimizing public discord and economic dislocation. Other governments resisted adaptation, holding back until the economic and political costs of not changing were too great. Many countries (the majority) followed a two-steps-forward-and-one-back approach to energy policy, but in the end, although by different routes, all did adapt to the higher prices and the shift to producer government (rather than oil company) control of supplies.

We characterize this up-down-up-down, price cycle as the M-shaped market. Extreme market volatility between 1973 and 1983 created very costly and unnerving conditions for everyone involved, since the fundamental need for market stability collided with the equally fundamental fact of market instability. Energy industries have among the longest lead times of any sector, and financial managers base their investment decisions on returns over a project's 30-year useful life. (It may take 12 years simply to move a project from the drawing boards to production.) The M-shaped market was also costly in political and capital terms for government officials unsure about which energy demand or supply program to underwrite. It was costly too for the individual consumer confronted with a bewildering display of conflicting information on everything from home insulation to automobile mileage. Market volatility made it tough on everyone in importing countries.

Governments were forced to react, whether they wanted to or not. So they scrambled, using whatever political and economic resources under their authority, to secure national advantage or to minimize losses during the swings between tight and loose oil markets. The balance (or imbalance) between demand and supply dictated how far and how fast the oil producer governments could expand their control, and how well consumers could retain some influence. When markets were tight, as in 1973 and the closing of the decade, the leverage shifted to exporters. When demand was slack, as in the mid-1970s and early 1980s, consumers had significant leverage and could work out bilateral and multilateral arrangements in world markets more in line with their own interests. Of course, the higher prices in tight markets were partly—but only partly—the result of OPEC countries' own actions.* They pushed prices higher and created supply uncertainties and higher logistical costs. But as both OPEC and the consumers eventually discovered, somewhat to their surprise, OPEC's ability to achieve these changes was made possible by the level of consumer demand. The world discovered it takes two to make a market.

---

*In keeping with popular parlance we employ the term <u>OPEC</u> as a collective shorthand to signify all major exporters who, like Mexico or Egypt, may not be formal members but who typically follow OPEC oil policies (Russell 1983, p. 2). Also the term indicates actions taken by individual and sovereign states. The separate governments actually take all pricing, production, and other key policy decisions; they meet in OPEC Vienna headquarters simply to debate, coordinate, and announce these national decisions through the Organization. OPEC itself has very little power to act.

The uncertain conditions of the 1970s oil market elicited increased intervention by governments with both political and commercial motivations (especially when exacerbated and mixed with regional conflicts in the Middle East or Southern Africa). The up-down-up-down M-shaped market forced a kind of stop-and-go policy response as governments grappled with the problem of deciding which was the 'real' oil market, but each consumer country was eventually forced by events to make certain minimal adaptations. And these national energy decisions were very much a product of politics. Politics made a big difference in the energy 'bottom line,' e.g., how much and what kinds of energy were produced where and at what cost, and how far national demand levels were reduced.

But more important than any single adjustment in a specific area of supply or demand were the changes that occurred worldwide in the way that governments were forced to go about making energy policy. For what occurred over the decade, slowly at first and at different rates in different countries, was a genuine energy policy explosion.

The Energy Policy Explosion

The single most important change in the 1970s was the universal, worldwide shift by governments away from passive energy policies to active ones. International and domestic pressures have forced these governments to get more involved than ever before in energy matters, to vie directly with the major private actors and other governments to obtain the most secure, reasonably priced energy supplies, and to obtain the capital necessary to pay for them. The new activist and inter-ventionist approach to energy policy not only encompassed oil and gas but also coal, conservation, renewables, and nuclear. The 1970s represented the beginning. The new movement was from less interventionist government policies to more interven-tionist. Just as all the countries in the 1970s began the inevitable transition to a post-oil economy, so the initial policy consequence was a transition to an activist government role in energy. In the 1950s and 1960s governments could, and did, leave most important aspects of energy to private actors. This ranged from exploring for oil in Canada by international oil majors to individual rural peasants collecting wood in Africa. Now, in the brave new post-1973 energy world, government officials felt obliged to get involved in the supply, distribution, and organization of energy in society. They did so because of their own notion of governmental responsibility in assuring national welfare, national security, or international competitiveness, and because of the boisterous pressures of politically active producer and consumer groups. The result was more government involvement in energy markets and an expansion of public policy.

The principal consequences of this Energy Policy Explosion are clear:

- More oil is sold directly from exporting country governments to importing country governments or their chosen agents, bypassing the private multinational corporations.
- Government-sponsored energy companies in importing countries have multiplied and taken on new roles, often at the expense of private firms.
- Energy planning by governments has become universal and efforts by government agencies to control supplies, prices and end-use of fuels have increased dramatically.
- Discussions and negotiations among governments and in international bodies grew in number and importance in all areas, from nuclear (London Suppliers Group), to renewables (U.N. Conference on New & Renewable Energy Resources), to petroleum (The International Energy Agency).

By the end of the 1970s energy was treated as an essential, almost precious commodity, necessary to a nation's well being and thus the stuff of high politics and national security. In the absence of any serious or sustained effort at formal international energy decision making to replace the former function of the oil companies, virtually every importing country in the world reacted to the new conditions and concentration of power in OPEC in a strikingly similar way, pushing deeper and deeper into national and international energy policy making on its own.

We argue that the changes in demand management policies were the most novel of any that occurred over the decade. In many ways the first two thirds of the 1973-83 decade were the years of the oil exporters, and the remainder the years of the importers. Certainly by the end of the decade the OPEC Revolution was nearly complete. Exporter control over almost every phase of production and crude pricing had been secured. The oil shock was transmitted, the ball served to the importers' court. The surprise of the first part of the 1970s was the new OPEC control of supply; the surprise of the 1980s has been the new importer control of demand. Consumers in the importing countries have cut back their oil use in the face of higher prices

and lower economic growth far more than had been expected.
Now the interesting political economic question is no longer
whether the exporters can seize full control over production;
it is rather if the consumer nations can maintain greater control
over consumption, at the same time that they try to expand
their own domestic production. We provide many of the answers
to this question in this book.

The separate national responses in the 1980s and 1990s,
as in the 1970s, will be shaped within the macroeconomic performance of the world economy. The world energy market
remains coupled to the rhythms of the world economy as a whole.
Despite vastly increased efficiencies, the greater the economic
growth, the greater will tend to be the worldwide demand for
oil and other energy forms, especially in the newly industrializing
countries, but also in the industrialized north. The real test
for the consumers will be their energy performance once economic growth restarts later in the 1980s and it is not clear what
the response will be.

In this book we argue that before analysts and policymakers
can construct plausible commercial and political scenarios for
future domestic policies and for international cooperation (and
conflict) we must know what happened in the recent past. This
must be done by analyzing the decade's change from the ground
up, as it were, rather than from the top down, reconstructing
the national responses of the main importing countries to energy
market structural changes. A total of 20 years between us,
working on this issue and traveling around the world has convinced us that the meaning of the 'energy crisis' is different
from country to country, and from specific policy area to specific
policy area. A discussion of a 'world' response must account
for national differences of economic development, region, and
of political system. It is true that all countries have adapted
in the 1970s to the same world market situation, but it is important to recognize domestic differences, and the differences in
the way countries fit into that changing system.

Finally, there are already many works that describe the
world-level changes; there are many that describe country or
fuel-specific responses. Ours is the first, however, to look
at the complex mutual interaction of world regime changes and
national policy adaptations in a broadly comparative policy
perspective. We present this interaction in terms of the policies
and institutions that all countries employed, though in different
ways, to mediate this interaction between domestic and international markets. Each country used a different mix of institutions and policies to achieve their national purposes. It is this

national variety within the universal need for certain basic adaptations of supply, allocation, and institutions that we try to capture in the phrase Energy Policy Explosion. The United States, for example, was unique in many respects, differing widely from other consuming nations and from the exporters. Because of this uniqueness the United States could not reassert its former international leadership in energy until it had adjusted its domestic energy system to the new price and supply conditions, and understood the motivations and actions of other importers. It needed to realize that its trenchant free-enterprise attitudes toward energy, and the great power which private U.S. oil companies continue to exercise both at home and abroad would post special problems since most other importing countries in the 1970s moved in opposite directions. The latest expression of U.S. uniqueness was the Reagan administration's campaign to abolish the Department of Energy and reduce government involvement in energy planning, research and development (R&D), and international crisis management at a time when almost all other countries in the world are expanding state activities in energy areas.

Complex international energy linkages will continue to provide opportunities for energy producers and consumers in the 1980s as in the 1970s. They also impose limitations on their freedom of action. It will therefore be imperative that public officials, private managers, and informed citizens in each country have more knowledge and insight into the results of the energy policy explosion in other nations.

The Special Role of Oil

The origins of the current energy policy explosion lie in the way oil exporting governments restructured the institutional core of the world oil market and thereby forced importing country governments to adjust. In the 1970s, as in the 1950s and 1960s, oil was the most important commercial fuel in the world. It has not always been so (its predecessor was King Coal), nor will it be in the future. But for the second half of the 20th century oil has enjoyed an unrivaled position as the most convenient, cheapest, and most desirable commercial fuel, and, up to 1973, also the cheapest.

From only 29 percent of world consumption in 1950 oil leapt to 46 percent by 1972, and much higher for individual countries. In developing economies today imported oil accounts for 76 to 100 percent of total commercial energy in at least 39

countries. During the post-World War II period oil has been
the single most valuable traded commodity, worth one quarter
of all commodities bought and sold on international markets.
And despite the brutal turbulence of the 1973-80 market, oil's
share of the total energy market slipped only one percentage
point down to 43.6 percent in that time (J. Cook, 1982, p. 100).
The international oil business accounts for many of the world's
largest corporations, and often the single largest company in
a given country.

Beyond its bigness in terms of assets and revenues, the
industry operates in every country of the world and has become
central to modern economic growth. This gives it unique political
and strategic aspects. For all these reasons oil's role is special.
The set of laws, administrative regulations, institutions, power
relationships and mutual expectations that went to make up the
international oil regime was the core of energy debate and
energy policy in the 1970s. All other sources of energy were,
quite literally, peripheral. Oil was the benchmark "fuel to
beat" for companies and governments considering other energy
resources. Its changing structure wasn't the only one, but
it was the one against which the others had to react. For this
reason we put the politics and economics of oil at the center of
our analysis, although we do not neglect the other key energy
sources: gas, nuclear, coal, electricity, and renewables, just
as we examine the expanding role of energy conservation. Still,
the decade of the 1970s was the Decade of Oil; energy policy
meant trying to buy, discover, or switch slowly away from oil
supplies.

While oil remained the preeminent energy source through
the 1970s, the decade marked a transition away from one set
of rules and structures governing oil to another. The outlines
of the new oil regime were only barely visible in the early years,
but by 1979 the new regime had begun to take shape and operate
along new lines. In the old regime, oil was clearly the dominant
fuel, cheap and dependable and under the reliable control of a
handful of vertically integrated corporations based in the importing countries. Managers and technicians in these companies
made the important production, price, and distribution decisions.
But the old system was more than just a market. Economic and
political power were closely entwined and the importer country
governments had a role to play. However, except in periods
of major crisis such as the two world wars, this role was mainly
passive. Importer governments usually gave companies wide
latitude to operate at home except when public or nationalist
pressures forced regulation. Abroad the governments aided

through diplomatic efforts to keep exporting countries compliant and find advantages for their own country's companies vis-à-vis the competitors. More important than any single component of this complex and daunting edifice of Western power was the stability of the structure as a whole. It was indeed greater than the sum of its parts, surrounded by an air of enormous power and efficient performance.

Then in the 1970s the market and political conditions changed. From the very first days of the decade the edifice was chipped away, dismantled, and finally shattered by the suddenly activist and nationalist governments of the exporting countries. A new regime emerged in which the exporters, whose political and economic interests differed greatly from the importers, came to exercise decisive control. The multinational companies became servants instead of masters of the market and the role of the suddenly high-cost oil as the dominant fuel was put into question.

The steady, quite literal disintegration of the old oil price and supply regime through the 1970s aroused dramatic new interest in governments and private firms in other fuels such as coal, gas, nuclear, and solar, which can be partial substitutes for oil. Energy conservation and the efficiency of energy using processes also entered the policy field. The doubts extended to the basic characteristics of the oil-based modern economic system, its methods of production and transportation, and its high standard of living.

In the decade of the 1970s the other major fuels also experienced significant changes in cost, availability, and attractiveness to the consumer. Some of these changes were directly caused by changes in oil, due to price linkages and fuel switching. Others occurred more autonomously, caused by events that were extraneous to oil. These included developments unique to the industry in question, such as technological change in gas transport and storage, or in nuclear reactor safety. Other factors changed during the 1970s, such as environmental concern, interest rates, and economic growth rates. These affected all industries, but did not affect them equally. Let us look at the nuclear industry as an example.

For government policymakers and for managers of private firms, the quick run-up of oil prices in 1973-74 combined with the uncertainty of supply led them to look much more favorably on nuclear power. The two fuels are not substitutable for most purposes, but they are in the key area of electricity generation. The consequence was that public and private managers in Brazil, France, and the United States among other countries began to speed up nuclear projects and to place more orders for nuclear reactors than they would have if the oil shock hadn't occurred. The perception of oil market instability made the nuclear market more attractive. Presidents as well as technocrats recognized the nuclear-oil connection.

In addition to these direct links between nuclear and oil markets, both were directly affected by strong underlying economic factors. In the mid-1960s and early 1970s high growth rates pushed up world demand for oil and nuclear power at annual rates of about 7 percent and 5 percent respectively. But when interest rates shot up in the second half of the last decade, lower growth brought down electricity demand and safety costs grew. This lowered demand for nuclear power and orders for new reactors plummeted.

Finally, there were other developments, which included industry-specific technological changes or commercial develop- ments. For example, nuclear markets in the 1970s were shaken when Westinghouse suffered a massive default on its agreement to supply uranium fuel to 25 nuclear generating companies in 1975. Although Westinghouse alleged that its multibillion-dollar failure to perform was entirely due to OPEC raising oil prices, and later claimed the fault lay with an illegal international uranium cartel, most disinterested observers feel that the fault lay in bad management decisions by Westinghouse executives responsible for covering short contracts. This was a series of events controlled neither by oil nor international stagflation.

As important as these kinds of developments were in nuclear, coal, or renewables, the fact remains that oil was the dominant fuel of the 1970s. Government policies in the 1970s had to be primarily directed toward oil in the short and medium term, even as they provided national incentives to develop and expand the future contribution of other fuels and conservation. Yet oil clearly cannot remain the dominant fuel forever. Our concern here is to identify and compare what governments are doing to retard, promote, or otherwise affect oil's passing.

The Good Old Days

Until the late 1960s, energy policy was very much a second- ary concern of governments in most importing countries. Defense, economic growth, industrial recovery and social serv- ices held their attention. Energy, of course, played a part in all of these fields, but high policymakers did not yet see it as a distinct issue, important in its own right. There were separate government interventions in one energy subsector or another, usually connected to industry-specific policies and guidelines. But there was rarely any overall idea of an inclusive energy sector. There were no elaborate "energy plans."

There were two reasons why energy policy failed to emerge at that time as an area of critical government concern, one economic and technical, the other more political. First, oil, the dominant fuel, was cheap, convenient, and seemingly plentiful from secure sources (the real price of energy fell between 1885 and 1967, the height of the "cheap oil" era). The vast oil concessions of the Middle East seemed ready to provide an endless bounty. These fields came to the fore as the crucial supplemental world supply in the mid-1950s, when the traditional fields in the United States, South America, and Europe began to level off. National planners, who needed rapid energy growth to fuel their prime objective of rapid economic growth, simply assumed the Middle Eastern reserve would be available when needed. Any occasional doubts about short supplies were dispelled by the large oil discoveries in the 1960s in Alaska and the North Sea, and the new liquefied gas technology which opened up large new natural gas resources to world trade.

At the same time, governments were permitting coal a gracious, though definite, decline to second place in their national fuel balances. Cheaper and more convenient oil could not be denied priority as countries pushed for sustained growth and international trade advantage. Coal mining was propped up because of local political and union pressures, not because it was seriously believed to have a future. Nuclear power was the wave of the future. It still appeared to be a simple, safe technology which could produce electricity more cheaply than coal or oil. The environmental movement, which was to have a profound effect on energy development in the 1970s was just gaining momentum in the United States and virtually unheard of elsewhere. The cheap oil and gas eliminated a small synthetic fuels industry in Europe, leaving only outcast, security-minded South Africa to continue serious coal liquefaction efforts. Low priced oil also prevented U.S. companies from making a serious effort to develop their vast U.S. shale oil reserves.

The second element which blocked national energy policy making was the character and locus of the control of oil. The dominance of the multinational companies appeared assured due to their vertical integration, high revenues, easy access to capital, worldwide operations, and acquiescence by home governments and exporters. The American, British, Dutch, and French governments intervened at critical periods (that is, after World

Wars I and II) to strike deals and bargains among themselves
that gave a political framework to subsequent commercial activities of the big oil majors. Governments thereby helped write
the "market" rules that private firms would follow. Under such
a system there was little incentive for a single government to
try to make itself independent of the system, even though some
disliked private sector control. Policy towards the oil market
was piecemeal and reactive, seeking to solve problems at the
margin while retaining the substantial benefits to consumers
that the system brought. Some nations tried to reduce the power
of the multinational companies inside their borders but, lacking
alternatives, found they could not do without them entirely.

The United States, which alone had the ability to curb
the power of the multinationals, was relatively well served by
them, and did not do so for ingrained political and diplomatic
reasons. Instead, the consistent U.S. policy was to encourage
expansion of U.S. company operations at home and abroad
through generous tax advantages. The big U.S. policy problem
in the 1960s was insuring that cheap Middle Eastern oil did
not undercut the politically powerful domestic producers. The
solution was a quota system which fixed imports as a small
percentage of production and kept prices and profits up. As
a legacy from the New Deal, natural gas was strictly regulated
and the political balance prevented gas price decontrol.

In Europe and Japan, two common policies of the period
were overseeing an orderly decline of the coal industry and
building up a strong national refining sector, generally dominated
by multinational firms. These activities, however, were better
categorized as industrial policy than energy policy. France,
with its tightly regulated domestic oil market, and attempt to
create an independent supply base in colonial Algeria, was an
exception. Many countries nationalized their coal, gas, and
electric industries and some created state-owned oil companies
to counter the private multinationals. These public energy
groups received tax aids and subsidies, but to a large extent
were left on their own by government ministers. The energy
market in general was stable and self-regulating, requiring
the serious attention of only a handful of government technocrats. Only rarely, in times of international crisis, such as
Suez in 1956, were prime ministers and presidents involved in
energy policy.

In many less developed countries (LDCs) which imported
oil, government policy was activist, but the scope of oil use
was small. Medium-sized countries like Thailand or Kenya
induced the major oil companies to provide local refineries so

that fuel import costs could be reduced; the smallest countries had neither the market nor political leverage to get refineries, and usually signed contracts with a single supplier. Large countries with domestic resources, such as Brazil and India, developed successful policies to reduce their dependence on the majors for imports, refining, and exploration, frequently seeking help from state groups such as Italy's Ente Nazionale Idrocarburi (ENI) or Soviet energy agencies.

Regional cooperation on oil matters during this period did not amount to much either, among the less developed importers or the Western industrialized countries. When the European Common Market was put together in the 1950s, it quickly agreed to liberalize the intra-European coal trade, which was dying on the vine, and to carry out joint nuclear research. Not only were these initiatives stunted, but efforts in the late 1960s to harmonize national oil policies also were unsuccessful. The differences between the liberal German oil market and the intensely regulated French system were vast, and while technocrats at the EEC headquarters in Brussels believed a common policy was worthwhile, the member governments found such unity was not worth the political effort. They perceived no outside threat forcing them toward such unity. The Organization of Petroleum Exporting Countries had been created in 1960, but the Europeans and other importers expected the oil companies to deal with the new group satisfactorily. No one saw the need for an organization of oil importers.

The Beginning of the End

By the start of the 1980s, this passive and disjointed approach to energy policy had changed drastically. National energy policy and management had become a priority concern of virtually all importing governments. Global oil policy was discussed in national and international forums once reserved for détente and high diplomacy. The promise of cheap, boundless energy supplies had been broken. The oil market structure, so long assumed immutable, had collapsed, giving way to something new and uncertain which was not only a more competitive market but also a political puzzle. Importing governments, starting in 1973, were constantly occupied with the economic dislocations caused in part by suddenly higher oil prices, and occasionally they had to manage actual fuel shortages. By the end of the decade, they were forced to take systematic policy steps at home and worldwide to insure they could obtain enough fuel to maintain their economies and national well-being. First gradually, and then with greater frequency, governments found themselves improvising new roles for themselves in the energy field. After the Iranian revolution of 1979, they saw clearly they could no longer depend entirely on the multinational companies to satisfy their needs on a secure basis. In lieu of conspicuously lacking agreement among themselves about dealing directly with the oil importers, the importer governments had to take on this task individually, even while continuing to rely on the majors for part of their supply. We return to this theme in Chapter 4.

The first major events which brought about this new situation were the parallel actions of the major oil exporting countries, starting in the late 1960s, to take full control of their oil resources. The 40-year-old practice of handing more than generous concession to the private oil companies was ended. Simultaneously, the producer states set up national companies to manage production of oil and gas. Gradually these governments moved toward effective control over key decisions of pricing, revenue and tax levels, ownership, exploration, and production rates. A common pricing arrangement was initiated within the OPEC framework to insure higher revenues for all. No agreement was reached on production rates, which remained the political province of each individual OPEC country. After the Iranian revolution, the pace of change quickened. The previous dominant alliance of moderates led by Saudi Arabia weakened with the fall of the Shah, and leadership passed to radicals such as Iraq, Libya, Algeria, and the new militant Iran. This brought on the new price hikes of 1979 and 1980 and also led several members to begin to reduce production. As world demand dropped in 1980, the moderates regained leverage, but at the same time the new hard-edged political attitudes brought increased efforts by all OPEC members to control who bought their oil and where it went. Instead of the short-lived production cutback and selective embargo of 1973-74, a less sweeping but steady process took place. The amount of world oil supply whose destination was controlled by the multinational companies fell from three-quarters to one-third during this time. By the end of the 1970s, the question of the amount of ultimate Middle Eastern reserves seemed to become irrelevant, replaced by the question of first how much the owners of the oil were willing to supply, and then increasingly, how much importers needed. Beyond the North Sea and Alaska, few new finds were made in areas where long-term access was considered "safe" to the Western importers. Hopes of replacing anticipated reductions

of OPEC production with finds in other developing countries
were chilled especially by the strong nationalist attitude taken
by Mexico to its large new discoveries.

The demise of the old concession system and the new
activism of the producer governments meant that the multinational companies had lost one of the two main pillars of their
former vast power: control of supply (Blair 1976). Because
of this, the other great pillar-control of marketing in consumer
countries—swiftly began to erode. With less oil available to
them, the companies could not guarantee everyone supplies
over the long term. Businessmen, individual consumers and
hence governments in most countries could not accept this.
Planning for energy contingencies could no longer be left predominantly to private firms. Oil became a national security
issue and not merely one of trade and commerce, and security
of supply superceded price as the key international policy issue.
In effect, the politicization of oil supply by the exporters forced
a political, as well as commercial, response from the importers,
and while the companies would continue certain market roles
where possible, these roles were more and more defined by
OPEC and the consuming governments.

As OPEC governments more frequently withheld oil from
the majors and sought to sell it directly, importing countries
found ways to buy it directly. National oil companies in importing countries, originally set up to compete in their domestic
markets with the majors and stimulate new exploration, were
pushed by events into new roles as agents. Several industrialized countries with major domestic oil resources such as Britain,
Canada, and Norway, set up national companies to better control their own output and revenues. Only the American policymakers, with their large domestic production and national
attachment to the major companies, refused to join the shift to
more direct government control over oil supply procurement.
They did, however, step up their attention to the related issues
of "regional security" in the Middle East, as well as strengthen
bilateral political relations with certain exporters.

But even the Americans could not escape the increase of
direct importer government involvement in the distribution of
oil products. The threat of sudden shortages eventually forced
almost all governments to develop planning and emergency allocation schemes. The United States responded with legislation in
1974 permitting the president to set prices and assign physical
quantities of oil in an emergency. However, government's main
involvement in domestic allocation came in through the back
door via President Nixon's oil price controls. Over the course

of the decade this involvement emerged as the single most
divisive energy issue domestically, and the source of extremely
acrimonious debate between the United States and its allies.
Designed originally as an anti-inflation measure, price controls
became the country's prime energy problem, pushing up consumption (and hence imports) while holding down domestic production.
The international structure of world oil had changed in the
early 1970s, but consumers (through their elected representatives) fought strongly against adapting. At the same time, the
United States, like all other importing countries, drew up energy
conservation schemes, sought ways to switch industrial fuel
use away from oil, and tried to develop long-term plans involving
use of alternative fuels. The failure of nuclear power to meet
its initial promise due to a combination of safety, environmental,
economic, and political problems heightened the urgency and
political complexity of the task facing all governments, especially
those with no domestic oil or coal reserves to fall back on. In
the importing developing countries, the problem of demand
management and government control over product distribution
was particularly difficult. Not only were commercial energy
markets scattered geographically, but government institutional
capacity to plan and execute policy was weak and underdeveloped
itself.

In the first half of the 1970s, the suddenly high oil prices
appeared to be the biggest threat to world stability, and received
the most attention from the public and from energy experts.
Price concerns drove public policy. The other problem of loss
of integrated control by the importers over supply and distribution, and a lack of consensus among them over how to
handle this, were originally less noticed but proved critical
over the longer run. Despite the fears of monetary and trade
collapse, by the middle years of the decade the importer economies proved they could adjust in the short term to higher prices,
with some difficulties, but without the anticipated disaster.
Essentially, countries either exported or borrowed or produced
their way out of the crisis. Collapse did not occur.

In fact, some argued that the sudden oil price shocks
proved beneficial by forcing all importing countries to take
immediate energy conservation measures and make serious
efforts to use alternative fuels. Some of the arguments in
favor of higher prices were made by an unlikely coalition of
conservationists, oil companies, and OPEC spokesmen. The
latter have consistently argued that in 1973 they righted the
long-standing wrong of Western domination over their resources
and also pushed the importers of energy to energy self-discipline

that was needed all along. The transition to post-petroleum
energy sources was surely inevitable sometime in the late
20th or early 21st century, but without the OPEC price rises
the gears would never have been set in motion as firmly as they
were by 1980. The OPEC nominal price hikes had a subsidiary
impact by impressing upon the man on the street and industry
leaders in importing countries that drastic changes were really
needed. This created an instant constituency for politicians.
The price rises and gyrations on the world oil spot markets
also revealed to the leaders themselves how little knowledge
they had about their own oil markets and the operations of
traders inside their borders. This brought changes in governmental practices and began a fundamental trend toward greater
transparency of oil sales. By the end of the decade, the governments and public were able to take sudden new price hikes in
stride, and questions of security of supply gained equal attention.

The Pressures for Change

We have discussed in a general fashion the new importing
government activism in energy policy, and will now look at
specific causes. Because of the international nature of the
OPEC revolution, the initial impulses for change came to importers
from the outside. The major international causes of the new
energy policy activism by oil importing countries are:

1. Response to greater activism among exporter country
governments which now demand direct political input into oil
dealings. The exporting countries sold an increasing amount
of their crude directly through their national oil companies,
bypassing the major companies. Such sales were strongly
conditioned by economic and political factors outside traditional
market considerations. Oil sales were linked to downstream oil
operations, trade and internal development packages including
nonenergy projects as well as broad political objectives such as
friendship with nonaligned nations and diplomatic pressure
against Israel. Also, more and more exporters insisted when
they held market power that prospective buyers have their
own national oil company (NOC) through which to purchase
and import their oil. These pressures led importers to respond
and seek out deals directly, and create or strengthen governmental institutions to implement them. Since oil trade and
political issues are increasingly likely to be tied up in the same
package, a certain amount of increased coordination inside

governments was needed to make a judgment on whether the
overall national interest is served by any given deal.

2. <u>Increased fears of energy supply cutoff due to international turbulence and desire to assure supply through direct
government actions.</u> The logistical and price troubles created
by the relatively minor amounts of oil actually cut back in 1973
and 1979 made energy supply security a chief governmental
concern. Government's ability to provide fuel for the domestic
economy and avoid a breakdown in production of goods and
services and in law and order during an international crisis
became a major component of national security thinking. Energy
security reports and proposals multiplied. The responses of
individual governments to this problem at the international level
went far beyond simply increasing direct dealings with the oil-
exporting states. They ranged from the post-1980 U.S. rapid
deployment force, a military unit trained for quick intervention
in Middle Eastern oil-producing regions, to large-scale diplomatic
efforts such as the "Euro-Arab" dialogue, designed to improve
relations between the EEC and Arab nations.

3. <u>Desire to reduce the role of foreign-based oil companies
in national energy matters.</u> The deep penetration of foreign
multinationals in most importing country energy markets was
unavoidable in the postwar era because of the companies' vertical
integration and especially their control of oil distribution. But
it was always tolerated grudgingly and under the post-1973
circumstances governments have several incentives to cut back
the role of the multinationals. The companies themselves were
less able to offer cheap, secure oil and have been, for certain
countries like Japan and Sweden, undependable in crisis situations. In addition, the strategic power of the United States
behind them seemed much less awesome in the post-Vietnam era.
OPEC oil sale policies strengthened the hands of the various
importer national oil companies against the large corporations,
especially in scarcity periods, and the increased intervention
by importer governments in oil policy made certain private
company operations less profitable. Finally, the gradual shift
away from oil to new fuels, more likely to be controlled by
domestic companies with state backing or control, has lessened
the majors' overall energy market role everywhere except the
United States.

4. <u>Efforts to avoid or control gyrations on the world oil
spot markets, especially for countries cut out of third-party
sales by the majors.</u> Countries which were denied sales by oil-
short majors in scarcity periods and did not arrange direct
OPEC supply deals, were forced to seek short-term supplies

on the highly speculative and expensive spot markets. At these times prices were substantially above OPEC official prices with rampant private profittaking and virtually no political accountability due to the international nature of the markets. Governments therefore had, temporarily, a huge incentive to work through direct deals with OPEC, where some political and economic leverage could be applied. Although these could become a burden in slack markets. Because of the pernicious role of the spot markets in the 1979 crisis, which grew from below 5 percent to 15 percent of sales and beyond, and acted as an informal price leader for OPEC, efforts by importer governments to increase the transparency and accountability of the markets, especially at Rotterdam, have increased.

5. Sharper competition among consumers, and therefore a perceived need for greater international cooperation among importer countries. The international nature of the oil market system and the major impact of energy supply problems on general international economic and defense policy making created severe consumer competition and some conflict, forcing several international agencies and conferences to address energy issues directly. The United Nations, Organization for Economic Cooperation and Development, North Atlantic Treaty Organization, the European Communities, the nonaligned nations conferences, and several others, have focused on energy, forcing member governments to develop national positions and attempt to negotiate solutions. There have been efforts to spread the risk through oil sharing and prevent any one country from being singled out for an oil embargo. Countries have also sought R&D, military, and diplomatic benefits from cooperation. The need for some solidarity against the exporters' organization in particular forced the hasty creation of the International Energy Agency in 1974. The energy question also greatly sharpened the debate over the role of the developing countries in the world political and economic order, and gave rise to, in effect, a continuous if not entirely successful "North-South dialogue" with the participants defined partly by their national energy postures.

6. Part of a broader trend toward economic nationalism and protectionism worldwide, driven by unprecedented inflation and economic stagnation. The economic difficulties exacerbated by the oil revolution of the 1970s—recurrent recessions, soaring inflation, unstable currencies and interest rates, and potentially overwhelming balance of payments deficits and credit defaults—have expanded general government activism in international economic matters. Import restrictions, export subsidies, and

heightened competition among industrialized countries for foreign markets have been fed by the unrelenting foreign exchange cost of oil imports and the need to contain their impact on the economy. In particular, increasing exports to pay the oil import bill and maintain economic growth have become a central government concern.

There are also several specific types of <u>domestic</u> pressures forcing a shift by importer governments to more activism in energy matters. Generally, they comprise the reactions of domestic groups to the impacts of the international pressures as they are filtered through different national channels. These domestic actors include specific consumer groups as well as energy-intensive industries, and representatives of energy rich or energy poor regions.

7. <u>Pressure on government to protect economic groups in the short term from suddenly higher prices and possible supply cutoffs</u>. The OPEC price rises after 1973 caused considerable economic dislocations and forced governments to take measures to soften the impacts, especially from sudden shocks, on vulnerable groups and regions. This included blocking product price rises or phasing them in slowly, and linking income support to higher energy prices. Besides protecting consumers from the direct effect of OPEC prices, the U.S. government in the extreme example, but West Germany as well, acted to prevent "windfall" profits on private oil holdings. In addition, the importer governments have had to assume the role of energy allocator in crisis periods, establishing a fair sharing of fuels among priority users. This latter role required major new planning effort for occasional curtailments and even rationing, and the assumption, at least on a standby basis, of strong power over stockpiles, imports, and refinery operations.

8. <u>The need to set long-term priorities and execute decisions for conservation and conversion to more desirable fuels</u>. The long-term world market trend toward higher energy prices contained a built-in conservation factor (i.e., demand elasticities) which governments attempted to guide through price, tax, and fuel use policies to bring the smoothest possible transition to a new energy balance. Taxes and tax breaks in particular were used selectively to increase the burden on "nonessential" consumption and reward conservation in industry and residences. Direct administrative mandates or subsidies to utilities and industry to cut oil consumption in favor of coal and nuclear became widespread.

9. <u>The desire to develop all possible domestic oil and gas sources and to introduce new energy technologies</u>, activities

which require higher risks and longer lead times than private industry can or will bear on its own. With the days of giant oil finds in accessible regions virtually at an end, adding new increments to the national energy supply became a highly complex, expensive, and lengthy industrial operation. In many countries, domestic private capital does not exist to do the job, and foreign companies are not welcome; in others private capital will not undertake the effort without strong financial support and political assurances from the government. Also the government may decide it is in the national interest to exclude private industry from important new initiatives. Even without its defense and environmental aspects, the nuclear industry would have developed with strong governmental involvement due to the uncertain and complex, but promising, nature of the technology. Government policies include stepped up oil and gas exploration at home and abroad through national companies and subsidiaries, large government-run energy research and development programs, and various subsidies such as guaranteed prices and markets for near-commercial ventures in synfuels, solar, and other areas.

10. Acceleration of past historical trends toward greater government control over the energy industry and treatment of energy supply as an essential public service. General doubts about the totally free market economy in most industrialized countries since World War II have been compounded in the energy field by the special market distortions created by OPEC pricing. Governments have tended to take actions to regulate or participate in the domestic market especially since lack of intervention normally would give free rein to the foreign multinationals. Only in the United States, despite its large public utilities sector, does the notion of a relatively free energy market and private ownership and control of the energy industry have overwhelming support because of the supposed incentive this creates for domestic production and efficiencies.

11. Demands of environmentalists sensitive to growing evidence of ecological damage due to use of various energy sources. The environmental groups, with their strong public support across traditional party lines in several countries, forced governments to pay greater attention to the pollution threats created by private industrial activities and their own energy policy decisions. The environmental impact statement in the United States is a remarkable self-policing device which has set a broad example for other countries. The essential impact of the environmentalists was to force governments to get even more deeply involved in on-going energy activities

through permit review boards and safety inspectors, and to require even more attention to planning for alternative fuels and conservation. On the heels of the political mobilization of youth and others in the late 1960s, it yielded an active, vocal constituency.

12. Perceived political need for some entity to assume overall management of energy policy. The public in virtually all importing countries now expect their governments to have some sort of overall energy "plan" and tend to hold their political leaders responsible for disruptions and hardships caused by increased energy costs and shortages. In response, governments have developed plans and new energy policy institutions to meet these expectations and made energy issues a highly visible part of the national political agenda. What was much slower to materialize was public awareness that their individual actions and habits as energy consumers are a key ingredient of national policy, and that under current circumstances there is virtually no room for a government to act without demanding sacrifices from the public.

None of these pressures acting alone would necessarily have forced the intense new government activism, this Energy Policy Explosion, but in concert their impact has been tremendous. At the same time, the national and international factors which had always been present in the past are now more closely intertwined, making policy decisions more complex. The turbulence of international politics starting in the 1970s had simply multiplied the complexity. Finally, the wide range of economic activities affected by energy means that changes in the international oil system produce impacts on the domestic scene through a wide variety of channels. The price of oil and other energy sources, as well as the availability of the supply are the broad avenues, but the impacts come through secondary paths including the price of industrial and consumer goods, changes in currency values and shifts in trade patterns favoring, for example, more energy-efficient autos. The multiple entry points of energy into the economy make effective policy extraordinarily difficult to implement and coordinate. The overall result is that the variety of energy impacts, policy responses and public perceptions is infinite, and the experience is unlikely to be the same in any two countries.

Market-Politics Interactions

A key question, given the diffuse origins and immense scope of energy use and production in modern societies, is how much control governments can actually exercise over them and whether governmental energy policy as such can have a decisive role. Our position is that the actions of governments to alter the behavior of energy producers, sellers, and consumers, are important influences on domestic energy markets and on international energy transactions. This is especially the case during periods of market turmoil and rapid structural dislocation, when old rules no longer work and new ones have not been widely accepted. At such points in time, political leadership is critical. We believe that energy policy will remain important over the coming decade. National governments separately or jointly will seek to provide the stability and guidance once furnished by oil companies in the world market. OPEC, with its fragile political consensus cannot provide a lasting basis and governments, burned twice since 1973, must be prepared for future turbulence.

We do not argue from this, however, that more government activism automatically means greater nationalization or government control of presently private actors. Policy encompasses a wide range of activities including decisions not to intervene, and to let market forces take their course. Further, more often than not the countries we are studying intervene to strengthen the market in certain ways rather than to supplant or eliminate it. Still, we recognize that there are certain areas where governmental policies tend to have a greater direct influence such as pricing, fuel switching, emergency allocation measures, and environmental regulation. Also, governmental policies at the international level, such as direct deals for supplies, regulatory or fiscal restraints on imports or exports, and strategic moves affecting energy geopolitics are especially visible and effective.

As one would expect, government policies are less able to quickly influence the structural features of energy demand. They take a much longer time to change. For example, the key non-policy factors such as the general performance of the national economy, sectoral balance between industry and agriculture, population growth and density, and climate, largely determine the composition and level of energy demand and account for most differences between countries. To alter the basic energy demand would require significant changes in the economic structure of the society itself. For example, dramatically reducing demand for auto fuel in the United States would imply vast changes in what has historically been one of its leading industries. On the supply side, there are important areas where government policies have altered energy patterns, not only in imports, but through a range of policies such as pro-

moting nuclear energy in France, coal liquefaction in South
Africa, gasohol in Brazil, and oil discoveries in India. To sum
up, governments can make changes in energy demand and supply
at the margin, and often "the margin" can make the difference
between soft or tight markets, and whether billions of dollars
stay home or move abroad. But the decade of the 1970s has
also shown us that normally big changes in energy patterns
take a long time; some energy projects begun in 1980 won't
have a national impact until 1995.

A further constraint on importer government power over
energy is that the new OPEC-centric oil market operates in a
world context. The actions they can take over price are quite
limited. It is OPEC more than the national government that sets
these prices, and they in turn do so only in a range set by
world interaction of buyers and sellers. The domestic governments of oil importers simply lack the leverage to directly reduce
world crude prices in the short term. This means they can
only play around at the margin with product prices. Sometimes
these margins can become politically sensitive as we see in
Chapters 6 and 7.

Why International Comparisons?

Our main purpose is to demonstrate the full range of
government responses and the organizational adjustments that
often accompany them, not to calculate their detailed impacts
on economic activity. We will illustrate the universality of the
external challenge, the instruments available to consumers to
respond, and the actual choices different countries make.

We found governments want to know what their fellow
governments are doing in regional and world energy markets.
Other governments' actions can affect price and availability in
one's own national market. This is especially the case when
governments agree to take concerted action. For example, a
general understanding among major importers to reject high
priced Iranian oil in late 1979 was a major cause for the reversal
of the crude oil price spiral at that time. In the mid-1970s when
a large importer like the United States (then importing about
8 million barrels per day, and spending about $1.7 billion a
week to do so) failed to reduce its consumption, it exerted
severe upward pressure on prices for all countries. Similarly,
because the USSR is expected to move from a net oil surplus
to an oil deficit in the 1980s or 1990s (though not in gas), its
domestic energy production and allocation policies are now sub-

ject to dramatically increased scrutiny by governments worldwide.
Also, countries are watching to see if France's accelerated
nuclear program succeeds, both for the nuclear lessons it may
bring and because it will reduce future French demand in the
world oil market. The anticipated rise of LDCs to one-third
of the total world market demand concerns all buyers. The
need to know about ones neighbors' energy policies is not
restricted to oil. Recent conflicts in the nuclear area over
uranium supply and the transfer of nuclear technology have
heated tempers and made headlines in Europe, the United States
and the third world. In the latter case of nuclear technology
transfer, West Germany's 1975 decision to sell nuclear plants
to Brazil in the face of considerable U.S. resistance symbolized
the collapse of American domination of the nuclear industry as
much as the 1973 oil embargo demonstrated their decline in oil.
There were serious failures by the Carter administration and
the U.S. Congress to appreciate the international resistance
to what were unilateral U.S. policy moves which affected domestic
energy policy choices in Brazil (and India). The domestic
politics of each country played a key role in the disputes, but
too often government decisions revealed a lack of information
about, and sensitivity to, other countries' energy policies.
In some cases additional information might have made a difference
in the policy eventually implemented (Darmstadter, Dunkerly,
Alterman). In others, additional information could have prepared officials to anticipate the kinds of responses their actions
would provoke. This book helps meet these needs.

Many of these national energy policies are now being watched
by the International Energy Agency. While it is unlikely the
IEA nations will be able to present a united front to OPEC on
oil purchases in the foreseeable future, recognition by each of
the market impacts of the others' actions is a fundamental first
step in this direction. The IEA secretariat in Paris has also
functioned as a clearing house for communicating data on energy
policies between members. Through annual reviews and critiques
of member policies, joint oil import targets and accords on long
term policy goals in areas such as coal use and conservation,
the Agency has provided useful information on trends and new
developments. These can help countries see how potential
policies have fared elsewhere. The example of American restrictions on environmental pollution from energy use and nuclear
safety standards has had a major effect on European thinking.
The London Nuclear Suppliers Agreements and the I.N.F.C.E.
did result in new policies as well as new information. While
the limitations of adapting policies of one nation to another's

energy system are great, the value of the learning process in each country cannot be denied.

The most obvious reason, however, for studying other countries' energy policies is because these misunderstandings tend to create major international tensions. Since 1973 energy policy differences were a major source of friction in themselves, and also fueled disputes in related areas of monetary policy, trade negotiations, and defense policy—especially among the Western allies. Although the intensity has been reduced in part through improved coordination of national policies, the record of misunderstanding and open acrimony over energy policy among the United States, Japan, and Europe since 1973 outweighs the modest cooperation inside the IEA, becoming for a time a leading headache at Western summit meetings. The United States, much more secure in its domestic supplies, accused Europe and Japan of selling out to OPEC blackmail by entering into special "sweetheart" deals. And by the 1980 Ottawa Summit, President Reagan had shifted the attack to a European sellout to the Soviets for gas.

Europeans on the other hand tended during the 1970s to harp about the lack of self-discipline in U.S. energy policy, saying the Americans lacked the political courage to raise domestic prices and cut wasteful consumption. As a side effect, the United States was said to be reaping considerable competitive advantage in lower export prices against other industrial countries by keeping industrial energy costs low (especially in goods like synthetic fibers with high energy content). This general attitude about U.S. policy was tinged by European and Japanese suspicions in the early 1970s that the U.S. State Department acquiesced in the raising of international oil prices, and then invented, through Henry Kissinger, the IEA to block any bilateral deals between Europe and OPEC by inserting a U.S.-dominated agency between them. Ironically, in 1979, when economic events had severely cut U.S. oil consumption, the Americans reversed roles and charged that the Europeans were refusing to set stiff import targets and instead wanted to keep oil consumption up to maintain their economic growth rates.

Suspicions steeped in oil also exist between the oil-importing less developed countries (OILDCs) and the developed "northern" importers. The OILDCs were very dubious of the sudden solicitude shown for their development problems by the north, which was anxious to have southern allies against OPEC. The importing south, reluctant to criticize OPEC suppliers, turned their ire on the north by accusing them of provoking the 1973 oil shock in the first place through their uneven support of Israel over the Arabs, and charging that all countries were now being forced to reap the whirlwind sown by the past unequal structure of the old economic order that vastly favored the rich over the poor. Led by the United States, the industrialized importers also firmly resisted OILDC demands to hold serious negotiations on energy and other development issues. This attitude softened somewhat under Carter; Reagan reasserted a hard line; and there remain considerable differences between the energy positions of the United States, Japan, Western Europe, and the OILDCs.

In revealing testimony to the U.S. Senate Energy Committee in July, 1980 former U.S. Secretary of State Henry Kissinger condemned the Europeans for their special oil deals with OPEC countries which he said not only disrupted the IEA, but also damaged the ability of moderate OPEC members to hold their own against radicals inside the organization. He feared in particular the injection of Middle East political demands into the oil market system, and called for bold U.S. leadership to head off this development. Kissinger's statement amounted to an invitation to all importers to engage in a political test of wills with the exporters, implying that if they lost, the Europeans would still have other options to protect their economies and populations from energy cutbacks. However, our interviews show that these countries, until 1983 heavily dependent on Persian Gulf oil supplies, and lacking large reserves of alternative fuels, believe they would be devastated by a prolonged oil cutback. They are already up against a very hard energy wall. The Europeans and the Japanese and many of the OILDCs simply do not have the range of policy options which Kissinger assumed. President Reagan's opposition to the USSR-Western Europe gas pipeline reflected these differences. It is this crucial need for nations to understand the limits of each other's policy options, and thus the degrees of flexibility they can bring to bear on world energy problems, which our study emphasizes. The lesson can also be a valuable aid to the Americans, who have for years been lambasted because of the Europeans' inability to understand why presidential energy plans do not automatically take effect in the United States once they are announced, but are instead mangled and even demolished by the powerful Congress.

The Kissinger attitude also betrays a deeper division between American and non-American perspectives which goes to the root of energy policy making. The U.S. approaches energy policy with the kind of latitude associated with military policy. If strategic superiority is threatened, one overcomes the threat by either spending more, producing more and/or developing new technology. From President Nixon's pie-in-the-sky "Project Independence" to President Carter's "moral equivalent of war," the attitude has been the same. Americans often supposed the only constraint was one of the national will to act, not the financial, natural, or human resources with which to do so. The American dependence on the free enterprise system for its energy supply (and its huge domestic fuel reserves) fosters this psychological approach with the endless refrain that America's energy problems would be solved if only industry were freed from government interference and allowed to get on with the job. Any time an energy policy fails, a search for scapegoats begins, because the initial assumption is that the problems can be solved with relative ease once, like enemy troops, they are confronted.

The Europeans and other importing countries, on the other hand, seem to view energy policy as a brand of industrial policy to be managed as well as possible given major difficulties. Options for domestic maneuver exist only at the margin, and mainly in the medium to long run. Outside forces such as OPEC and the foreign oil companies severely constrain the range of policy objectives. The goal is not to "win" the energy war, but rather to make whatever national adjustments are possible to ease problems and maintain a minimum of national security. Influencing the energy industry is considered no different than restructuring the automobile industry or aiding economically depressed regions. The Europeans shied away from making oil policy a central part of the Common Market precisely because changing national policies was so difficult. In sum, during the 1970s the Americans have learned through repeated policy failures that they have less control over their energy future than they like to believe, while the Europeans have increasingly tried to exercise more control over theirs. But the two come from very different directions and must recognize this before reaching an understanding on where they both should go.

The Energy Policy Explosion was much more than simply finding a new way to solve old problems. It was more than a quantitative change in the number of new policies. Not only were new policy instruments and governmental entities needed for energy matters, but the very activism of the governments created new public awareness and interest groups. Finally, governments began to find direct linkages between energy and nonenergy matters. Countries were made to reevaluate fundamental issues such as the role of multinational companies, the

value of postwar international alliances, the need for state
enterprise and the proper balance between economic growth
and environmental values. The pervasive, intractable energy
problems forced governments to change significantly their own
concept of their economic and political role. This was a quantum
leap into an unfamiliar area, and there were no easy answers.

The main purpose of this book is to document, compare,
and explain how the oil-importing countries have tried to adapt
to the new oil regime. The book will first examine the policies
used by importing nations to acquire supplies through imports,
and through expanded domestic production. We then study
how governments in the 1970s allocated those supplies. Finally,
we analyze the institutional adaptations that were made.

2

COMMONALITIES
AND DIFFERENCES

INTRODUCTION: WHAT ALL GOVERNMENTS WANT

Whether in Riyadh or Rio, in New York City or Mexico City, two constant themes ran through our interviews with energy officials. The first, a sense of awe at the profound and unanticipated changes that wracked the energy world after 1973. Officials knew they faced a new world after that year, and had to make their peace with it. The second theme, often more implicit, was that national accommodations were very different from country to country. Said one energy ministry official, "Whether we are socialist or capitalist, large or small, we must learn to live with these changes, each in our own way."

In this chapter we show how the international challenges faced by each country were similar, and why different oil importing countries, when faced with this common dilemma, responded with different kinds of public policies.

The demise of the old international oil structure posed common energy problems for the 130-odd countries which imported oil. New and radical external events meant that they could no longer take their energy supply for granted and therefore had to manage carefully both supply and demand. From our interviews and analysis of the documents the following five policy objectives were absolutely central:

> to obtain secure energy supplies from abroad at reasonable prices in the short term while promoting increased domestic production, efficient use and fair allocation of energy in the long term.

29

These five objectives—secure supplies, reasonable prices, increased domestic production, efficient use, fair allocation—may have been present in whole or in part before the 1970s. However, the OPEC revolution made each element of the equation more urgent and forced governments to try to weld them together into a consistent whole. This was no mean feat in the middle of a disruption of the magnitude of OPEC I. Foreign supplies overnight became less secure and prices more volatile. New energy sources had to be developed but were untried and expensive. Conservation, beyond the initial squeezing out of obvious waste, grew more and more costly and the consumer-citizen resisted. Domestic allocation for many countries posed severe problems in emergency situations. Political and economic ends and means merged, and few could sort out the exact short, medium or long term priorities nor say what their social impacts would be.

Each of these objectives represents the adjustments of national policy making to external conditions. This is especially the case for the two shorter term goals—secure foreign supplies and reasonable prices—which presented the most immediate headaches for public officials.

Supply Security

Perhaps the most striking commonality was the intense drive by importer governments to improve short and medium term energy supply security. We treat this extensively in Chapter 4. They pursued this premier goal by seeking more firm arrangements for oil deliveries and by diversifying sources of oil and other imported fuels. This search was initially defensive, aimed at protecting the nation as much as possible from the tumultuous international markets. Eventually it became more active as governments learned more about the working of the market.

All importers faced this dilemma because in the years and months leading up to October 1973 the exporting governments grew keenly aware of the high value of their scarce resources. They grew quite reluctant between 1973 and 1983 to make iron-clad supply deals during volatile periods when price jumps were common. Exporter interests lay in a series of short-term deals to take advantage of and encourage the ratcheting up of oil prices. It was better than being locked into longer term contracts with lower rates of economic return. At the same time, the value of dollars they received for their oil consistently dropped through much of the 1970s, making them even more reluctant to sell through the old term contracts. Finally, the rate of production and exports in many exporter countries has been tied to domestic social demands and OPEC diplomacy, making them more political. The upshot is that the oil-exporting governments were far less willing to provide customers with the long-term concessions and contracts of the past. This too contributed to market instability. The private companies were still able to obtain a large amount of oil from the OPEC producers, but with no guarantee they would continue to receive supplies if it became economically or politically inconvenient for exporter governments to deliver them. The net result was tremendous uncertainty on the part of importer governments.

Realizing this, in the 1973-80 period the majority of oil-importing governments sought out direct bilateral deals with exporter governments, searching for greater energy security. Direct deals became the rage, with high hopes for importer security. They did reduce the intermediary role of the private oil company, and most importer governments, who trust the foreign companies little more than OPEC members, saw this as an advantage. But there were costs too, as we see below. And in the buyer's market after 1982 these deals diminished.

Oil importers also diversified the types of energy imports. Many industrialized countries planned major coal imports from relatively secure areas such as the United States and Australia. Japan, Europe, and the United States took increased volumes of natural gas imports from countries including Algeria, the Soviet Union, and Canada. Even though some of these suppliers were no more dependable than those supplying oil, the mere fact that the gas supplies were only indirectly linked to the oil market made them marginally more attractive.

Besides direct deals with established producers, importer governments tried to increase security of supplies through state-supported exploration for oil in non-OPEC countries. These oil "proliferation" efforts operated on the theory that any new oil find will add to the available world pool of oil and make all efforts to obtain crude somewhat easier and perhaps exert downward pressure on prices. There was ample room as major oil companies devoted only 2.5 percent of exploration activities to non-OPEC developing countries and West African drilling increased partly for this reason as the lessons of OPEC sunk in.

Reasonable Prices

A second commonality among all oil importers was the goal of paying "reasonable prices" for oil imports and to adjust their domestic economies to the new high world market prices. The outflow of money for oil imports has caused severe balance of payments pressures in all importing countries. At the same time the large sums paid to OPEC each year were not available for domestic investment. The tenfold increase in official OPEC prices over the decade (in nominal terms) had a direct impact on oil consumption, raised the price of most alternative fuels and had a ripple effect throughout importer economies causing disruptions and adjustment problems. The situation is similar worldwide since OPEC members have shown little favoritism in oil pricing, giving few major price discounts beyond those demanded by normal commercial practices in glut periods. They have preferred to charge the poorer oil-importing nations the official prices paid by everyone and then grant financial aid to selected countries in a separate operation to help to ease their burden.

In response most governments took the attitude that there was little they could do to avoid the increasing world market prices outside of reducing domestic demand and refusing extortionist-type price offers. Some oil-producing countries such as the United States and Canada tried to shield consumers from the full impact by controling the price of domestically produced oil. But such policies have proven counterproductive and after 1980 were being abandoned. The most successful countries, such as the newly industrializing countries (NICs) adapted by passing through much of the increase directly to consumers in the short term and then revving up their exports to pay for imported oil (World Bank, 1980).

Reduce Import Dependence and Increased
Domestic Production

A third goal shared by all oil importers, which was the mainspring behind long-term energy policy, was the desire eventually to end national dependence on imports of oil and other energy forms by expanding domestic supplies (discussed in Chapter 5). If this was not practical, the goal became cutting imports back to more politically and economically manageable levels. Some countries, blessed with large domestic energy sources, were closer to this ultimate goal than others. But no country was prepared to depend over the long haul on the world market or individual foreign countries to supply energy using the traditional international concept of a division of labor between exporters and importers. The long-term trend everywhere was for governments to push toward greater energy autarky and away from the liberal trading system which existed for several decades. This meant policies to help find new oil, gas, coal, and hydroelectric resources in their own national territories, and also research into and development of new energy forms such as solar energy conversion technologies and synthetic fuels, even though potential domestic production from these sources remained commercially limited.

Efficient Energy Use

A fourth goal (which we take up in Chapter 6) was important economically if ambivalent politically: promoting more efficient energy use. Importing governments tried to eliminate wasteful uses of energy in their economies through price pass-throughs, regulations, and other incentives to consumers to save. Transportation, home heating, and industrial consumption were three key sectors where savings were sought, and in many cases found. In general, any reduction in oil use was translated into a drop in burdensome oil imports. However, in many countries with significant domestic oil production energy officials faced a real political backlash from consumers who felt entitled to reduced prices for their national domestic oil, and who resented the high returns or "obscene profits" that private oil companies gained through unexpected windfall price jumps. This meant price rises, which increased efficient energy use, ran afoul of political demands for price control. Still, this search for efficiency remained the most novel objective of the decade.

Allocation Formula

Once energy is imported or produced domestically all importing governments have a fifth common objective, finding an economically and politically sound formula to allocate supplies inside the country. This too is discussed in Chapter 6 and again in Chapter 7. Domestic groups, whether industries, regions, or government bureaucracies, will seek politically sanctioned advantages in the allocation of energy, either by pricing or direct government mandate. Energy-producing groups will want a higher share of the price paid for energy to be returned to them as profit. All actors promoted their demands by identifying themselves with the "national interest." The fact that a considerable portion of supplies are imported stamps energy politics with a particularly unsteady pattern as officials must jockey between often contradictory international and domestic pressures. Finally, prudence dictates that governments prepare standby plans for allocation and controls on energy during crisis periods when shortages could create a chaotic situation.

This allocation problem has led virtually all oil-importing governments to increase regulation of energy and in many cases to participate in the domestic market as an importer, producer and distributor of fuels. These roles required a buildup everywhere of government energy bureaucracies and semi-independent agencies such as national energy companies and energy advisory boards. This is of course the core of the energy policy explosion. Previously nationalized energy sectors such as coal, gas, and electricity suddenly became much more involved in and important for national energy policy making.

Five main common objectives form a coherent whole which is generally the basis for an overall energy plan. In many ways they are complementary. By becoming direct importers of energy, governments can have increased control over price and allocation. Conservation and new oil finds reduced world price pressure by 1983. At the same time contradictions arise. A government which negotiates relatively stable and cheap supplies may find conservation efforts at home hampered. Failure to find cheap secure supplies may help conservation efforts, but jeopardize domestic political support and stable economic growth. It is easy to answer that the theoretical objective is to find secure imports in the short term and reduce all imports in the long term while achieving a perfectly balanced mix in the medium term. But in real life policies are seldom so discrete and coherent.

Common Concerns

There is a final set of common concerns for all oil importers, based on the character of world oil, which shapes national energy policies and makes life more difficult for government policymakers.

The first is the interaction between national energy policies and the overall health of both the world economy and the domestic economy. In buoyant economic periods oil demand will be high, supplies tight, and prices will tend to rise faster. At the same time countries will find it easier to export products and pay for the increasing oil import bills. In periods of world recession, such as those that followed 1973 and 1979, oil demand slackens and price pressures diminish. However, exports also diminish and countries earn less money to pay for oil imports. In the period after the price surges of 1979, this phenomenon was accompanied by a new trend of high interest rates, which slowed general growth and made it more expensive to buy new energy related equipment.

At the same time energy is only one component among many in a national economy. Energy represents a small part of overall production and consumption in both industrialized and developing economies although that part is very strategic. It is nevertheless not an end in itself (Darmstadter, Dunkerly, Alterman). Governments strive toward a more general, overarching objective of national welfare and security however defined, and they will rise or fall on a wider set of policies. A government may, for example, find that general economic growth is desirable even if it means continuing a high level of energy imports or maintaining foreign political commitments, such as U.S. support for Israel, despite complications for energy policy.

Another common fact of life which had to be addressed by the importer governments was the still considerable influence of the multinational oil companies. They continue to sell a sizable portion of OPEC crude plus large production of their own from non-OPEC areas and remain entrenched in most domestic energy markets through refinery and distribution networks. In the current transition period, with its inherent instability, few countries are either ready or able to replace completely the major oil companies with other arrangements for obtaining and processing crude oil. The oil companies have also been quick to move into other energy fields including coal, gas, nuclear, and solar, often being ready with new energy sources and technology as soon as the price is right. At the same time there is widespread distrust of the private oil companies in almost all importing countries. While governments often share this attitude, they must at the same time deal with the companies, risking political embarrassment.

Another factor faced by all importers in the 1970s was the heightened competition for supplies. This problem, which is implied by the search for autarky in energy policy, was prompted by the decline of the old oil structure based on plentiful supplies and the middleman function of the oil companies. In the tighter energy market of the late 1970s, even at times when short-term supplies are plentiful, each national capital looked carefully, and with good reason, to see what other importing governments were doing. Are they trading in the spot market, building stocks, taxing consumption or developing alternative supplies?

In the past these concerns were less pronounced and when something went wrong, anger was directed more toward oil companies than toward other importer nations. But with the greater direct government involvement in energy, the potential for friction between governments is greater.

The oil companies were indeed for decades a superb buffer for such friction, not only between producer countries and importer countries but among the importers themselves. They functioned to keep all parties at arm's length. The companies supplied the managerial talent to keep oil flowing from where it was produced to where it was refined and consumed. Except in crisis periods, the importing governments needed to do little beyond maintaining "normal" relations with suppliers. This buffer function played a role during the crisis of 1973 when the major companies took it upon themselves, to the relief of most importer governments, to ration out equally to all customers the cutbacks imposed by the Arab producer states. This meant that the United States and the Netherlands, although totally boycotted in theory, received approximately as much OPEC oil as France which maintained good relations with the Arab producers. But since then the buffer role has crumbled, as we explain in detail in Chapter 4. When the 1979 Iranian shutdown occurred, the major companies were caught in the squeeze and could not manage. They were forced to end third party sales in almost all importer countries, driving those governments in many cases to direct dealing with OPEC on a significant scale.

A final common concern, perhaps the most important for policy over the course of the decade, was the volatility in the world oil markets. Price and supply fluctuations had a deleterious effect on public officials' ability to make tough energy decisions that should not be underestimated.

The interaction of these factors—fluctuations, the role of the oil MNCs, heightened international competition, and the interaction of energy and economy—together with the need to meet the common goals listed in section one of this chapter, led to what we have called the Energy Policy Explosion.

The Reasons for National Policy Variety

Despite the common conditions and objectives of importer governments the specific policies adopted by each varied widely. Each country's policies were a unique blend of domestic factors interacting with international market and political conditions. The most important of the domestic factors are the national resource base, the level of economic development, political structures and attitudes, and the geography and climate of the country.

We found to our surprise that the greater the amount and variety of domestic energy resources the more complex and, in many ways, difficult, will be the energy policy-making process. Domestic resources are a boon for energy-hungry nations seeking greater autonomy from troublesome world markets. But they bring their own headaches. Generally, the more resources, the more choices; the more choices of which fuel to develop where, when, and at what price, then the greater the threat of acrimonious and disruptive domestic political conflict. Resource-rich Canada's National Energy Policy is a good example. The presence or absence of resources also greatly affects the national position on international energy issues. France's small resource base and Britain's big oil reserves have certainly shaped these two countries' combative behavior in EEC energy councils.

Politics and economics play their roles. The level of economic development will structure final demand and set the broad outlines of government policies to promote different forms of supply. A higher gross national product (GNP) may enable a country to import more oil at less aggregate costs to other nonenergy sectors of the economy. The political structure can influence policy in several ways as we explain in detail in Chapter 7. The way government structures access to its courts will greatly affect the success of environmental challenges to energy projects. Political rules can allocate more influence to producer or consumer interests; national institutions can simply be inefficient or factionalized, letting energy problems drift. National attitudes about the proper role of government in energy development, and the fundamental issue of whether energy should be considered a public good or an object of private exploitation will vary greatly from country to country. Each country's previous economic experiences and the way its coal, oil, gas, and nuclear industries developed are unique and can also widely vary, especially by the influence exercised by foreign interests. Finally the climate and size of a country will influence for example its transportation infrastructure, its housing stock and heating and cooling needs.

These factors together explain the variety that one finds in the adjustment of oil-importing countries to new international conditions. International shocks will be differently received by each country and be met with different adjustment policies. In these responses importer governments may be genuinely adaptive, making required changes in the organization of their energy sector; or they may be narrowly defensive and blind to opportunities for change. Governments may anticipate and initiate change, as did India and Italy with their early 1970s decision to promote government-to-government oil deals, or Brazil's gasohol projects, or they may steadfastedly refuse to allow external changes to alter their domestic operations, as with U.S. pricing policies through the 1970s. Even among countries with similar economies, as one author noted in discussing the Atlantic Alliance, the common element to most problems is the "delicate interaction between the rigidities of domestic social, political and economic structures and the dictates of the international system" (Makins, 1980, p. 492). These rigidities are usually expressed through politics, and in energy as in other areas what a government can do rests in large measure on what powerful domestic interests will allow it to do before they throw up roadblocks and vetoes. The play of politics largely determines the specific policy mixes that a government will adopt.

International Energy Relations

Not only do countries tend to have rather different policy mixes, but the Energy Policy Explosion in each nation and heightened international energy competition have tended to bring these differences to the fore. The divisions among importers over energy policy, which frequently repeat general political attitudes, have long been present. But energy policy questions since the OPEC revolution have been more urgent, directly affecting important national constituencies, while at the same time having wide international implications. Governments were frequently on the spot and could not wait for an international "consensus" to develop even when countries appeared to have common objectives. In several cases, deep political divisions made it clear such a consensus was unlikely in any case.

International differences and local politics interacted with the M-shaped market fluctuations to make international cooperation difficult among both consumer nations and producer nations, as well as between the two groups.

The possibilities for intragroup cooperation at any given time in the 1970s reflected the current state of the world oil market. From 1970 through 1981 the market was rising, despite a temporary dip in mid-decade. This underlying market pressure made it easier to sustain OPEC unity and reap the benefits. On

the way up there was an expanding pie for the exporters and
serious divisions were few. It is always easier to allocate surpluses than deficits. But for the importers the situation was
reversed. A rising market meant allocating pain, and conflict
abounded between the United States and the Europeans, between
the Japanese and everyone else, and among the Europeans.

In the subsequent falling market of the early 1980s consumer cooperation was much easier, if less necessary, than in
the rising one of the 1970s. Conversely, this was the time when
the exporters needed unity but there was often little to be had.
For them the question was how to allocate cutbacks (and hence
revenue shortfalls) across the 13 OPEC members, and who would
try to enforce the necessary discipline on the group.

Cooperation among the Western oil importers was crippled
immediately after the 1974 embargo by a spectacular fight between France and the United States over the proper approach
toward OPEC and the role of the major oil companies. The
European Common Market, already suffering from a fundamental
dispute between France and West Germany concerning liberal
market versus state-controled energy policy, was weakened
further by the lack of solidarity shown to the Netherlands
during the 1973 boycott and by persistent British demands that
its North Sea oil be treated as a national and not community
resource. The International Energy Agency after almost a
decade of existence, has proven unable to rise beyond its
emergency sharing function and take an activist role toward
OPEC on the basic price and supply issues. Its major achievement during the decade was to arrange a set of oil import targets
for each member and to check members spot market purchases.
The IEA essentially became a diplomatic device for keeping countries talking in civil tones about each other's energy deficiencies.
The IEA has no common energy policies beyond general recom-
mendations which members may or may not accept. In the final
analysis each member was allowed to set its own import target
and decide what policies to use to meet the import goal.

The industrialized and developing oil importers have been
even less effective in defining or meeting common problems.
Discussion about the "new international economic order" became
an awkward and always changing dance of the cranes involving
not only the major importer groups, but also OPEC. The talks
culminated in the 1978 Paris Conference on International Economic
Cooperation which produced many words and virtually no policy
agreement. The collateral talks between OPEC and the OILDCs
produced only slightly more concrete cooperation and at least
momentarily a sense of political solidarity.

We conclude there cannot be a single ideal answer to the many problems raised in each importing country. This book explores differences sytematically without trying to prescribe a single policy approach for all. Instead any national energy policy must be and will be adapted to unique local conditions, politics and social priorities. Our objective is to provide the reader with a clear understanding of the national energy policy processes—supply, allocation, and institutional—in major importer countries. Then and only then can nations consider "borrowing" solutions; then and only then can a carefully constructed international consensus begin to take shape. Indeed, in the key policy division discussed in this book—private company versus state control of oil supply—there may be no common ground. The United States may never be capable of setting up a national oil company just as the Europeans and developing countries may never move to a predominantly private system. This too should be understood by both sides before any real unity can be achieved.

In order to describe the key policy divisions among oil importers it is convenient to break the importers into three groupings: the United States, other industrialized importers, and the developing importers.

Unique Americans

The United States is by far the most unique and perplexing of the three groups and during the decade after the first oil shock it retained, and with the arrival of the Reagan administration reasserted, this uniqueness (Kash and Rycroft 1984). This does not come from its continental size, federal system, or vast bounty of energy resources, features it shares with Canada and Australia. It lies instead in the way that energy is owned in the United States and the way the political system handles it. Virtually nowhere else in the world can a citizen who finds oil, coal, or natural gas on his property take immediate possession of the resource as he sees fit or lease it to an energy company with only minimal interference by the government. In almost all other countries subsoil resources are automatically considered state property.

This system of massive private ownership of energy resources has been upheld for over 100 years by the principal components of the U.S. political system. As a result, private individuals, small companies and large corporations can own and sell energy resources for a profit and the profits in energy have historically been large. These high stakes in the energy arena have in turn led, because of the pluralistic American political system, to the establishment of a powerful pressure group representing the oil companies which can act effectively to protect private energy interests. They have also taken advantage of the political emotions associated with "free enterprise" in the United States to reinforce their position. Aside from wartime or military-related actions there has been no successful attempt to create a national oil, gas, or coal company or find any other systematic way to get government into the fossil fuel business as an actual producer. The federal synfuels corporation, established in legislation passed in 1980, can only own its own production facilities under severely limited, last-resort circumstances, and even this was bitterly opposed by the energy industry. The major exception to this rule is in electric power—the TVA.

The fact that since the 1960s most untapped fossil fuel resources in the United States happen to be on federal property has not affected the dominant private enterprise system. The government continues to grant private firms exploration and production rights on its lands and offshore tracts on a straight business basis, reserving some environmental policing powers but virtually no political control over the use and pricing of the resources. In the electric power and nuclear fields, the federal government does have a limited direct energy production role. But even with the success of agencies like the Tennessee Valley Authority—always the famous example—there is no general move toward government control of the power industry. Government-owned utilities account for a small percentage of total U.S. installed capacity. At the same time proposals have been made to turn the government nuclear fuel enrichment role, which dates back to the Manhattan Project, over to private enterprise.

Alongside this unique system of resource ownership in the United States stands a dense array of public regulations affecting all energy forms which in its own way is equally unique. Other countries, where the government participates directly in energy production, often use regulation as a secondary means to control private energy groups. In the United States, regulation is the principal means of control. As a result, interest groups from environmentalists to Mobil and Exxon wrangle over regulations to gain power in the energy market. A Brookings Institution study of over four decades of U.S. energy policy found that a flight from market forces via regulation has been one of the most frequent strategies of the private sector and public sector alike (Goodwin 1981). As often as not corporate energy interests were able to capture the government agency nominally regulating them to gain stable prices, profits, and markets.

The complexity and arbitrariness of U.S. energy regulations makes them an imperfect if widely used tool. Hammered out between the administration and innumerable congressional committees, regulations are often overly-complex and unwelcomed by industry and the bureaucracies which must carry them out. They are applied in an adversarial fashion and with different degrees of vigor and various interpretations depending on the party in power. Also, since a majority of Americans tend to believe that a deregulated market where private enterprise has a free hand is desirable, regulations are often geared to have an indirect effect. They do not tackle policy problems directly, but try to influence the balance of market forces which will in turn bring about the desired policy objective. This contrasts strongly with the more direct approach to energy control in several other industrialized countries and the developing oil importers.

As a general rule in the United States, the older the energy form the less regulation (Davis 1978). Coal remains basically unregulated except for environmental problems with mining and coal burning. Oil was not regulated until the 1930s when large producers sought production restraints to keep prices up. This was repeated in the 1950s when the domestic producers won rules to limit imports. But more recently oil price and allocation regulation has served to protect consumers and small operators from the large companies. Electric power regulation came with the New Deal and regulation of both the price and transportation of natural gas flowing between states was established in the 1940s. Finally in the 1970s the strong system of nuclear power regulation was established mainly because of safety concerns.

Another key political factor in the way energy decisions are made in the United States is the strong system of constitutional checks and balances. This coupled with the existence of active local pressure groups on all sides of energy issues virtually assures that quick, clean decisions are nearly impossible on major energy problems. If the president makes a proposal, opponents can try often with success to block it in Congress and as a last resort in the courts. In early 1980 for example, Congress and the federal courts were simultaneously the scenes of successful attempts to kill President Carter's oil import fee.

The fact that the private oil companies have such an entrenched position and high stakes in the U.S. energy system adds a ferocity to the energy debates not found in other countries. The debate in the United States during the 1970s over crude oil price controls, for example, often resembled a theological discussion of pure good and pure evil. While the companies were charged with making "obscene profits" and holding back supplies, they in turn charged their critics were trying to dry up U.S. oil production. Our interviews overseas showed that foreigners viewed this endless wrangling as a particularly vivid example of America's inability to formulate energy policy. Recently both the oil companies and the consumer groups have toned down the rhetoric as each has recognized some value in the other's positions, and the post 1981 "glut" dulled public attention. The companies have acknowledged other energy goals besides higher oil and gas production, such as conservation, while consumer groups have recognized that a long term tightening supply situation exists and all shortages are not necessarily contrived. Some learning occurred on both sides, but the current glut has papered over many splits that will be politically rancorous again when the tight market part of the cycle returns.

There are several areas of potential conflict in oil company involvement in other energy activities such as coal, solar and nuclear. The specter of an "energy cartel" has replaced the old "oil trust." At the same time the fundamental issue of whether the oil companies should be treated as public utilities or, in the words of one Texaco executive, as "just another chemical company" has not been resolved. Suggestions for a national oil company to explore on federal lands, a federal oil importing agency or even a system of national chartering of oil companies have not found wide support in Congress. At the same time few Americans would accept the extreme oil company position that the government should leave them alone and trust them to do what is best for the country. This inability to come to grips with the fundamental issues posed by the existence of private companies is a major cause of ambivalence throughout U.S. energy policy.

The other crucial feature about the American energy system is its vast influence on the rest of the world. This is due to both the historic international role of the major American oil companies and to the very substantial amount of U.S. domestic oil production and consumption.

While the United States has been a prime supplier to the world of nuclear technology and uranium enrichment services

and a growing exporter of coal, the greatest impact in the past
and at present is in petroleum. Drilling for oil was invented in
Titusville, Pennsylvania in 1857 and the basic pattern of the
oil industry developed in the United States during the late 19th
century. It was from the start a privately owned affair with
a strong tendency toward monopolistic practices. U.S. influence
spread abroad as John Rockefeller's Standard Oil Company and
later the companies created by the 1911 breakup of the Standard
trust sought export markets and foreign supplies. Up until
World War I the United States was the world's major oil exporter.
As oil was found in colonial areas and Middle Eastern principali-
ties British, Dutch, and French-based companies followed the
U.S. companies into the production and trading business. However, the pattern of operations, both in technical and business
matters, had already been set by the Americans. After World
War I, the U.S.-inspired world trading system, based on the
large Middle Eastern concessions, flourished. By and large
the producers and non-American consumers accepted it. When
countries such as Britain, Norway, and Canada developed oil
resources at home, they adopted domestic arrangements with
industry which did differ from the American model, but these
existed side by side with U.S.-style trading operations.
Mavericks such as Italy's Enrico Mattei carved out special
niches in the system for state-owned companies, but no one
was really "independent" from the prevailing system.

The OPEC revolution presented a successful challenge to
the vast influence of American companies, achieved through a
kind of implicit coalition between exporter country officials and
the management of some of the smaller "independents."

Also, as the single largest consumer of imported oil, the
United States dramatically influenced world oil markets on the
demand side. During the middle 1970s when Europe, largely
due to price pass-throughs, was able to reduce its oil imports
by about 1.5 million barrels per day, the U.S. imports increased
by the same figure, effectively undercutting the potential price
easing that reduced world demand could have achieved.

The United States also exerts great influence in the world
market for nuclear fuels, know-how and equipment. It created
a set of international rules for which it got the concordance of
other industrial nations, and has acted for a generation as the
"enforcer" of last resort of these nuclear rules. As we will see
below, there were very dramatic changes in this world market
caused both by falling demand, supply failures by private firms,
and much greater policy activism by the U.S. Congress. Here
too U.S. power, U.S. policy, and U.S. instruments were unique.

However, despite these American singularities the Americans themselves, for the most part, did not recognize their own uniqueness. They believed that it was the other importers who were out of step when they resorted to the use of state oil companies, government-to-government deals and state participation in offshore oil finds. The Americans considered such moves misguided, inevitably leading to politicization of oil and economic inefficiency. As long as so much of the world's energy supply was effectively controlled by their own major companies, the Americans' faith in their system was not unfounded. But as OPEC and the other importers departed from the old pattern, the American position became more isolated and the chance of international misunderstanding grew apace. This gap between the American and non-American perceptions of reality was one of the basic divisions hindering real accord among the industrial importers on how to deal with OPEC.

The American tendency to see the world from an insular perspective is partially due to the country's bigness and its relative isolation from the push and pull of world economic forces. The foreign trade sector of the overall U.S. economy is a small percentage compared to that of most other countries, and general economic policy making does not turn on it. The U.S. companies have long been major international oil traders, but most of their international business up to the 1970s was selling non-U.S. oil to non-Americans. Oil imports into the United States only became an important factor after 1970 and when the 1973 oil crisis hit most Americans were simply unaware of their growing dependence on foreign supplies. Americans found it hard to accept this situation and adopted a particularly virulent brand of chauvinism in regard to OPEC. Ironically, it is they, not the actually more dependent Europeans, who moan loudest about "oil sheiks" and sport "Let them eat oil" bumper stickers. This coupled with the powerful pro-Israel sentiment in the United States made it nearly impossible for American politicians to take the moderate attitude toward OPEC which would be necessary to bring about a long-term agreement on oil trade.

Ideological differences aside, the United States by its sheer size and vast resources is de facto a key element in any calculation of world energy supply and demand. While the role of the U.S. oil and gas production has diminished, the country remains the world's third leading oil producer. At the same time the U.S. market for oil is the world's largest by a factor of four. Any significant U.S. energy action affects the entire world system. The U.S. decision to restrict the flow of cheap foreign oil into its own market in the 1950s had profound effects on

Europe as the diverted crude hastened the decline of coal and the construction of the European refining industry. In the 1970s, the sudden growth of U.S. oil imports was a major factor in tightening the world market situation. The notion that the United States was "hogging" oil was a key irritant in Western energy relations and weakened the overall U.S. leadership position. By 1984 the readiness of the United States to use its 400-million barrel Strategic Petroleum Reserve, which represented a volume of oil vastly larger than any other private or public reserve in the world, had become a major topic of IEA discussions precisely because of the major effects release of such a stockpile would have worldwide. Starting in the late 1980s the U.S. ability to transform its coal and shale resources into usable alternatives to petroleum may be equally significant.

In summing up the U.S. policy posture based on five key factors the United States has (1) extremely large and varied natural resources which provide wide flexibility in energy development, (2) a narrow range of policy tools which excludes direct participation in oil development by the government and restricts other forms of regulation, (3) an essentially inefficient system for making policy decisions, though one which allows wide participation by interested parties, (4) poor relations with other countries on energy matters due to distrust of OPEC and misunderstanding of policies of other importers, and (5) a generally friendly attitude toward the private multinational oil companies despite public and official fears about company abuses. The combination of these factors means the United States has high confidence in its ability to solve the energy problem by itself using its traditional private enterprise system. It has less inclination to adapt to shifts in the international oil system by changing its own ways of dealing with the outside world on energy. Its oil companies, while losing clout overseas, will probably maintain their political position unless a catastrophe forces the government to take direct control of energy resources and markets.

The Industrialized Importers

The second grouping we deal with in this book is the non-U.S. industrialized importers. (See Kohl, Lindberg, Mendershausen, Nelkin and Pollack.) They include most prominently Japan, West Germany, France, Italy, Canada, Sweden, Benelux, and Britain before 1980, as well as Australia, Denmark, and other smaller consumers like Portugal and Spain. These countries, despite their diverse geographies and resource bases, have several points in common. They are the world's largest energy consumers as a group although none is as big as the United States either in absolute demand or per capita use. They have mineral rights regimes which tend to retain ownership by the state and their mineral leasing laws reinforce this state control. They have mixed energy sectors with major public entities alongside private companies in oil as well as gas, electric power, and coal. Their oil industries have developed as a reaction in one way or another to previous U.S. market dominance and most still have large U.S. company operations inside their borders. They tend to have parliamentary government systems which produce timely energy policy decisions with more ease than the American system and give less opportunity for activity by private pressure groups. Several of these countries, however, have a division of power in energy matters between the central government and regional or provincial governments which cause headaches similar to those in the United States, and at times even greater.

One key tendency of this group is that its members more readily accepted a broad and consistent government role in national energy policy and relations with the oil producers than the Americans. Several of them, including Japan, West Germany, France and Italy who are heavily dependent on imported oil and will be for the foreseeable future, actively avoid strident positions which could interrupt the flow of oil. But even those with substantial domestic resources have come to see OPEC as a necessary component of the world energy market at this time and try to avoid confrontation. They are accustomed to existing in a world market for commodities which they do not control and adapting themselves to its demands. Thus there were few attempts among these countries to prevent the full force of the OPEC price rises from being passed through to consumers during the 1970s. At the same time most of them, including small countries with normally passive import-export policies, set up governmental groups to seek out deals with oil producers. These price and supply policies were adopted without the sort of raw public debate and political trench warfare that either issue would raise in the United States. On the whole these countries see their problems as greater and their options more limited than the Americans. This more scarcity-oriented, pessimistic view has the additional benefit that when things go wrong no public debate is needed, such as occurred during the 1970s in the United States, over whether an energy "crisis" existed in the first place.

This does not mean that nuclear policies were easily implemented by this group. On the contrary, the nuclear politics
of Germany and Britain resemble the partisanship of the United
States. But the big difference lay in petroleum politics and
policy.

On the whole these governments seem to be able to move
quickly on policies affecting external supplies and OPEC relations.
If major energy debates arise they tend to concern domestic
issues such as fuel taxes, the power of national energy companies,
or nuclear power. In countries such as Britain and Canada
with substantial oil resources, questions of how much of the production will be sold abroad and how the revenues from the
resources will be divided up in society also play a big role.
In the non-U.S. industrial countries, once a policy decision
is taken, especially toward outside forces such as OPEC or the
multinational companies, a general national solidarity tends to
build behind it. Government makes policies to protect the local
oil companies and sometimes, as in Italy in the 1960s, it becomes
a patriotic duty to support the national company against foreign
oil groups. In all countries foreigners can become scapegoats.
Psychologically it is always more convenient for the public to
blame problems such as pollution, price gouging, and shortages
on OPEC or the international oil "cartel" than domestic groups.
However, this occurs less in other industrialized importers
than in the United States.

This does not mean the energy policy debate in these
countries is nonpartisan as we see in detail in Chapter 7. For
the most part it is simply carried on within more narrow boundaries and policy is implemented more efficiently. The domestic
financial stakes for private businessmen are smaller, there are
fewer interfuel choices, and a more limited number of avenues
are open for political maneuver. Much day-to-day decision
making is done by the government ministries with intensive
bureaucratic debate. Also, an increasing number of decisions
are made by officials in the semigovernmental energy companies,
usually with ultimate responsibility tied to a government minister.

There are valid questions about whether this dual system
of ministry and state company is in itself efficient. However
this form can vary widely depending on how clearly the role
of each is defined by the particular political system. The interaction of the Italian government with Mattei's ENI would defy
the analytical powers of Machiavelli while the relation of the
British national energy groups to the government seems clear
even in political-transition periods. In most of these countries,
politically controversial energy issues are often decided quickly

and the lengthy debate is stored up for the next parliamentary elections. In extreme, but increasingly frequent cases, a major energy decision can help bring on the elections. This contrasts strongly with the pluralist U.S. system where the president, Congress, bureaucracies, and pressure groups are involved in policy, but no one has decisive power to push programs through.

All countries with discrete, subnational administrative units run into efficiency and political problems. This is especially true in nuclear and environmental matters where state boards and agencies seem to make life difficult for central governments everywhere. A key factor is that in many countries, such as Canada, West Germany, and Australia, subnational units have strong powers in the mineral leasing field and tend to develop their own energy supply programs. Canada's Alberta, with its vast oil and gas wealth, acts like a state within a state in dealing with the federal government in Ottawa on several issues. For example the price of oil and gas flowing over provincial borders is negotiated with the provinces—not decided by the national parliament. The U.S. counterpart to Alberta, Texas, does not have an oil policy in the same sense. It regulates only production rates and leases only land it actually owns. The real battleground for regionalism in U.S. energy politics is Congress where the "sunbelt" and "frostbelt" states often clash on production, taxation, and allocation policies. In several industrial countries the greater attention to energy policy has exacerbated the long-simmering regional issues. The reawakening of Scottish nationalism was fueled by claims to a fair share of the North Sea oil wealth, and energy has played a key role in Canada's ongoing constitutional debate.

In almost all the non-U.S. industrial countries, the system of mineral rights holding gives to the government primary say over exploration and development. Because many countries have so little onshore oil and gas there has been little opposition to laws, in most cases passed after World War II, transferring sweeping rights to governments. Domestic groups have little to lose from government ownership. Some countries such as Canada maintain the U.S.-type system for mineral rights on private property but this is meaningless in practice since only 15 percent of oil-rich Alberta, for example, is considered private property. At the same time all these countries use "discretionary" leasing systems under which the government retains wide supervisory control over drilling operations. They also maintain more flexible tax and royalty systems so they can capture more of the benefit when exploration is successful. Generally, leasing terms are easy until something is found, then they are toughened to suit the situation. This contrasts with the United States where the leasing system is more inflexible and an oil company, after it pays an initial bonus, is protected against confiscation of vast profits if the exploration results in a big find.

In almost all the non-U.S. industrial countries, the political system as a whole accepts the use of state-owned enterprises as a valid public policy tool. Intense political debates, based on classic socialist versus conservative party ideology occasionally occur about the size and influence of such entities in the energy field. But there is a majority opinion across party lines which accepts state enterprises for general policy purposes just as there is a majority in the United States which rejects them, except in very specialized and limited roles. The Conservative government in Britain, which took power in 1979, has not tried to eliminate totally the British National Oil Company, while the short-lived conservative government in Canada in 1980 found dismantling PetroCan an insoluble political problem. Virtually all of the non-U.S. industrial countries which have found substantial oil and gas in their territories have organized state enterprises to fully or partially exploit their resources. In countries with little domestic resources a major incentive to establish such entities has been the weakness of the domestic oil refining and marketing industry in competition with the multinationals. This played a key role in Italy and France in the 1950s and was a major factor in the Japanese government planning in the 1970s which led to the greater government intervention in the private oil market system. Even West Germany, which is inclined to use market instruments when possible, was forced to create a state-backed group, VEBA, in the mid-1970s to retain a minimum 25 percent oil market share under direct national control. By 1960 most European countries had already been forced into heavy state ownership in coal, gas, and power industries due to the need for vigorous industrial reconstruction after World War II.

This group of industrialized importers also shares a similar energy demand pattern which is different both from that of developing importers and the United States. Per capita energy consumption is high but relative to the United States more "efficient." The traditionally high energy costs in Europe and Japan have encouraged the development of an energy-efficient infrastructure. This includes a good public transport, small cars, and a very energy-sensitive industrial sector. Consumer prices, except for subsidized coal and power, tend to be based on world market prices with revenue-raising taxes added on top. At the same time the sophisticated economic structure allows for substantial flexibility in shifting demand among different types of fuels if supplies are available. This structure differs fundamentally from the developing countries which have a much lower per capita income and also less ability to shift demand among fuel sources. The difference with the United States is one of degree. Historically, lower U.S. energy taxes have kept U.S. fuel prices lower and there has been less incentive to use energy sparingly. U.S. gasoline consumption for transportation is particularly conspicuous, outdistancing average per capita consumption in Europe and Japan by a factor of four. Since 1979, when U.S. energy policies began to make prices reflect world market trends, major demand reductions occurred, narrowing the former disparity. On the whole the United States has had more fat to trim and has begun to do so. Thus despite similar national economic structures among industrial countries, the intensity of energy use has differed. Now that conservation has become a direct policy goal for most countries, national differences in per capita consumption rates are narrowing.

The most obvious difference within the group of non-U.S. industrialized importers is domestic supply availability. Some countries have major domestic energy resources to fall back on while others have virtually nothing. As a result, long-term supply strategies differ widely, and these in turn influence allocation and institutional policies. Britain, Canada, and Australia, like the United States, have major coal, oil and gas resources and can pursue energy supply development on several fronts. Others have limited resources such as coal in Germany and gas in Italy and the Netherlands, but not enough to provide real hope of energy independence. A third group including France and Japan have minimal conventional energy resources and must immediately look to nuclear and other alternatives to provide any significant domestic supply input. While most of these countries continue to carry out strong domestic exploration efforts, the potential amount of conventional resources likely to be found is rather low. This forces future planning to be more important and realistic. Especially for the resource-poor countries, the supply options are narrow and there is less margin for experimentation or involvement in questionable projects and technologies. Also tough decisions on nuclear energy cannot be put off. Most governments in this group are involved in development of new technologies, often through state enterprises. Although working mainly from the incentive of promoting national energy policy instead of the pure profit motive, industries in this group have competed with success against U.S.

companies in several fields including liquified natural gas, synthetic fuels, and to a lesser extent nuclear power engineering.

This group also by no means has a uniform view about the role of government in energy policy. While all countries have adopted some form of state participation in the energy industry, the conception of how much leeway should be given for normal market forces in the energy field varies widely. The overall tendency is to leave a large scope for decision making to the market and also to expect the state-owned energy enterprises to respond to market signals and to operate on a traditional profit/loss basis. This is more pronounced in the former British empire countries, Benelux and Germany. In Japan, France, Italy, and other southern European countries state intervention in the normal market system is more accepted and tight controls on fuel marketing to protect local enterprises from outside competition is widespread. Also attitudes toward the major U.S. oil companies differ. The British and Dutch, who provide the home base for two of the "Seven Sisters"—Royal Dutch Shell and British Petroleum—are hardly in a position to condemn the Americans for their activities on international markets. But all countries with resources which American companies are interested in exploiting—either supplies or markets—have grown increasingly wary during the last decade. The Canadians and Australians for example have introduced strong rules governing foreign participation in energy ventures, and the British have kept a tight rein on U.S. company activity in the North Sea. Countries with little domestic oil and gas, where the main activity of American firms is refining and marketing, have tended to become more critical of the companies and offer a stiffer challenge through their own state-owned firms.

The non-U.S. importer states also tend to have differing views on international energy cooperation based on several factors. Oil-rich Britain has been a major stumbling block to energy cooperation in the European Common Market because it fears losing control over North Sea oil. Norway decided to stay out of the EEC altogether in part for the same reason. Britain, however, has been a key member of the IEA, where sovereignty over domestic supplies is not threatened. For years France has sought in vain to get the EEC to adopt a strong system of oil import and marketing controls but has refused to join the IEA because of objections to U.S. international policy. Germany and Japan have cooperated in international energy programs to a point, but have always resisted actions which could adversely affect general economic growth. Germany has also been skeptical of EEC activities to restrain the northern

European spot oil market which is a key supplier to German industry. Each member of the group subscribes politically to general energy cooperation with other members and the United States through the Western economic summits, IEA, and EEC political systems. But all have consciously developed individual relations with OPEC and other suppliers such as Mexico. As yet no country has been willing to depend on joint action with other importers to secure direct oil supplies. They are unlikely to do so until general efforts such as the North/South dialogue or the EEC talks with Arab states begin to show some progress.

In summing up this group we find: (1) resource options vary widely; (2) countries make use of a wide variety of policy tools but tend to be interventionist; (3) the ability of the political system to take decisions on energy policy and carry them out is high; (4) relations with suppliers and other importer nations vary but are generally nonideological and positive; and (5) the private oil companies are tolerated but, except for Britain and the Netherlands, are seen as foreign groups which cannot be trusted in the final analysis to carry forward the national interest. The group is similar to the United States in economic structure but has affinities to the developing importers in use of state enterprises and attitudes toward producers and the multinational companies.

The Developing Oil Importers

The group of approximately 100 developing countries which are oil importers have become increasingly important actors on the world energy scene (World Bank 1983; Dunkerly, Ramsey, Gordon, Cecelski 1981). Now about 12 percent of world oil demand, it is the fastest growing segment of world energy markets. While LDC debt and depression news fills the headlines in the early and mid-1980s, in the post-recession world when the supply-demand situation is likely to be tighter the less developed countries' faster growth rates will make them an important set of actors.

Through the 1970s this group had a faster rate of energy demand growth than did the United States or the other industrialized nations. This growth was all the more dramatic since it occurred despite sharply higher energy prices and supply uncertainty. Between 1973 and 1978 oil consumption in these countries rose from 5.7 million barrels per day to 7.4 million barrels per day despite the price increases.

Because the developing oil importers are clearly a new
and growing factor in the world market, over the 1970s they
have received much more attention from both the industrialized
countries and OPEC. There are several reasons for this new
concern. One (certainly not the only one) was a humanitarian
concern that the poorer of this group were crushed by the oil
bills and hence unable to invest in economic development.
This could lead to a "fourth world" of nations with deepening
stagnation and a potential for escalating violence. A second
is that the LCDs went deep into debt to finance needed imports,
raising fear among governments, commercial banks, and the
I.M.F. that a string of oil-related defaults were just around
the corner, defaults that would rock Western economies. In
1980 for example, the largest LDC importers devoted the following percentages of their total export earnings to oil imports:
Brazil, 51 percent; India, 75 percent; South Korea, 32.2 percent; Thailand, 29.5 percent, and Turkey, 102 percent (Ghadar
1982, p. 12). Third, the more rapid growth of oil consumption
in the LDCs could put real pressure on world prices during a
recovery.

In a longer perspective the third world was also judged
an important factor in future world energy supplies.

Third World Differences and Commonalities

Just as there were differences and similarities within the
industrialized countries, so there are also in the developing
world. For example, Brazil in Latin America and Tanzania in
Africa are very different in many ways, including along our
four energy-relevant dimensions listed above. Tanzania has
few domestic energy resources; Brazil, many. Brazil has a
dynamic economy with a huge industrial sector despite its recession; the Tanzanian one is in a recessionary shambles, over-
whelmingly agricultural, and extremely poor. Brazil has a
federal system, while Tanzania is unitary and centralized.
Brazil alone imports more oil than all of Black Africa.

There are certainly huge disparities in energy consumption
between the rich and the poor countries. Only a handful of
countries are responsible for most of the group's total energy
demand. Brazil, India, Egypt, Mexico, Taiwan, and South
Korea together account for 75 percent of the total rise in LDC
oil consumption between 1974-1978 (Central Intelligence Agency
1979, p. 31). At the same time, combining the annual oil imports
of the 70 poorest developing countries gives an amount roughly

equal to India's annual imports. This means that many of the smallest countries play an insignificant role in world supply-demand balances even though the overall state of that balance can be absolutely critical for their own domestic economies.

In summary we can identify the newly industrialized countries (NICs) like Brazil or Korea, the middle level importers like India at the upper end and Kenya at the lower, and the poorest LDCs like Tanzania. They differ by their economic structure and their size as much as by their domestic energy resources. They will also differ as to the policy problems faced by their governments. This poorest group has little industrial infrastructure, low incomes, poor credit ratings, and small export earnings to pay for oil. They are often victims of deforestation and could benefit more than others from new technology such as solar energy, but lack the wherewithall to launch effective programs. The government role in such countries is especially large in part because of the minimal private markets. These conditions confront officials with limited choices, and very limited policy tools with which to implement public choices.

Still, despite these differences of scale, this group does share certain basic features important for energy policy such as heavy reliance on external loans for oil imports. The domestic energy systems of most developing countries are dualistic and externally dependent, and international oil shocks were received and transmitted to local consumers through this kind of structure. A modern, urban industrial sector dependent on imported oil and coal exists alongside a rural, traditional sector which relies on local noncommercial fuels such as wood, charcoal, and animal wastes. In the latter sector 80 percent or more of the energy will be used for household and subsistence farming purposes. Thus the oil crisis situation familiar in the industrialized world is paralleled and worsened in developing countries by a second crisis—fuelwood. The declining supply of non-renewable fuelwood can have a much greater impact on a rural LDC family's daily habits and economic life than increased oil costs in a modern industrial society. In the Sahel region of Africa, for example, what was once a short walk to find cooking wood may now take a half day.

The two problems—supply of commercial and noncommercial fuels—are directly linked and pose a serious policy question for many developing country governments. As consumers are forced out of the noncommercial fuel by shortages, they will turn to modern fuels, especially kerosene. Such a shift can cause a significant increase in oil demand and create an even greater burden on foreign exchange. But high kerosene prices hike up demand for woodfuels, worsening deforestation and cropland loss. The energy choices are not easy. All developing countries are going through this type of transition and furiously building an oil-based industrial structure. For the larger countries such as Brazil and Korea the process included shifting an existing industrial base from coal to oil. The present group of industrialized countries went through a similar stage of high growth in energy and oil use in the 1950s and 1960s when fuel was very cheap and the transition therefore easier.

Like the industrialized countries, the governments of the developing oil importers have responded to the new world oil market conditions by seeking supply security and price relief from exporters and making some domestic adjustments. However, in many countries policy making is hampered by the underdeveloped state of the governments which have insufficient or inexperienced persons in energy policy positions. The Energy Ministry of Zaire for example had only two trained engineers during the mid-1970s to oversee the entire energy sector. State energy institutions are generally weak and unable to enforce decisions outside the capital city. Thus government-sponsored demand management is problematic. At the same time reliance on the market as a policy instrument is also difficult since markets tend to be very shallow and imperfectly integrated. Also, reliable statistics on both private and public sector are often hard to come by. On the whole, developing country governments try to intervene widely and forcefully in energy matters, but, especially in smaller countries, with little effectiveness. At the same time there is little popular political input into energy policy decisions. Regional political differences can play a major role in policy as will the general balance of priorities inside the government between issues concerning the modern sector and those connected with the subsistence economy.

In most oil-importing developing countries, public ownership of the power subsector and of domestic primary fuel resources is the norm. State control of oil, gas, and coal resources is not a contentious political issue. Instead the key policy question is how much the state should share operations and revenues with private companies, either domestic or international. This is often linked directly to the urgency with which the developing country government wants to exploit potential resources and try to break out of the cycle of increasing dependence on energy imports and crushing foreign exchange costs. The large multinational companies capable of large-scale development projects will seek as liberal an arrangement as possible with host governments and, especially in highly specu-

lative exploration ventures, may refuse altogether if the terms
are too stiff. Trying to develop energy resources without the
aid of Western companies can be a long, painful process as
countries must build up technical expertise and industrial
capacity from scratch, although India has had a fair amount
of success. The World Bank has begun to play a mediator role
in this area, offering developing countries oil and gas exploration funds so that foreign expertise can be used with fewer
strings attached.

The oil-importing developing countries as a group actively
pursue government-to-government deals. This has occurred
across the spectrum from stronger countries like Brazil and
India to poorer ones. Some smaller countries have successfully
negotiated both guaranteed supplies and below-market prices
with oil producers, particularly with those in their region.
Mexico and Venezuela have aided Central American countries
in this way and Nigeria has given special treatment to African
states. The improvement in regional stability helps the oil
producers as well as consumers. Also the developing oil importers as a group have come under consideration by OPEC
for special treatment through loans and grants to help cover
oil bills. In 1980 an OPEC working group had developed a
general system to rank developing countries according to economic strength and to make financing available through a central
OPEC fund. But OPEC-OILDC tensions still remain.

In summing up, the developing importers have (1) a wide
variance in domestic energy resources and, except for the very
advanced, major problems in assuring exploitation of that which
is found; (2) a theoretically wide range of policy tools with a
general tendency toward the politically easier path of direct
state intervention; (3) difficulties in taking policy decisions
and carrying them out due mainly to lack of energy experience
and political cohesion; (4) an "us-against-them" attitude both
toward OPEC and the industrialized importers with some political
solidarity with the producers; and (5) a generally negative
attitude toward the multinational companies who are nevertheless
important in many cases for future energy development. Overall,
political ideologies and attitudes toward OPEC are similar, but
the regional separation and the vast disparities among the
economies of the group make concerted action difficult beyond
the rarified level of third world political forums.

3

ENERGY IMPORTS
AND GOVERNMENT POLICY

I

INTRODUCTION

In the last chapter we saw that officials in importer nations
confronted the same new energy goals irrespective of their
levels of economic development, their governmental systems,
or even their levels of energy production or capacity. Yet
achieving these goals was far more difficult than simply announc-
ing them. And once attention was given to the full problem
the goals were not easy to put in order of priority.

Yet by far the biggest and most immediate headache over
the decade was oil imports. While official concern did eventually
spread to cover production and conservation, the principal
factor driving national concern was the problem of imports,
which was the tail that wagged the energy policy dog. In
this chapter we go into some detail on exactly how importer
governments tried to rank these goals and mesh them into a
coherent whole starting from a basic calculation of import needs
and realities.

With the new post-1973 oil regime, the need to import
energy, especially oil, came to be seen as a political weakness
and an economic liability. Governments were expected to "do
something" about the problem using all available means. For
many countries the fact that oil was their national lifeblood but
remained outside their control, was a profound psychological
shock. Suddenly no country wanted to become more import
dependent without very compelling reasons, and all wanted to
reduce if not eliminate imports. Relying heavily on imports

could still be considered a necessary expedient, but no longer the desirable or neutral policy it once was—before 1973.

This new attitude toward imports held even through the ups and downs of the oil market. This aspect of the Energy Policy Explosion proved quite consistent. When prices fell, public officials continued to key in on this import problem, even if with somewhat less urgency in some countries.

The awakening to this new post-1973 point of view came in two stages for most governments. First payment and price were the principal enemy; that shifted by the end of the decade and security of supply took center stage as concern number one.

At first glance the problem seemed to be mainly a financial one. The 400 percent price rise, not the brief oil supply cut-off, was the focus of governments' attention after 1973-74. They had to cope with economic dislocation due to higher oil costs and the sudden need for more foreign exchange to meet oil bills. Countries with domestic oil production such as the United States, Canada and Australia also acted to hold down by government controls the price of domestic crude to take some edge off the inflationary impact of the OPEC oil supplies and to prevent profit windfalls at home. Several countries also recognized the decisive shift in power over oil supplies and prices toward OPEC and made initial diplomatic and trade adjustments with producers. But there was no mad scramble for supplies because after the brief initial boycott, supplies became easily available and none except the dire pessimists believed a supply squeeze would occur until the late 1980s, if then.

However, at the end of the 1970s the question of security of supply came dramatically to the fore as the key question facing government officials. Security replaced price as the central theme of political speeches, government investigations, and consultants reports. Our interviews with officials during this period revealed a new attitude: almost "oil at any cost." Needless to say, this attitude was not lost on the oil-exporting governments.

What the Iranian crisis and the subsequent confusion showed was that reducing imports to a manageable level was not an isolated oil sector goal; governments had to see cutting oil and other energy dependence as a sine qua non for overall national security as well as economic well-being.

The difficulty before governments was predicting market behavior. There was tremendous apprehension among all importers that the highly charged and hair-trigger period at the top of the oil market in the late 1970s and early 1980s had become a permanent condition. Governments had to act accordingly to take necessary security precautions. And even when

prices started to stabilize and decline in real terms, most governments continued to see the world oil market as a far less dependable mechanism than they once believed and import factors
continued to provide an organizing principal for long term
planning. Some professional economists like M. A. Adelman
railed against the security hysteria, but most officials felt
they could not take the chance of ignoring the security factor
(Adelman 1978). Even when surpluses grew and prices continued to drop after 1982, import concerns continued and
governments maintained many of their special import programs,
which we describe in detail in Chapter 4, such as government-
to-government oil deals and diversifying imports.

Because of these developments, by the end of the 1970s
most consumer countries had devised a definite energy import
strategy. Due to the central role of imports in their energy
balance—providing the missing link between domestic supply
and demand—this import policy usually formed the focal point
of the country's entire energy policy. The public also saw the
problem of reducing imports or continuing to pay high prices
to the OPEC cartel as the main energy issue facing their governments, giving the import policy a basis for popular support.

National import strategies, whether set down in a precise
statement or elaborated piecemeal through separate decisions,
usually contained some or all of the following seven elements.
We present them here in an idealized and sequential fashion:
in real-world situations they may appear sequentially, bunched
up, or only in pieces. This checklist should help correct the
nearly exclusive focus on one or another component of overall
import policy that is found in so much of contemporary writing
on energy policy.

A National Import Strategy

The seven main components of a national import strategy
are:

1. A general calculation of the amount of energy imports
that are desirable given the country's overall economic, political
and resource situation. This might be expressed as an import
target, usually for oil. In 1979 the IEA members formalized
such targets by establishing national oil import "quotas" for
themselves after a long series of negotiations. Besides import
volume targets, several countries and the EEC as a group set
goals for reducing the percentage of imported oil in overall
energy consumption. The French used a monetary quota based

on the annual cost of oil imports. The common denominator in all these was the creation of a measuring stick to guide import policy and gauge its success.

2. A series of general policy measures designed to reduce overall energy demand and/or increase domestic supply. In this way the government hoped to manipulate domestic energy production and domestic demand so that the gap left between them matched the desired import level. In most cases the mainspring of these general policies was to be the market effect of rising energy prices which directly encouraged conservation and domestic energy production. Government policies then normally enhance this impact or make corrections where the market is somehow distorted, since most governments feel that price alone will not provide enough incentive for desired outcomes. Such measures included special incentives for oil, gas, and coal production, fuel taxes to discourage consumption, incentives for consumer conservation, and switching to domestically available fuels. Probably the key initial decision by any government is whether to let the international price levels for oil and other fuels prevail. The link to import policy may not be explicit in these policies, but in some countries the connection was made clear for political reasons. In the United States during the four years of the Carter administration virtually every energy policy put forward was accompanied by a well publicized calculation, not necessarily dependable, of how many barrels of imported oil would be saved by carrying it out.

3. Measures to directly influence energy movements across national borders, discouraging or encouraging imports and exports depending on specific policy goals. These measures, which supplement the general energy policies by providing a more direct means of control, included import taxes and quotas to force consumption down and prohibitions or taxes on exports of domestic energy supplies. Export restrictions are generally popular since the government is seen protecting the national energy endowment by keeping it at home. Taxes and quotas on imports are usually unpopular since by definition they cause instant economic dislocations. While governments frequently discuss such moves, they are hesitant to really take action unless forced by a crisis situation. President Carter's politically disastrous attempt to impose a fee on oil imports in March 1979 was a grim warning to any government considering such plans.

4. Direct actions to insure that the amount of imports needed by a country will be available from producing countries. This especially pertains to oil supplies which are the most vital for day-to-day economic activity and also the most prone to disruptions and cutbacks. Policy in this area begins with a

judgment of how much of a country's needs can be reliably met
by the traditional supplier role of the major oil companies.
Based on this, governments make direct contacts with producer
governments to assure access to oil supplies. This frequently
occurs through the national oil companies of consumer countries
which are deliberately built up to compete in world petroleum
markets and carry out special deals. Also in this category are
general diplomatic actions and contacts designed to maintain
friendly relations with producers, avoid boycotts, and pave
the way for direct deals. Consumer countries also must carry
out what amounts to diplomatic relations with the international
oil companies to maintain as much as possible their share of the
companies' worldwide pool of oil and force local subsidiaries of
the majors to act in the national interest of the host country.

5. Cooperation among consumer countries to protect themselves as much as possible from the effects of sudden supply
cutoffs and price rises. These policies are based on domestic
planning for short-term crises as well as longer term diplomatic
strategy. The major Western consumer nations established
emergency oil sharing schemes in both the IEA and the EEC,
in which existing supplies would be pooled in a major shortfall
situation. These systems in effect create a political framework
to replace in a grave emergency the informal apportionment
system carried out by the major oil companies in October 1973
and subsequent shortages. In noncrisis situations this sort of
consumer cooperation includes actions to provide oil for countries
with local shortages, monitor international spot markets, and
pressure consumer countries to avoid expensive spot market
purchases which could drive up prices. In the third world,
the Association of Southeast Asian Nations and the Latin American
Organization for Energy Development have moved toward similar
consumer cooperation. Also, on a long-term basis, the consumer
countries have made very tentative efforts to arrive at a common
diplomatic position among themselves vis-à-vis OPEC which would
allow eventual multilateral talks on oil supplies and prices. So
far, such efforts have failed because of a lack of agreement
among Western consumers and an ongoing fear on the part of
the developing oil consumers to align themselves with the developed consumers.

6. Measures to insure that the country will have the financial resources available to pay for oil imports. This problem
is especially critical in developing countries where energy imports
can form a substantial part of total imports and where export
earnings can be dependent on unstable commodity markets.
However, the oil payments problem has forced all consumer

countries to become more export conscious and find ways to cover the large payments made to suppliers. For countries with major indebtedness problems, especially among developing countries, this side of import policy generally included reliance on large international loans and credit from the International Monetary Fund and other agencies.

7. Efforts to diversify the sources of oil imports to reduce reliance on present suppliers and to encourage imports of other fuels besides oil. One facet of this is government promotion of oil exploration and production in non-OPEC foreign countries usually by consumer-government supported national oil companies or through international financial agencies. Such efforts expand the overall world oil supply and give a chance for sponsor countries to win ground floor concessions from emerging oil producers, even though these may turn out to be of limited value in providing a long-term steady flow of oil.

Most consumer countries have developed plans to diversify fuel use and import other energy forms including coal, natural gas, and uranium. All these fuels present some drawbacks compared to oil. They can be less flexible to use, harder to transport, and pose major environmental and safety problems. Frequently they come from sources no more reliable than the major oil exporters. But they offer the advantage of not being directly linked to the volatile world oil market and thus are not likely to be dramatically affected during an oil crisis or a long-term tightening of the oil market. In all diversification policies the common aim is to spread out as much as possible the many risks inherent in energy imports.

THE SEARCH FOR POLICY INTEGRATION
AND COHERENCE

Long Term Versus Short, Domestic Versus International

Comparison of the above points reveals that any national energy import strategy operates in a variety of time frames and toward a variety of domestic and international goals. In general the first three points are aimed at eliminating oil imports or keeping them as low as possible. They are generally domestically oriented and long-term in nature.

The second four points mainly attempt to obtain necessary imports, acknowledging the crucial part they play in the nation's day-to-day existence. They are usually internationally oriented and tend to be short and medium term. The two halves of the strategy equation are not contradictory in principle. A well balanced energy import policy can and should accommodate both without confusion. But the vagaries of real-life political and economic events make it rare for energy policy to develop in a rational progression. We will next examine the potential contradictions among the various policy points, stressing the importance of maintaining distinctions among the components of import strategy. The remainder of this chapter will then examine in detail the first three points—import targets, general policy measures, and specific import and export controls. In Chapter 4 we examine the critical and difficult short term policies of arranging immediate imports, especially through government-to-government transactions. Countries tend to vary in their relative emphasis on domestic or international policies to form their energy import strategies, depending primarily on the key factors pointed out in Chapter 2—such as availability of domestic resources and relationship to the major oil companies. Countries with major domestic resources such as the United States, Britain, and Canada have been less vociferously pro-OPEC. They have tended to rely more on domestic measures to enhance home production and discourage export of needed energy resources as the main approach to import strategy. They still can depend on substantial supplies for home consumption, despite the loss of ownership rights to production in most overseas countries. U.S. and British officials have made virtually no attempts to win specific supply guarantees from OPEC countries in the post-1973 period, instead fighting a rear guard action to preserve "friendly" operating conditions for their private companies where possible. Despite the major blow to British and American efforts in this regard caused by the fall of the Shah of Iran, the Americans have maintained a crucial supply line through the ARAMCO arrangement with Saudi Arabia. This situation also colors the view these countries take of the IEA, making it mainly a means to preserve the overall status quo including the position of the major oil companies and to influence other consumer countries which might be more inclined to pursue different, government-to-government strategies.

Countries without large resource bases and with less established links to the major companies have tended to put a higher priority on short-term international actions to secure supplies and diversify sources. Countries like France, Japan, West Germany, Italy, and most developing countries have had little choice but to seek direct deals for their growing national oil companies. This has forced them to be more attentive to day-to-day political demands of OPEC members and the general vicissitudes of the world oil supply system. Experiences such as those of Japan in 1979, losing one-third of its foreign oil supply when major companies cut back third party sales to cover Iranian losses, or France in 1980 seeing an Iraqi commitment for 400,000 barrel a day dissolve due to the Iraq-Iran war, force policymakers to focus on short-term supply issues. Without back-up domestic resources the response can only be more pursuit of elusive foreign supplies. The IEA is either not much trusted as in the French case, or seen as an unproven backstop in an overwhelming crisis. The pressures on these countries due to their more tenuous foreign supply situation can give powerful impetus to domestic measures to find new energy sources. The French and to a lesser extent the Germans have grimly stuck to their nuclear energy development programs because they feel there is little else they can do in the long run domestically to make a major difference in demand levels and thus imports.

The ability to carry out an activist import policy will also be affected by other factors. A country needs a credible national agency, whether a government office or national oil company, to carry out an oil or gas importing program independent of the major companies. This in turn requires a tradition of political consensus which encourages government involvement in the oil business. The Americans have no agency to carry out a major crude import program and proposals to create such a body, routinely made by liberal Democrats and trade unions, are immediately embroiled in ideological battles and make no progress. Also a country must have an infrastructure to handle crude purchases, or be able to negotiate deals to process crude in foreign refineries.

Domestic Implications

On the domestic side, the core of the public energy debate hinges on the various opinions on how to reduce imports. As we discuss in Chapter 7, consumer groups and the public will oppose stiff taxes and seek some protection from world oil price rises. Governments will welcome the direct pass-through of real market costs as a means to induce conservation, but may be forced to use controls to curb inflationary or equity side effects. In cases where the economic system is already tightly controlled, world market pricing can cause problems. In 1979 a revolt erupted in the Sudan when President Nemeiry permitted an oil price rise, and his order was soon rescinded.

Finally the general public expects the government to reduce imports and break the supposed grip of foreign oil producers on the domestic economy. In general, energy targets and plans got a positive public reception but follow-through measures which demand actual sacrifice to attain import reductions were less welcome. Also if the government had to bow to political pressure from one of the above groups and pull back from an earlier target or promise, public criticism was likely to be intense. The general feeling in the United States that President Carter "failed" to handle the energy situation persisted mainly because imports refused to drop substantially until almost the end of his term. In fact Carter, in a zigzag fashion, had developed a set of major compromises between key interest groups which opened the way for the more-or-less manageable import situation by 1981.

International Implications

A government's selection of one international energy strategy over another can also become highly politicized at home. At the same time it forms one of the fundamental divisions among the various consumer governments. On the domestic scene governments are judged closely on whether they can deal effectively with OPEC and they can be burned just as easily by giving in too much to oil producers (or too publicly) on price or politics or alternatively by failing to handle the producers diplomatically and thus losing supplies. In 1980 when Colonel Qaddafi announced that ELF-Aquitaine had been granted oil exploration leases in Libya within days of his disputed "annexation" of part of neighboring Chad, the French cabinet felt it necessary to order work on the leases "deferred" to avoid giving the impression of a French-Libyan political deal. The French press nevertheless roundly accused the government of muting criticism of the Libya-Chad fusion in exchange for exploration rights. Interviews we conducted in Paris at the time confirmed French government efforts to avoid undue domestic criticism on this international oil deal. The injection of the Arab-Israeli dispute into oil deals also causes frequent headaches back home for politicians and not just in the United States where the pro-Israel lobby is active and influential. In 1981, West Germany sought firmer ties with Saudi Arabia to assure substantial oil supplies but agonized mightily over sales of weapons to the Saudis which might be used against Israel. In part due to the war guilt issue, Chancellor Schmidt finally turned down such sales in May 1981 during a dramatic visit to Riyadh.

At the same time if the importing government decides to move toward more government control over import deals through a public agency or national oil company, a major and potentially divisive debate over public versus private enterprises can easily occur at home as has occurred in Kenya, Korea, and the United States. Also the oil import activity of ENI has caused a major political scandal in Italy because of mysterious commissions on deals. Finally if the importing government decides to remain dependent for supplies on the major companies, criticism will tend to be particularly intense if the companies do not come through with necessary supplies and are seen acting against the national interest. The policy of diversifying fuel imports can also become a major political issue because of the dangers and pollution potential of liquified gas, nuclear energy, and coal. Thus, we find that the import problems cut both into domestic as well as international policy imperatives. Nationally the choice of strategies almost inevitably puts government officials in a squeeze between the producers, the large companies, and the U.S. government with its staunch pro-IEA, anti-special deals attitude. Domestically, different policies will hurt or help different sectors and constituencies as we see in Chapter 7.

In the following two chapters we pursue these themes by concentrating first, in Chapter 4, on government import strategies, and then in Chapter 5, government policies to promote more domestic energy production.

II

Energy Imports from Guestimates to Targets

In 1973 when the problem of high-priced OPEC oil hit the importer governments, few had any real experience with energy import planning. The Americans had gone through a series of reviews of oil import policy during the 1950s and 1960s which formed the underpinning for the oil import quota system which was in effect in one form or another from 1956 to 1973. The focus of these reviews was the impact on national security and domestic production of then low-priced Arabian crude. For other nations energy planning by governments focused on other things besides oil imports except in the immediate postwar period where getting and paying for oil imports with scarce hard currency became a major concern. Several countries periodically produced plans and targets for reduction or stabilizing coal production and some like Britain in 1967 made a major effort to

decide whether nuclear power was really needed. Oil figured
in these as the key substitute fuel with which coal and nuclear
energy had to compete to survive, but since oil was cheap and
easy to get, no specific oil import plan was needed.

During late 1973 and early 1974 oil imports suddenly became
the focus of attention, but governments in general had very
little grasp on the fundamentals of the new energy situation
and were not prepared for import planning. Instead reports
and studies simply drew rough pictures of how much imported
oil was being consumed at present, how much would be needed
in the coming 10 or 15 years, and what it would cost at the
new price levels. For most countries the rapid first glance was
appalling. The projections assumed continued high economic
growth, and thus foresaw continued high levels of oil consumption which would be intolerably expensive at the new price
levels. The growth-energy ratio was erroneously assumed to
be constant.

There were other miscalculations which affected this
pessimistic picture, especially hopes for a major contribution
by nuclear energy to replace oil by the early 1980s, as well
as some pure wishful thinking. The U.S. administration, for
example, reacted to the 1973 events by declaring that through
its grandiose "Project Independence," oil imports could be cut
to zero by 1980. By 1974, this objective was quietly discarded
as import trends moved in the opposite direction. The euphoria
of "Project Independence," however, remained in the public mind
and forced the Carter administration to launch its much less
ambitious energy plan in 1977 with what amounted to scare
tactics about imports to force a public awakening. The key
tool was a very pessimistic CIA report on the world oil outlook,
leaked by top energy adviser and ex-CIA chief James Schlesinger
two days before the plan itself was announced. In 1981 the CIA
openly admitted its bleak prediction of falling Soviet oil production by the early 1980s was mistaken and therefore its entire
shortage scenario was overdrawn.

The two key problems with most energy predictions during
the mid-1970s was overestimation of demand due to the failure
to foresee the conservation effects of higher prices and the unanticipated world recession. This was an underestimation of
the demand elasticity in the face of much higher prices. A
comparison of official U.S. government reports on energy trends
published from 1976 to 1980 shows a steady decline in demand
predictions for the 1985-to-2000 period as awareness of these
features sunk in. Despite the fact that domestic supply was
also generally overestimated because of the new optimism over

nuclear energy in most national plans, the general effect was
to predict a wide gap between total demand and home supply
which meant a relatively high demand for imports. Early in
the decade these high import predictions were not targets,
but instead benchmarks of what would happen if no action were
taken. Later on, when governments had developed a better
sense of what policy actions to reduce imports were feasible,
they created targets with government actions factored in. The
actual plans to reduce imports were frequently wish-lists and
were not fully implemented, when targets were met it was
generally due mostly to changes in underlying trends.

Among consumer countries, the Americans with their wildly
careening energy politics in the 1970s were among the vaguest
on import predictions. The developing countries, many of whom
lacked the managerial wherewithal to make serious projections
and who had the most volatile oil import patterns because of
the high growth rates, also missed widely. The main exceptions
in this tendency to vagueness were the French and the Commission of the European Communities. Both very early on proposed
specific targets for oil imports based more or less on dependable
projections. Also the British, who by 1974 were busily planning
how to exploit their North Sea oil wealth, were in a position to
make reasonably sound import projections based on a gradual
move to self-sufficiency by the early 1980s.

The French government starting in 1975 established yearly
targets for oil imports based on the cost for imports in French
francs for the full year. The 1975 target was 51 billion francs
gradually rising to 58 billion by 1979. Though dubbed "quotas,"
the import figures were really targets for use by the French
official planning machinery. The government, through its tight
controls on oil movements, had the power to enforce the targets
if it wanted to, but it never did. In 1976 a severe drought
reduced Franch hydroelectric output and the government
officially upped the annual oil import target from 51 billion to
53 billion francs late in the year to accommodate the needed
increase in oil use. The target for 1977 was raised to 55 billion
francs to adjust for OPEC price hikes, but the actual oil costs
came in more than 1 billion francs below the target. In 1978
the same pattern prevailed as monetary market shifts reduced
oil costs to France causing the target to turn out too high.
The actual amounts of French oil imports dropped from the 1973
level of 2.6 million to 2.2-million barrels a day by 1979. This
is approximately the same import trend observed in most major
European importing countries and thus it is difficult to make
the argument the target system actually imposed a discipline on
French consumption.

The Commission of the European Common Market moved very quickly after the 1973 crisis and by May 1974 had proposed a set of targets for the Community as a whole designed to drop dependence on energy imports from 61 percent to 40 percent by 1985. The ambitious plan was trimmed by the nine members of the Community in December 1974 when they agreed on a target of 50 percent dependence by 1985. The Community targets did not contain specific objectives for each member government since the members feared that adherence to a fixed target level of oil use could mean a sacrifice of economic growth. If that situation arose, few governments would stick with the target, so they believed it better not to be pinned down to one in the first place. Through the decade import targets in both the EEC and IEA remained joint targets. By 1979, however, the Western consuming nations reached the point in the wake of the Iranian scare where they did agree to individual import goals as part of an overall international arrangement. Nevertheless the targets remain an attention-getting device to warn of a dangerous trend; they were never implemented by direct government policies.

After the first shock in 1973-1974, import volumes for most consuming countries stabilized because of the price rise, recession, and short-term boycott. By 1977 however, actual import trends once more began to move up, seeming to fulfill dire long term projections. In January the IEA secretariat reported that little real progress was being made in cutting oil imports due to the slowdown of nuclear energy, the weak dollar which made oil relatively cheap in Europe, and the U.S. price controls which encouraged overconsumption there. The IEA said the group's total oil imports, which were 24.3 million b/d in 1975, could climb to 35 million b/d by 1985. In February the EEC Commission reported that its target of reducing energy imports to 50 percent of total consumption by 1985 would not be met and that the nine would be lucky to reach 55 percent. Events proved these wildly pessimistic but at that point no one foresaw a sudden oil price jump from $13/barrels to $40/barrels.

Because of these problems, several nations began revising their energy plans in 1977. The West Germans produced the "Revision of the 1974 energy plan" which aimed for a more restrictive growth of imports but also took a much more realistic view of the limits of nuclear power. The Japanese produced a major new energy plan designed to greatly increase conservation efforts and hold 1985 imports to a level about 15 percent below previous projection. The new American administration of President Carter came out with its initial "national energy plan"

which was designed to roll back the recent increases in U.S.
oil imports which had become a major irritant to Europe. Carter
hoped to cut 6 million b/d from projected U.S. imports of 10
million b/d by 1985. As the countries moved ahead with these
individual planning actions they also began to take planning
as a group more seriously. In 1975, when the IEA had just
been organized members took an informal pledge to immediately
cut total imports by 2 million b/d, but this has faded fast in
the face of mounting U.S. imports. Carter, seeking international
support for his tough energy plan, pushed for a more disciplined
IEA action and by June 1977 an informal accord was reached on
a target of 26 million b/d oil imports for the entire group by
1985. No individual targets were set but it was understood
the United States would account for half of the savings needed
in the projected level for that date of 35 million b/d. The
system of yearly reviews of each country's policies was started
to check on progress toward targets.

In 1978 the tables turned on the United States as Carter's
crude oil equalization tax failed in Congress along with a standby
gasoline tax plan. The Europeans began to use the joint import
targets as a weapon to pressure the American president into
another effort to end oil price controls and thus reduce imports.
In June the EEC countries agreed on a pledge to hold 1985
imports to 1978 levels and challenged Carter to do the same at
the July summit in Bremen. Carter promised to produce a plan
to cut the U.S. imports by 2.5 million b/d by 1985 which eventually emerged as the phased-in oil decontrol proposal, put
into effect in May 1979 and accelerated by President Reagan
later on. By early 1979, however, the Iranian revolution had put
a scare into all consumer governments and finally opened the
way for broad international agreements on specific short term
oil import targets.

In March 1979, the IEA board asked members to undertake
a crash program to cut 2 million b/d of 1979 import levels.
This swiftly conceived effort which amount to a 5 percent cutback eventually proved unattainable in most countries and had
become a dead letter by the end of the year. At the same time,
however, a concerted diplomatic push developed to set specific
import targets for 1980 and at the Tokyo summit in June the
major Western nations agreed to targets. The summit accord
among the seven major nations paved the way for agreements
on individual country targets both in the EEC and the IEA by
December. The targets remained only a set of planning objectives
and the only enforcement power came from the fact that any
nation exceeding its allotted target would be severely criticized

by the other IEA members especially if the sudden increases appeared due to hoarding.

The Americans, by late 1979, had transformed themselves into champions of import targets, especially since they were active in dissuading other countries from rushing headlong into unwelcome deals with OPEC governments. In early 1980 the United States tried to put some teeth into the system by proposing automatic downward adjustments of the targets based on conservation efforts and the emerging market trend of dropping import levels. This attempt stalled however. Most IEA member's imports were lower than the IEA country targets in 1980 because of the sudden fall off in demand for oil at the new high price, but governments believed it wiser to leave the targets alone just in case a sudden economic resurgence pushed up imports. At the same time the more stable oil market situation by late 1980, when the sharp losses of the Iran-Iraq war had been overcome, once again lulled consumer countries into the attitude that the energy situation was taking care of itself. Import targets and quotas were invoked infrequently. Even massive purchases by the United States for its strategic oil reserve went ahead with little comment from other consumers who two years ago had feared such an action would destabilize world markets.

DOMESTIC POLICY ACTIONS

After 1973, when domestic energy plans began to be formulated, the natural focus was on reducing oil imports. But policymakers were only dimly aware of the difficulties of reducing oil use, and thus imports, in complex societies through regulation and government incentives. The initial programs were timid and did not in themselves bring substantial identifiable results in cutting imports in the short term. At the same time the market forces based on the relative oil price had a surprisingly strong effect on consumption and imports in the short term. In general the OPEC price rises in 1973 and 1979, tempered by a period of real price drops for oil in between due to the weak dollar, were the key determinants of oil import levels, with governmental policies relating to conservation, rational use of energy and development of alternative sources playing a marginal but important role through the decade. In the mid and late 1980s however, such policy programs initiated by governments in the 1970s should bear results and become even more significant. In general terms oil imports had dropped by 1979 below

1973 levels in most developed countries and no further growth in imports was expected between 1980 and 1985 even with renewed economic growth. At the same time virtually all countries had recorded some growth in total energy consumption, creating a clear trend toward less dependence on oil, and substitution of other energy sources.

The single most effective short term policy that government officials have used to reduce imports in the post-1973 period was simply to let oil prices rise, based on world market trends. In principal, countries with high import levels had little long-term alternative to this policy since their oil supply has to be purchased abroad for its full market value and this cost is naturally passed on to the ultimate consumer. However, many countries held national prices well below world levels. Such countries, especially those with a tradition of government control of prices like France and Italy, frequently keep a hand in oil pricing by controlling refiner margins, as we discuss in Chapter 6. Some attempts to hold prices low led to disputes with the major oil companies and a potential loss of supply. By contrast, countries with substantial domestic energy resources can hold down the domestic component of the total energy cost by artificial means, but they cannot control foreign supplies. Such domestic price controls may be useful in the short run to fight inflation and soothe public concerns about windfall profits but they can cause more long term problems than they are worth. These problems will be discussed in Chapter 6.

The strong conservation and thus import dampening effect of higher energy prices was not evident through most of the 1970s and only became a dominant factor at the end of the decade when oil prices had risen over 1000 percent compared to the pre-1973 period. In comparison to this, direct government policies to drop long term demand or solve acute oil import shortages have proven less effective unless supported by the underlying market situation. Government drives to reduce imports through conservation and enhanced supply policies tended to follow a cycle in which long term programs are begun and stepped up on a crash basis when an oil shortage suddenly develops, a reflection of the cyclical market trends.

Direct Controls on Imports and Exports

Governments have imposed direct controls and fees or tariffs on energy imports for several decades for various policy reasons. Up until 1973 the main objective of such controls has been to protect a domestic coal or oil industry against cheap foreign energy supplies, especially oil. Also governments have regulated imports to insure deliveries of oil from a specific foreign source or a colonial area controlled by the consuming government. Controls on energy imports have also been used as a means of controling foreign exchange outflows in periods of currency shortage like that following World War II. Finally some countries like France, Brazil, Spain, and Japan have controlled who has the right to import oil as a means of controlling the domestic petroleum market itself. Generally these controls did not serve to implement established energy plans, but instead were means to carry out separate industrial or financial policies.

The foremost example of this traditional type of control was the American oil import quota system which was in effect on either a voluntary or mandatory basis between 1956 and 1973. The quotas, which fluctuated between 9 percent and 12 percent of U.S. consumption were mainly used as a means to protect the domestic oil industry from being forced off the market by cheap foreign oil. The basic effect was to insure that prevailing U.S. crude oil prices did not drop below a minimum of about $3/bbl. The protection was made politically acceptable by the controversial notion that it contributed to national security by preserving a strong domestic petroleum industry. The quota system was enforced by issuing import tickets which gave the holder the right to import a certain volume of oil. These tickets, assigned under a complex system of grandfather rights, became a powerful policy tool for officials of the Interior Department which controlled distribution. They were used for launching new refineries in selected areas for various political and social purposes. The U.S. quota system was thus an industrial policy brought on by the existence of a large domestic oil industry with a very powerful lobby in Washington. Its geopolitical aspects were secondary when it was being implemented but its effects on future energy policies worldwide were enormous. The quotas created the economic climate which produced the Alaskan oil finds of the 1960s which in turn played a key role in slowing the U.S. production decline in the mid-1970s. The high (for that time) oil prices also encouraged a massive switch in the United States to gas. The quotas also forced cheap Middle Eastern crude onto European markets. This hastened the decline of coal production, initiated Europe's heavy reliance on oil imports, and eventually loosened the grip of the major companies on the European market as the oil glut spawned competitors.

The main user of quotas and tariffs in Europe to protect domestic coal production during this period was West Germany.

The Germans instituted oil and coal import quotas and then charged a tariff premium for further imports. In the mid-1960s Bonn abandoned this approach because of Common Market trade rules and shifted to heavy domestic taxation of heating oil and fuel oil to prop up coal. The question of coal protection was a major economic issue for a decade as the coal industry and unions fought inside the German government against other economic groups which wanted cheap oil to fuel the nation's economic boom. The eventual winners were the cheap oil forces who insured that the protection was never enough to cause real economic damage. Japan also instituted a substantial tariff on crude oil to protect its weak coal industry using the proceeds from the import tax to pay coal-mining subsidies. Because of this fiscal link, the Japanese crude tariff remained in place through the 1970s and has been put to new uses. Tariffs on imports of refined products, unlike crude oil levies and quotas, are a universal phenomenon, used by most countries with refining capacity to protect the home processing industry. The creation of the Common Market brought with it an elimination of such barriers inside Europe. This boosted the position of the Rotterdam oil market as the hub or "turntable" supplier for all Northern Europe and also encouraged a major Italian export refining industry.

The OPEC oil price revolution of 1973 caused major changes in the approach importer governments took toward control over energy imports and exports. The new, high oil prices meant domestic energy industries did not need protection since oil was now much more expensive than coal. Thus controls and tariffs on crude oil and coal were generally unnecessary. However, the oil price rise and slowdown of growth in product demand created immediate overcapacity in the refinery sector, so tariffs on oil products remained in place. The drive by OPEC to increase its downstream operations and provide finished oil products instead of just crude oil to importing countries gave product tariffs further importance. The Common Market on several occasions considered using proposals to give special reductions in oil product tariffs to certain OPEC countries as part of a deal in which European companies would participate in refining ventures in the producer countries. The poor health of the home refining industry, however, made agreement of such concessions among the nine virtually impossible. A key victim of this indecision was the German-Iranian refinery complex planned for Bushir. The United States had maintained only minimal tariffs on refined product imports during the 1970s since the price control scheme in place there served indirectly as a protectionist instrument for refineries. But, with the end of controls in 1981, the product tariff was a possible option for the Reagan administration as it attempted to formulate refinery policy.

Also after 1973 importer governments started to develop new, clearly defined energy strategies and they found that traditional controls on cross-border energy movements suddenly had several new uses.

Countries with domestic energy production took actions to insure that their energy resources were used at home unless it was clearly more advantageous to export them for reasons of regional or fuel balance, or to earn foreign exchange. These actions included direct bans or taxes on exports as well as monitoring policies under which energy exports needed government approval to take place.

Additionally, countries seeking to adjust demand to policy guidelines considered import controls to force reduced consumption of a type of fuel or fuel from a certain source. This type of control was used infrequently and mainly as a form of fine tuning for the more general government policy designed to insure sufficient in flow of imports. In 1979 and 1980, when oil supplies were short but consumption still high several countries looked seriously at some type of import quotas or taxes to depress demand and force the conservation effort needed to meet IEA and EEC targets. Only the United States actually attempted such an action, creating a political firestorm and no savings. The other countries stood pat and the 1979 price rises eventually produced the savings through normal market mechanisms.

Export Controls

Canada—After 1973 Canada's Liberal Party government undertook a major effort to overhaul the nation's energy strategy by forcing its Western energy production to flow to its Eastern markets. The key to this was choking off exports of Canadian oil and gas to the United States, building West-East pipelines, and as a result reducing the need of the Eastern provinces for imported oil. A quota was instituted on crude and product exports to the United States which started at 500,000 b/d by the mid- to late 1970s and dropped to 50,000 b/d over six years. At the same time a variable export tax on crude and product was instituted to insure that the Canadian oil would be sold in the United States at the equivalent of U.S. domestic prices and there would be no special demand for Canadian oil induced by lower Canadian prices. Gas exports were also subject to national policy considerations in the National Energy Board licensing procedure. This policy, undertaken in the name of greater national self-sufficiency, was strongly disputed by the Western provinces which saw restrictions on the U.S. market outlet as restrictions on their incentive to produce. While the provincial governments controlled their own production, they were only consulted on export policy, and this dichotomy of power led to the major struggle between the Ottawa government and the Alberta provincial government in 1980 and 1981.

United States—When the U.S. Congress approved a measure to build the trans-Alaska oil pipeline in 1969 legislators from Eastern states won inclusion of provisions to make export of the Alaskan oil difficult. Despite longstanding Japanese requests for Alaskan crude and periodic oil gluts on the West Coast, no administration has been able to overcome this opposition and arrange exports or even swaps. In 1980 the legislation was amended so that the findings needed before exchanges could take place were virtually impossible to make. Japan has imported small amounts of Alaskan gas for several years with no problem. Also the Carter and later Reagan administrations have aggressively pushed U.S. coal exports as a means to boost the domestic coal industry and provide export earnings. Legislation to improve coal export ports was a priority item in Congress in 1981. Apparently because coal is not directly used by consumers and abundant in the United States, little of the anti-oil export sentiment transferred to coal exports.

Great Britain—When North Sea oil began to flow in 1974 the British Labour government set up guidelines for export levels under which companies would not export more than one third of production. But the policy was not strictly enforced during most of the 1970s since the North Sea oil commanded excellent prices abroad and British refineries needed a mix of domestic and foreign oil to operate efficiently. Public demands to keep British oil home were dampened by the expansion of production and prospect of self-sufficiency by the early 1980s. The sudden loss of foreign supplies by British Petroleum (BP) and Shell in 1979 and shortfalls in North Sea output forced the Thatcher government to reconsider this flexible policy. Export limits were more carefully monitored and the British National Oil Corporation—North Sea (BNOC) took a lead in keeping more North Sea oil at home. The British also consistently throughout this period resisted any action which would tend to lessen their sovereign right to control oil exports to other Common Market members. North Sea oil was simply not included in the "free trade" concept of the Community. The closest to a breach of this was agreement under strong American pressure in 1980 to include British North Sea exports to the continent as "domestic" EEC oil for purposes of the IEA quota system.

Australia—The Australian government starting in 1974 began a systematic policy to review the national interest served by any energy exports. In that year the Labour government halted uranium exports contracts until 1977 when the Fox Commission completed a report on pricing and equity issues. At that time new orders were again allowed. At the same time the government stepped in to strictly control the amount of gas which would be exported from a planned development of wells on the western continental shelf, allowing exports of only 53 percent with the rest reserved for home use in the western part of the country. Like the United States, Australia maintained a policy of coal export expansion.

European Community—Theoretically under the EEC's free trade rules, oil products like other goods normally flow freely across borders. But differences in taxation and pricing policies of national governments sometimes bring major price differentials between countries and encourage supplies to move across borders to the more advantageous markets, causing local shortages. France and Belgium, with oil product price control policies, have lost oil to the German market this way and have asked Community authorities in Brussels for aid. The EEC Council of Ministers has traditionally refused to grant waivers to allow export restrictions among members and the normal policy is for Brussels to allow the affected government to issue pro forma export licenses which allow at least close monitoring of supply movements.

Import Controls

United States—In March 1980 President Carter, as part of a last-ditch economic package to save his administration, proposed a fee on oil imports designed to increase retail gasoline costs 10 cents per gallon. The object was to cut 250,000 b/d of U.S. oil consumption and raise $10 billion a year to help balance the national budget. Carter proposed the plan in such a way that it was not a normal tax and thus did not need special legislation. His action was, however, subject to congressional approval and in May both House and Senate voted it down by overwhelming margins. While the action was proven unnecessary by subsequent events, at the time the politicians were simply seeking not to offend voters with a new gasoline tax so close to an election. While Congress was voting, the plan was also struck down in federal court because of its odd structure, which had been devised to get around congressional interference. While the U.S. government has no power to ban oil imports directly, it can block natural gas imports under the 1978 legislation which set up the Department of Energy. In 1979, this power was used decisively to block two major proposals to import LNG from Algeria. DOE Economic Regulatory Administrator David Bardin ruled that the gas was not needed given several other potential supply sources including Alaska, Canada, and Mexico.

European Community—In 1979 the EEC Commission put forward a plan similar in purpose to the failed U.S. oil import fee plan. A fee would be put on all EEC oil imports to dampen consumption and the money would be used to finance the EEC budget. The fiscal side of the plan had particular allure. It would in effect excuse Great Britain from a part of its EEC budget burden since most of the oil consumed there was domestic. The plan was discussed but never brought to a formal decision by the nine members once it was seen market forces were having a similar effect.

Brazil—The Brazilian government, with its economy acutely threatened by soaring oil import costs has used oil import volume quotas together with its crash alcohol fuel program to curb imports.

Several major Western countries have programs which control the companies which import oil and attempt to influence the sources of imports. The French and Japanese in particular maintain a tight governmental control over imports and use their powers to encourage or force importers to bring in crude from certain countries. But these policies do not limit imports overall and instead attempt to enhance security of access to crude, a problem which will be dealt with in the next chapter.

CONCLUSION

Actions taken by consuming governments on the domestic side of import policy thus appear to be relatively uniform, with the major difference based on the size of the home oil resource base. All importer countries tend to have an energy plan and oil import targets, although this is less evident in surplus supply periods. Countries with little domestic supply will have little choice but to allow rising oil prices to drive their domestic import reduction programs. Crude oil producers have on the other hand tended to use price controls to soften the impact on consumers. Such countries have taken the step of imposing quotas and taxes on imports only to meet acute situations.

The major divisions among importing countries springing up in this area have pitted the nations without resources against those with. The Americans and others have taken criticism for their price controls which increased import demand and provided a general trade advantage. Japan has attacked American export restrictions on Alaskan oil and the U.S. northwest has been severely hurt by Canadian export cuts. As will be shown, the differences occurring among consumer nations over the domestic portion of import policy are minor compared with differences arising from their international import strategies. In this latter category government relations with the major companies, world political posture, and attitudes toward state-controlled companies all play a major role, setting the United States apart from the other developed countries and the LDCs apart on their own.

We now turn to policies to secure foreign energy supplies especially from the major oil companies, state corporations and foreign exporting governments.

4

SECURING ENERGY IMPORTS

INTRODUCTION

All governments wanted to reduce their dependence on imported energy through the kinds of long and medium term strategies discussed in Chapter 3 (import targets, and others), but until these took effect, the exigencies of the changed world oil market forced consuming governments to pursue more immediate objectives to ensure that imported energy was available in the short term when needed. Consuming nations, especially those with limited domestic resources, had to make critical decisions to ensure that international supply channels would remain open. Energy security had become tantamount to national security.

To ensure national energy security in the short term more activist policies were needed. Unlike earlier periods, oil and other energy forms were less easily and less immediately available in international markets. Therefore, starting in the 1970s, government officials had to be prepared to go beyond traditional market and concessionary arrangements and act directly to assure energy supplies from abroad. But confronted with nearly overwhelming uncertainty and unprecedented turbulence the paths were not clear and improvisation was the order of the day.

In this chapter we examine what public officials did in the 1970s when faced with the problem, "How can I assure that my country gets adequate oil or oil substitutes in the weeks and months ahead at prices that seem manageable for the economy?" In contrast to the last chapter the primary focus here in on the next two quarters, not the next two decades and beyond.

In rough and tumble day-to-day decision making, the pressing problem was what could be done right then. The usual short term immediacy of policy making was reinforced in the 1970s by the rapid and nearly hysterical pace of energy market changes, by the compressed duration of oil contracts, and by the unpredictable midstream alterations of producer country export policies. Even as they kept an eye on long term supply problems, public officials had first and foremost to worry about short-term contingencies and try to please their various constituencies.

Public officials took steps to reduce the market uncertainty and their exposure to risk by acting individually and collectively to make the existing market structures work in their favor if at all possible, and if not, to assume some of the market functions themselves. Usually, in different areas of the market, they did both simultaneously. Since change in the market did not affect all parts equally (the OPEC revolution hit exploration and production more quickly and thoroughly than distribution) new hierarchies and channels were created or old ones expanded. Such post-1973 actions by importers assumed that in certain cases, and in certain sensitive activities, neither the producer nor multinational firms, nor yet the domestic final consumer could or would act by themselves in the national interest to guarantee a steady flow of energy supplies into the country.

The kinds of short-term policy steps governments took to protect their consumers from the new unstable supply conditions ranged from the highly interventionist and novel, to the more modest and temporary improvisations needed to make the traditional market mechanism work smoothly. The more modest steps included expanded government information gathering and monitoring of prices, volumes, origins, and destinations of petroleum, coal, and nuclear flows into and out of the country. Also, some governments sought more detailed data on the worldwide commercial operations of the big companies, or on spot market behavior.

On the more interventionist end, some European and LDC governments pursued semiofficial diplomatic arrangements with producer countries to assure supplies. At the farthest end of the arsenal were consumer policies of direct government intervention and ownership to obtain 100 percent of foreign supplies. These changes represented the most radical consumer alteration of the world energy markets since the 1930s. All this tinkering, tugging, and pulling at the market's operation eventually changed its structure in unexpected ways.

The Same but Different

By 1983 a consumer who pulled his automobile into a service station found ample supplies and stable prices for gasoline. A young teenage driver might well ask, "What was all the fuss ten years ago during the so-called 'energy crisis'?"

The fantastic machine that is the world oil system was still quite capable of delivering millions of tankfuls of gasoline to distant points all over the globe, from Rome, Italy to Kisumu, Kenya, in the quantities and the grades desired. Crude oil still went into the front of the international energy machine in Mexico or Oman, and products were delivered downstream to billions of consumers who wanted kerosene to cook their dinner or Number 2 heating oil to warm their houses. Ten years after the first oil shock, in 1983, the oil machine seemed to work perfectly.

Yet if we awakened a Rip Van Winkle who had been sleeping for a decade and asked him to look inside this marvelous machine, he would have a great deal of trouble recognizing the system that he knew 15 years ago. To a surprising extent it does function as in the past. But the seeming surface normalcy for the consumer at the pump belies a subterranean and still fragile reordering of the great machine's parts.

Underneath is a jerry-built contraption that works well during periods of calm but like a make-shift engine might blow up under serious external stress. Ten years of constant tinkering and resistance has rearranged the parts and stretched them out of past proportion. For example, the spot market has increased tenfold in size, while the oil majors' role is slashed by half. Our awakened mechanic might inquire how prices are set, demand and supply matched, indeed, how oil is moved from one place to another through this altered system. And like our Rip Van Winkle, no one today is sure how to fix it, if it even needs fixing, or whether it will hold up under the next period of stress in the volatile international oil market.

Let us turn now and see how this machine was put together in the 1960s and how it was overhauled to mixed effects in the 1970s. How did we come to a point in the mid-1980s when there seemed a return to normalcy, when only a few years earlier there was talk of invading the Middle Eastern oil fields to guarantee "security of supply?" Have we indeed returned to normalcy, or is this yet another period of false promises with more market turmoil ahead?

THE CHANGING ENERGY MARKETS: 1970-1980

The basis for the substantial rise in consumer government involvement in international energy markets was the dismantling of the old oil concession system, particularly in the Middle East, a consequence of new producer government activism and their control over how, how much, and on what terms crude oil would be made available to consumers. These OPEC-led policy choices of the early 1970s were in turn made possible only by the prevailing tight conditions in the world market. John Lichtblau of the Petroleum Research Institute reminds us that OPEC only accelerated certain underlying market trends.

> Market trends in the late 1960s and early 1970s
> were such that a substantial increase in the real
> price of oil would have been inevitable even without
> OPEC from the mid-1970s on. [Lichtblau 1981, p. 198]

The most far-reaching changes occurred in the oil market. But important changes also occurred in nuclear and coal during the 1970s. In all three cases the background for the changes was strong worldwide economic growth which pushed up the demand for primary fuels and electric power. Then sharp price increases occurred in nuclear power through episodes of commercial supply insecurity, probably precipitated by changed U.S. enrichment policies compounded by Westinghouse's contract noncompliance and the actions of the international uranium cartel. Other shifts occurred in coal, though far less dramatically. We discuss these changes in detail in Chapter 5.

CHANGING CONTROL AND OWNERSHIP
IN THE OIL INDUSTRY

By far the most important change to which public officials in oil importing governments had to respond was the appropriation of ownership and control over the industry by the exporting country governments.

Industry Tasks

In all markets, oil included, there are certain activities that some agency, whether public or private, must perform if the market is to function properly. Typically in oil these activities have been performed by a mix of public and private, national and foreign actors. In the 1970s OPEC nations changed the balance and locus of ownership and control dramatically.

Oil industry tasks can be divided into upstream and downstream activities including exploration, production, pricing, exporting, transportation, refining, and distribution to the final consumer. This sequence of interrelated tasks must be performed by, and for the benefit of someone, and the producers-versus-consumers fight in the 1970s was over who would control what. Prior to the 1973 OPEC revolution, control over these tasks was the province of the seven major oil companies: Exxon, Mobil, Standard of California, Texaco, Gulf, Shell, and British Petroleum—the Seven Sisters. Each was successful in integrating these tasks vertically within the company; they also determined all business strategy. And as we see in Chapter 5, they actually owned the oil itself through concessions granted by the host country all of which resulted in a very profitable business.

These features of the system—company control of business policy, company management of the oil, company ownership of the oil and company profits—were precisely what OPEC governments called unfair and colonial and wanted to change. The way they did so had dramatic implications for public policy in the importing countries.

Four Channels of Distribution

There were four channels through which oil could be moved from seller to buyer: the private independent companies; the state controlled national companies; the spot market traders; and, most important, the major oil companies.

Through the 1960s the great bulk of the oil traded in the world moved through the majors. They owned the oil they traded, they managed it, and they set prices. Of the four potential channels this one was widest by far, and it was the one that experienced the most change during the OPEC revolution of the 1970s, as we can see from Table 4.1.

Thus, over 20 years the producer governments effectively seized control over management (including pricing and sales) and ownership. Some of the radical exporters took that power and insisted on a kind of quid pro quo: If consumers wanted access to OPEC oil, they had to buy more through their own nationally owned, government agency. In other words, don't go through the majors. This theme ran through our interviews with several exporter governments' officials. For many con-

TABLE 4.1

International Oil Companies

Year	Management of International Oil Flow (in percent)	Owned Crude International Oil Flow (in percent)
1960	100	100
1970	70	40
1980	50	17

Source: Compiled by authors (from Conant 1981).

sumers, this provided a welcome opportunity for direct oil. In this way, the newly-powerful exporters and some consumers hoped to bypass their nemesis—the majors which had been the main channels of world oil.

The other channels had of course smaller shares of world oil flows, but the shares grew over the decade of the 1970s. European state companies had some access to crude through earlier colonial arrangements and domestic regulations which forced national control of a certain amount of a nation's oil imports. Then, in the late 1960s and into the 1970s the state companies and the smaller independents (like Occidental Petroleum—Oxy—or Phillips) moved in to seize a greater share of the markets as the OPEC governments used them as foils against the oil giants.

The spot market channel also widened over the decade, increasing tenfold. Historically, the spot market operated very much at the margins of the world oil system, accounting for only about 2 to 5 percent of the total volume. It consisted of oil brokers in Western Europe, Singapore, and the Gulf Coast that bought and sold small lots for companies and consumers who had small surpluses or needs. It was a kind of balance wheel that fine-tuned the larger sales of the other channels. By the early 1980s, as buyers sought to avoid higher contract terms, it ballooned to nearly 50 percent of world trade volume.

Finally, as we will discuss further below, new channels appeared once the deintegration of the majors' ownership and control had been accomplished. Customers hedged against the market's volatility by developing futures markets for oil products.

They operated in Chicago, New York, and London next to the older markets for other commodity futures like soy beans or pork bellies.

By 1970, Algeria, Libya, and Iraq began to take control out of the hands of the companies and nationalized the oil concessions. This happened almost simultaneously with disputes with the majors over the price of oil that culminated in the Teheran Agreement of 1971. This decision involving company-government codetermination of prices revolutionized decision making in the industry and was recognized by both sides as the beginning of the end. This new system of national control was already partially in place by the time of the 1973 embargo and price hike by the Organization of Arab Oil Petroleum Exporting Countries. It was implemented more fully in the succeeding years of the decade. The magnitude and scope of the changes meant that oil-importing countries and their governments would have to adjust their policies and their institutions. The Energy Policy Explosion followed apace.

For example, the reduction in crude quantities available to the majors had critical consequences for many importers. Perhaps the most important change was that the majors in turn were forced to reduce their usual resale of excess crude not needed by their own affiliates. These sales outside the company to nonaffiliates were called "third party sales." The cutback in third party sales began in the early 1970s but came to a climax in 1979 when the events in Iran caused a temporary shortage, and, more importantly, a logistical tangle, leading most big companies to issue force majeur notices and cut back even long-standing outside customers. This was especially severe for some customers like Japan which depended heavily on such sales. The crisis left them with a loss of roughly one-third of their entire crude supply, and a major crisis on their hands. Private Japanese companies, coordinated by the trade ministry, immediately responded by seeking out other import channels. They plunged into the spot market and sought new exporter government sales, but at high premium prices. This precipitated the 160 percent jump in prices after the Shah fell.

It is important to stress here that the necessary volumes of oil were available in the world market. However, the logistical interruptions meant that the instruments to obtain them cheaply and easily were not yet in place (Neff 1981). It is as if an irrigation water pump broke down, and farmers were left with buckets and straws. Even the U.S. refining companies, also cut off from their major suppliers, were led to deal through spot traders for any available crude, and to pay spiraling prices. Prices mounted. They went from about $12 to $36 between 1978 and 1980 and continued up for a while thereafter. In Europe, British Petroleum suffered particularly in 1979, being shut off from Iran and Nigeria and then cut back in Kuwait by two-thirds; many BP customers were left high, dry, and in search of new supply channels. Other companies with more secure access, like the ARAMCO partners in Saudi Arabia, were less badly affected.

This experience in the late 1970s left a great psychological scar on all buyers for the next two years. Access, not price, was the top priority for importer government officials. It seemed oil at any price was the rallying cry. While slightly overstated, this does capture the desperation we sensed in consumer capitals the world over. State and independent company managers alike told us they placed tremendous weight on the goal of finding and keeping major OPEC supply contracts at almost any cost. Rumors circulated of middlemen paid millions of dollars to obtain "secure" oil contracts. Company officials trod gingerly, afraid to say or do anything that could conceivably jeopardize their fragile relationship with suppliers. Our interviews with officials in the United States, Europe, and the third world confirmed that such fears were widespread. Our talks with OPEC officials showed their awareness of the situation and their eagerness to exploit it. Eventually, however, importers and especially exporters fell victim to their own worst fears and hopes—the exporters failed to appreciate that such power was theirs only so long as the market allowed it.

OPEC soon got caught by the M-shaped market. The fluctuations put the exporters on the receiving end of what they had dished out only a year or so earlier: term contract cancellations in order to buy on the spot market. Consumer government officials and other buyers were first reluctant to cancel contracts as the spot market price fell and the exporters kept their contract prices high, even though they might be losing on each barrel bought. But as the glut took hold and the spot and contract prices grew farther apart buyers overcame their reluctance and a wave of contract cancellations occurred. Soon oil refused by one buyer could not be sold elsewhere and production was shut in or cut-rate prices offered. Now it was OPEC's turn to complain that unilateral abrogation of contracts was "unfair." The end result was softer prices, a substantial drop in OPEC production and revenues, and by 1983 an OPEC agreement on production quotas after several false starts. However, the trend toward government-to-government transactions did not appear to be significantly reversed, and the spot market remained strong with one-third to one-half of the market volume.

Clearly, the decade's OPEC revolution did not wholly replace one distribution channel with another. Instead, their relative width changed and evened out somewhat. The logistics became more complex. For example, the numbers of buyers purchasing from OPEC shot up from 100 in 1975 to about 400 in 1980. There were also more players in the game, and perhaps ironically the market had actually become more competitive. It was arguably this greater competition that helped account for the increased instability.

Still, as in all revolutions, there was as much continuity as change. As we said at the beginning of this chapter, the world oil market still retained a remarkable degree of constancy. The majors continued to exercise power through the amount of crude to which they still had secure access. They were still the single largest buyers of crude oil, and the largest trans- porters by far. The Seven Sisters still hired most of the talent in the industry, and had the ability to switch gears in order to find and manage new oil and new energy sources in other "safer" areas less politically volatile than the Middle East. Despite the changes, the majors managed to hold their own rather nicely as an important channel for oil supplies. Neither the exporter nor the importer governments could afford to ignore them.

The importer governments responded to the OPEC revolt with the Energy Policy Explosion, pressed to make conscious choices about how best to import oil—through which of the four channels, from what countries, at what costs to their economies, and their political positions. But they could not choose freely. They had to develop clear-cut relations with both OPEC govern- ments and the major oil companies, and with one another. They were forced to become more interventionist. This was rather a far cry from the previous arrangements where the private oil companies did most of the work. Now new conditions forced their attention to securing energy supplies from abroad.

CONSUMER GOVERNMENT OIL ACQUISITION

When governments got involved in acquisition of oil from abroad there were two principal routes available: first, efforts to arrange for oil to be traded directly between the producer government and a state-controlled or state-designated company in the importer nation—this is the state-to-state oil channel;

and, second, oil acquisition efforts by state controlled companies to win exploration and development agreements with producer governments—that is, go drill for oil. Governments did both. And in both cases, importer government officials took over some of the roles of the majors by substituting public for private control of acquisition channels. Now the importer national "chosen instrument" oil companies performed a growing number of these functions. This pull from the consuming governments, combined with and responding to the push from the exporting governments, meant cutbacks in the majors' market role.

There were four standard contributions governments typically made in the acquisition of overseas oil under the new system. They were:

1. An overall rough notion (held by policy makers) of the desired amount of oil which should be imported directly by government without the involvement of the majors.

2. Capital transfers to the national company via direct government investment or subsidies. This is particularly important for foreign exploration companies like ELF or ENI or BrasPetro, which have major upfront risk capital costs without secure returns.

3. Diplomatic assistance either to arrange agreements on a direct government-to-government level or to provide a conducive "friendly atmosphere" to allow the national companies or negotiators to deal effectively on their own.

4. Domestic regulation and intervention to improve the competitive position in the home market for the crude and products obtained through government deals, and/or to abide by exporter government destination restrictions.

The relationship between direct government oil purchase policies and exploration policies is indirect. The purpose of both is to obtain oil from overseas. Yet they are different in many respects. Exploration and development require huge amounts of risk capital, and results are highly uncertain— companies can spend anywhere from 10 to 100 million dollars to develop a field with no guarantee of commercial success. As a consequence, only a handful of industrially powerful and sophisticated countries can afford state-backed exploration efforts overseas. However, most countries now pursue some form of purchases of oil. While government purchase deals can also appear as fair bargains for export goods, as we explain below, they can also appear one-sided, with the producer using his control of supply to take advantage of the consumer in tight markets.

A national company with a history of drilling in a producing country may be better able to conclude purchase deals than other companies. Clearly in both purchasing and exploration policy the state companies in the late 1960s played a key role in creating wider negotiation and participation flexibility for the exporting and importing governments alike. However, of the two, the direct state-to-state purchases brought about the most immediate changes in the way that all importing governments do business. But exploration policy in the long term can also be crucial. By 1984 successful exploration by France's state ELF company especially in Gabon and other West African countries had allowed it to cut back strongly on earlier state-to-state purchase deals arranged by the French government with Saudi Arabia and also provided high profits to offset refining losses in France.

Government-to-Government Transactions

Generally, government-to-government deals can be defined in two ways, with one definition a narrower category of the other (Mohnfeld 1980, p. 329; Neff 1981, p. 27; Wilson 1983). The broader concept includes all oil deals concluded between two state-controlled or state-influenced entities—the producing country national oil company on one end and any consuming country oil-buying group with state backing on the other. This broad meaning can stretch to the day-to-day operations of the large established state companies like ELF, ENI, and VEBA which operate in most cases like private major oil companies, seeking supplies as part of their normal operations. This meaning also contains plenty of gray areas, such as the activities of British Petroleum, in which the government owns shares but is operated independently of (and sometimes in spite of) government mandates, and the Japanese private oil buying companies which operate under government umbrella but with no public ownership.

The narrower definition covers transactions where the main impulse comes from government officials on both sides who are carrying out a partially commercial-partially diplomatic action. Also included here were barter arrangements (for example, Brazilian iron pellets for Mexican oil) and sales with restrictions preventing resale to third parties.

In our interviews with state company officials in Europe most felt that the narrower definition should hold since the broader one takes in actions that are in essence commercial, and that indeed some commercial firms operate with the same restrictions. In this narrower understanding of government-to-government (G-G) deals the technical aspects were dealt with by experts from the respective national oil companies, and the actual delivery arrangements also carried out by these groups (sometimes private firms were used if the importer lacked a state company). But the deal was presented as part of a political agreement between high government officials and could be part of a larger technical assistance, diplomatic, or trade accord. A classic example was French President Giscard d'Estaing's numerous voyages after the Iran-Iraq war to the Middle East, Mexico, and elsewhere in search of government oil deals which were then implemented by CFP and ELF. Less eye-catching but increasingly frequent were the trips by foreign or trade ministers and other high officials from consuming countries to arrange deals and maintain friendly contacts in case a deal would be necessary in an emergency. Saudi Arabian and Algerian officials told us of third world leaders literally dropping out of the sky unannounced at their airports, seeking preferred prices and guaranteed supplies through state-state deals.

Thailand presents an interesting case where a country without a national integrated oil company pursued a G-G deal with mixed results (Far Eastern Economic Review, March 6, 1981, p. 40. Platt's Oilgram News, various issues, see especially, March 21, April 19, September 10). This case illustrates several points, including the continuing prominent role of private oil companies even in state-to-state deals, and mostly the murkiness of international oil trading.

After negotiating a 100,000 barrel G-G deal with the Saudis, the Thai government arranged to have the crude shipped by Summit Oil, a private group, which landed as much crude as Thailand's small refinery could handle, and processed the rest at a plant in Singapore. It was not clear where the Singapore-processed 40,000-odd barrels ended up, nor was it clear in whose name, and for whose account, the oil was sold. Soon some Thais believed that Summit had ripped them off by over-charging for its services, while some Saudis apparently felt their relatively less expensive G-G fixed price oil was being resold on the open market for a profit. They remained skeptical until Thailand increased its capacity to process all 100,000 barrels of the crude.

The OPEC preferences for state-to-state oil transactions forced all the other market actors to respond to the challenge, but they did so in different ways and with different degrees of enthusiasm. Most were simply put off because the proposals were new and meant yet another basic instability in an already turbulent market. The oil companies feared the deals would eat into their own operations and profits. The LDCs hoped to exert fraternal pressure by appeals to third world solidarity for cut-rate prices. The Europeans were more ambivalent; on the one hand, even the smaller countries had years of experience with state companies domestically and internationally and thus had the requisite instruments and know-how; on the other hand, they recognized the potential for political blackmail state deals might bring in tight circumstances.

The Americans were fully opposed to the growth of these transactions on free market ideological as well as material grounds. Materially their companies stood to lose the most in a new world market dominated by state deals. Also the Americans had the luxury of large domestic supplies to fall back on.

Despite the hesitancies of major importers there was a veritable stampede toward these transactions that revolutionized the industry. By the end of the decade the state transactions were at least as important as the commercial ones for many countries. The overwhelming evidence from the 1970s and 1980s is that consuming governments decided that government-to-government deals were in their overall national interest. In less than a decade they became a respectable component of the national policy arsenal of consuming nations.

But what exactly were the reasons that led the consumers to employ state transactions? We will explore the various reasons for consumer acceptance before going on to analyze the mechanics involved and then the various national experiences with G-G deals in the United States, the other industrialized nations, and the developing countries. Finally, we will give a preliminary assessment of whether this greatly expanded oil channel met the expectations of the parties concerned.

WHY G-G TRANSACTIONS?

In trying to untangle these complex issues we feel it is most useful to focus on three principle areas where these kinds of transactions were generally believed to make a difference for exporters and importers alike: the oil market itself, commercial deals, and the political arena.

The Oil Market

Naturally most of the interest in state transactions was focused on the benefits they could bring within the international

oil market. Some importer officials believed that government-
to-government deals could achieve the following: cheaper prices,
greater supply security, supply diversification, and both circumvent the majors and gain greater oil market leverage in
general for national firms.

Cheaper prices and better security of supply were the two
main motors of the G-G process for importers. They believed
that closer political ties between traditional (or new) friends
could moderate the higher prices. Since many consumers
initially felt that high prices were only the result of political
manipulation and not market forces, they reasoned that political
favoritism would drop the price. This was especially the case
for the poorer third world importers. If consumers couldn't
get cheaper prices, the next best thing was some guarantee of
continued supply. Remember that the 1973 embargo meant
importers feared a cut off of their precious oil supplies. The
fact that the targeted embargo failed to discriminate because
the majors cut everybody equally was not widely recognized
outside the circle of oil experts. By the time politicians began
to learn the lesson, the Iranian crisis made the issue moot
since the majors no longer controled the crude and could not
very well repeat their balancing act. With Japan and Brazil
suffering severe losses from both the Iranian collapse and the
Iraq-Iran war, access to secure supply became critical. When
there is only a limited amount of oil to go around, so it was
argued to us in several national capitals, we want to make sure
that we are on the list of friends and brothers who get oil, and
not on the list of enemies who don't.

Also, since very few trusted the majors with their history
and reputation of self-interested and rapacious behavior, some
governments guessed that they would be better served by dealing
directly with the exporter governments and avoiding the tender
mercies of the Seven Sisters altogether. As Middle East instability
continued, state transactions were taken as one means of diversifying one's supply sources to new areas like Mexico or West
Africa. Finally, creating a generally good political climate
between one's own country and the exporter's was just a good
general insurance policy on behalf of one's national firms.

Commercial Deals

While reaping oil market benefits was the key prize, consumers did not fail to recognize that G-G deals could be two-way
streets. The importer country could use the G-G oil deal as a

lever to sell national products to the OPEC countries from which
it bought its oil. From shoes to surplus steel to supersonic jet
aircraft the consumers sought to balance out their growing
trade deficits with the exporters by selling anything and everything they could.

OPEC wanted to use their so-called "oil weapon" in commerce
to create beneficial cross-market links. Oil sales were sometimes implicitly and sometimes explicitly tied to purchases of
goods or services from the importer, often at apparently favorable rates for the oil exporter. This could be set down in a
contract, or, far more likely, set out in a separate series of
parallel letters of intent and understanding. This worked less
well for poor countries with little to sell. OPEC countries in
trouble also found such deals very helpful. For example, Iraq,
hard pressed for cash during its drawn out war with Iran was
grateful to be able to pay for vital French military supplies
directly with oil. The French government managed the transaction in which money payed for the oil by French state
companies ELF and CFP was transfered straight to the French
arms suppliers.

Political Arena

Given the prevalence of intense and divisive conflict in
some of the major producing areas—the Middle East, or Africa—
it is not surprising that consumer government officials were
anxious to secure political points wherever possible, and G-G
deals were clearly one means of bringing oil and politics together.
In the tight period after the Iranian revolution the politics of
oil deals were in the producer's favor. The Iranians themselves
took what they considered the most advantage, selling oil only
to those outsiders which remained friendly to the new regime
in Teheran. This boycott effect worked for a while, but as the
oil market swing to surplus and consumers preferred to avoid
fixed price, long term deals for commercial reasons, the advantage changed. It became a political favor on the part of the
consumer to conclude such deals. Consumers at this point could
begin to use deals for political damage control in the Middle East
and elsewhere, hoping to create a community of interest with
key states and cool hot tempers.

THE COSTS OF GOVERNMENT DEALS

If there were plusses there were also potential minuses to
such deals. In the oil market, for example, more secretive

government-to-government transactions might bid up the cost of oil. With the market more opaque and tied up in a countless series of bilateral bidding arrangements there was an even larger incentive than before to jump into the market to outbid your neighbor. Under the old system the companies had balanced world supply with demand so there was less incentive to hoard supplies. What might seem to be in the interest of one government could work against the interest of all.

Second, the system lost flexibility since companies could not shift supplies as readily since oil was locked up in these one-to-one deals, with destination restrictions limiting the switching and balancing that could be done. Among other drawbacks this problem made the IEA emergency sharing scheme appear worthless in a scarce supply scenario.

Third, the other side of supply security was overreliance on one producer government, just as one could rely too heavily on one commercial supplier. A coup d'état, a war, a shift of national priorities could leave the customer with a sudden supply loss.

NATIONAL EXPERIENCES

Having described these goals and the potential costs of trying to achieve them, we will examine the actual national experiences that different importer countries had with state transactions. Immediately after the 1973 embargo some European countries led by France and Italy actively sought direct deals with OPEC countries. They pursued the objectives cited above, especially security of supply, lower prices, and commercial deals to help compensate for the suddenly higher balance of payments problems.

In December 1973 French Foreign Minister Michel Jobert reached an accord with Saudi Arabia to deliver 27 million tons of crude over three years at the established price for Saudi "buy back" crude. The action was taken despite public warnings by U.S. officials, and it struck directly at the heart of the American "special relationship" with the Saudis which had virtually excluded oil companies from other nations. The French spent much of the next three years trying to win a much bigger supply deal, but this effort ran ahead of the Kingdom's own plans to phase in non-U.S. sales and eventually the original deal was merely extended (the Saudis finally established an oil-trading agency outside Petromin in 1983). During the late 1970s France moved aggressively to win crude supply deals

with Iraq, Mexico, and several smaller exporter countries.
Typically, the deals would be arranged during state visits by
President Giscard d'Estaing with both French companies ELF
and CFP getting access to the direct oil. The French put a
heavy emphasis on oil-for-technology deals, supplying Iraq
with one nuclear reactor and bargaining with Iran for the sale
of two more.

The Italians moved into the direct deal market almost as
quickly as the French, arranging in the mid-1970s major barter
deals with Iran, Iraq, and their former colony Libya. Typically
the Italians dealt through ENI itself, with backing from government officials, but with less fanfare than the French. In 1979
ENI reached a 12.5 million ton, three year deal with the Saudis,
but the sale was canceled by the outraged Saudis in 1980 after
a scandal erupted in Rome over sales commissions given to
mysterious third parties. In these deals ENI has drawn heavily
on its strong presence in OPEC countries through joint exploration ventures and its general policy of openness toward the
third world established by Enrico Mattei in the early 1960s.

Italy and France were able to move quickly into these
deals because they already had large state companies in place
and the diplomatic and industrial muscle to bargain effectively
(smaller countries lacked these plusses). They also had a
strong tradition among senior government and industry officials
both of state intervention in commercial arrangements, combined
with distrust for the major Anglo-American oil companies and a
desire to win advantage over them on the international scene
(an important difference with the American government). The
creation of the IEA in 1974 was little deterrence. France refused
to join precisely because she believed the organization would
restrict her independent dealings and political policies toward
OPEC. Italy joined the IEA but paid little heed to the U.S.
warnings against "excessive bilateralism" (Schneider 1983,
chapters 7-8; Doran 1977, chapter 5). As it turned out the
IEA took no actions as a group to limit direct deals until the
end of the decade, when the sudden price spiral caused virtually
all consumer countries to agree, at least informally, to dampen
spot purchasing. The IEA meetings became a sort of clearing-
house for such informal restraints.

Japan and West Germany were slower to move toward direct
deals because of their political traditions and their need to first
build up coherent domestic-based industry groups capable of
handling large deals. Also these countries did not want to
contradict U.S. Secretary of State Kissinger's announced policies
flagrantly, and thus chose a more low-profile approach to OPEC.

These countries did, however, possess large markets for oil and excellent industrial goods for trade with OPEC, and thus eventually became major players in the direct deal system.

The Japanese government has been committed to increasing direct deals since 1971, but this policy was complicated by the fragmented nature of the Japanese oil industry and its relation to the government. There are over a dozen private Japanese firms actively engaged in oil importing and a typical government-influenced deal with an OPEC producer may include several companies either joined in consortium with other Japanese firms or negotiating separately. Government ministries have provided political and/or commercial coordination and sought to entice companies to participate in politically advantageous deals. Still, Japan's operating style is to put together a multitude of small deals, with the private firms doing the actual negotiating.

The Japanese made important purchases from Saudi Arabia, China, Indonesia, and Mexico in the mid-1970s, but the real upswing came in 1979 when the Iranian revolution caused a swift cutoff of third party sales by the majors to Japanese buyers and wholesalers. Japan lost 520,000 b/d of supply in April 1979 and was able to come up with 780,000 b/d of new supply, mainly from other Persian Gulf suppliers. The Japanese importers were nevertheless still short, and were among the first to negotiate with the new Iranian regime. These deals, done under duress, often at exorbitant prices, caused new headaches for the Japanese government, which was pressured by other Western countries to curb its buying, which was having a spiral effect on world prices. Its own joint oil-for-petrochemical investment-and-technology deal with Iran proved however to be a white elephant.

During this post-1978 period, the Japanese government also tried to recast its mechanism for performing government-government deals. The newly reorganized Japanese National Oil Company was given a backup role under which it would purchase direct-deal oil when necessary to follow through on arrangements in which private companies did not want a certain quantity of oil, or in which the producer government wanted to sell to an importer state agency. Also, the JNOC was asked to become more active in setting up umbrella consortia to handle major direct-deal contracts. Such groups had been established for Mexican and Chinese deals. The Japanese government refused, however, to create a consolidated, single "Japanese major" such as CFP or ENI, perhaps because of private sector opposition. Only in 1984 did an effort to consolidate the Japanese oil groups start up under government tutelage.

The West German effort to enter into state transactions
was much slower and less fruitful than France's, Italy's, or
Japan's. The Germans did act strongly in 1974 to reorganize
and strengthen the large partially government-owned energy
company, VEBA, to enable it to assume a larger role in foreign
direct deals (and also foreign exploration through its subsidiary
DEMINEX). But VEBA made only limited progress in deals with
Saudi Arabia and Libya. The company was hampered by money-
losing refinery holdings in Germany (finally sold to BP in 1979).
and the entrenched role of the majors in the liberal German
market. VEBA was designed to assume a 25 percent share of
the domestic oil industry, but by decade's end it remained below
this figure. By 1983 the new Kohl government in West Germany
had begun divesting government holdings in VEBA. In 1980
Saudi Arabia increased its small flow to VEBA and also concluded
a 100,000 b/d deal with AVIA-Mineroel, a group of 25 independent
distributors with no refining capacity of their own. Also
Deutsche-BP, the largest oil company in Germany after its takeover of some VEBA properties began in the early 1980s to operate
somewhat anomalously as an individual German company in
government-inspired deals. In 1980 Deutsche BP was opening
contacts with Saudi officials for a 100,000 b/d contract.
    Thus the percentage of oil acquired through state-inspired
deals became considerable, as the figures in Table 4.2 indicate.
    Other smaller, southern European industrial countries with
étatist traditions have built on their national companies' existing
networks to win and implement direct deals, with even higher
percentages through state channels. Portugal went from 25
percent through this channel in 1978 to 40 percent only a year
later. Over the same time Greece increased its percentage from

TABLE 4.2

Share of Oil Imports through Government-to-Government Deals

Country	1978	1979
France	30	40
Italy	15	25
Japan	19	27

Source: Adapted from Mohnfeld.

28 percent to 48 percent, while Spain jumped from 35 percent to 55 percent. By 1978, for example, Greece had signed direct arrangement contracts with Iraq, Saudi Arabia, Libya, and the Soviet Union, and officials were promising eventually to use 100 percent direct deals to fill demand.

Some European countries with different traditions of state control in the oil sector made less significant efforts. Belgium, Denmark, Ireland, and Sweden created national oil-importing bodies to begin direct deals. Even the Dutch, who have traditionally relied on Royal Dutch Shell for domestic oil supplies considered such a national buying group. The efforts resulted in several false steps, and generally brought only minor deals, but even into the early 1980s the trend was upward. The Irish national company, for example, brought much of its direct-deal crude to refineries in Britain for processing before importing finished product. The Danish company's director ran into a firestorm of political protest at home after negotiating a contract with the Saudis which seemed to lock Denmark into a strongly pro-Arab political course. Sweden found it necessary to move toward direct deals through Svenska Petroleum in 1980 because price controls were causing the traditional major companies to cut supplies to Sweden, especially during tight market periods. The Belgians encountered similar problems both with the majors and with the ability of their small traders to find supplies on the Rotterdam market at certain times. In 1980 a major supply deal between 50 percent-government owned Distrigaz and the Saudis was finalized with some of the oil destined for the national stockpile program.

Since 1973 the U.S. government, under Democratic and Republican presidents has opposed direct sales with OPEC by all consuming countries, saying they weakened the common consumer front against the exporter front. The U.S. Congress has consistently shown little interest in proposals for a national oil-purchasing company. Some key figures, like the former Senate Energy Committee Chairman the late Henry Jackson, had called attention to the moves toward direct government purchasing by other countries, but politically there was no realistic chance for the creation of such a government company.

Part of the reason has been that most proposals made in the United States are primarily aimed at driving a wedge in OPEC by creating monopoly for a new government company over all U.S. imports. The European-style thinking that a national company would be helpful to handle some of the nation's imports without a monopoly has not been presented and would make little sense to most U.S. politicians. But in 1981 a remarkable departure from this norm occurred when the U.S. Strategic Petroleum Reserve, an arm of the Department of Energy, concluded a major crude deal with the Mexican national petroleum company. The import arrangement, a genuine government-to-government deal, did make sense to American officials because it allowed the junking of a cumbersome system of swapping California U.S. naval reserve oil for crude delivered to the strategic reserve, all in the name of national security. The Mexicans were delighted because the deal came just at a time when other customers, including earlier direct deal buyers such as the French, were pulling out due to price pressures. Both sides were pleased because it helped overcome the hostilities surrounding the on-and-off gas import deal blocked earlier by then-Secretary Schlesinger. Finally, the Mexican sale was linked by some to U.S.-Mexican negotiations over immigration policy. The deal got little publicity in the United States, in stark contrast to the large splash which direct deals make in other countries, and the U.S. political system continued to operate in the firm belief that private oil purchasing as the only acceptable method.

For the developing consumer countries, the gains from government-to-government deals were probably the greatest of any group, since they were the most devastated by the direct and indirect impacts of the oil price jumps.

The LDC movement to direct state purchase of oil supplies was a natural trend given their patterns of business-state relations, their dissatisfaction and past conflicts with the majors, and the willingness of OPEC members to make such deals for political solidarity reasons. For the larger LDCs like India, Turkey, and Brazil this was especially easy since many already had national oil companies. Brazil's PetroBras (and its international relations adjunct BrasPetro) was an old, well-established, and sophisticated oil firm. PetroBras brought in 100 percent of the country's crude through its import monopoly, and had long dealt with OPEC state companies. Even when these kinds of countries had to develop a state oil company de novo it was not terribly difficult since they had more skilled people and stable governments. Thus, capitalist (though state-guided) Korea was easily able in 1978 to create a national oil company to explore overseas and import G-G oil, and by 1980 brought in 34 percent of its oil this way. However, Korea demonstrates that doing G-G deals does not mean inevitable state takeover. During this same period the government also liberalized its policies to allow private trading groups to import oil. In the past, only the majors like Gulf or local refiners could import crude. In 1980 the latter contributed 24 percent of total imports, and the majors 42 percent (Korean Herald, October 3, 1980). By thus drawing on the experience and networks of the private companies the government could diversify as widely as possible the national oil import channels.

The use of G-G deals as a package yielded some price, security of supply, and commercial results. They were not necessarily impressive in achieving geographic diversification of supplies. For example, despite quite explicit government exhortations to diversify, and despite the growth of G-G deals, the 1979 source picture was more concentrated by the end of the decade than before. In 1977 for example Saudi Arabia, Kuwait, Iran, and Iraq contributed 57.8 percent, 29.3 percent, 10.4 percent, and 2.2 percent respectively of Korea's oil imports. By 1979 the figures were 56.7 percent, 37.5 percent, and 5.8 percent, with no imports from Iraq or the Neutral Zone. In the early 1980s when the Persian Gulf war became a major threat to supplies, the desire of Western consumers to avoid concentrating supply sources in that region reinforced commercial reasons for avoiding government-to-government deals. By 1984 most European countries and the United States had drastically reduced supplies from the Gulf and were much less troubled by the periodic flare-ups in the Gulf fighting including Iraq attacks on shipping. Japan, which did not cut back government deals in the same way, remained highly exposed (Petroleum Economist, November 1979, p. 448).

If India, Korea, and Brazil had an easy transition to a world market packed with G-G deals, this was not the case for the smaller and poorer LDCs. Most of these countries relied on one or two large multinationals to obtain imported crude and product. In Africa, for example, CALTEX, Shell, or BP often acted as the sole or principal importer. Responsibility for government-company relations often lay with an overworked accountant in the Central Bank or Treasury. OPEC insistence on delivering secure cheap oil through national companies sometimes caused these nations problems.

In Kenya there were administrative as well as political problems in creating a new national oil company. According to the head of the new Ministry of Energy, planning for the company was directly prompted by "Iraq's insistence on exporting through a government organization. Kenya will import half of its yearly 46-million barrels of purchases directly from Iraq at below-market prices" (Energy Resources and Technology, Vol. 8, 32, August 8, 1980, p. 318). Some domestic opposition from more free market forces arguing for continued reliance on

the existing oil majors apparently snagged creation of the proposed company. Zambia, to Kenya's south faced fewer political
problems but did confront severe manpower shortages and relied
on Indian, Sri Lankan, and European expatriates to run its
small national import company.

These instances, like Thailand cited above, are not unique.
They point up the dilemma of G-G deals for the poor countries—
they most need the payment and price relief that G-G deals can
bring, but they are most unlikely to have adequate infrastructure
to create and staff a national oil company. Still, these deals
provided a wider window on the market activities of the companies
and perhaps offered greater control.

For their part, the exporters encouraged, and often insisted
on, these bilateral arrangements through governments. They
also used various intergovernmental means to soften the economic
blow for selected importing LDCs. During 1978-80 in particular
several OPEC members appeared sensitive to the international
equity problems caused by their price hikes. Iraq, for example,
extended long term interest aid to LDCs for loans to pay the
new post-1973 surcharges. Most of the aid was initially given
along regional and religious lines. There were also multilateral
steps to help LDCs, through organizations like the OPEC Special
Fund. OAPEC countries gave aid to other Middle Eastern and
Muslim nations. Nigeria and Algeria organized joint guarantees
of secure sales (though at market prices) to Africa, and Venezuela and Mexico launched an energy assistance program of
preferential sales and loans to small countries of Central America
and the Caribbean.

State Oil Transactions: A Preliminary Assessment

Virtually every industrial and developing importer country
made some use of G-G arrangements in the 1978-81 period. The
ability of a consumer to do a G-G deal successfully seems to
hinge on carefully coordinating the following conditions, all of
which must be met:

1. a desire on the part of government to avoid dependence
on the traditional majors or the spot market;
2 a governmental mechanism to make the actual purchases
and carry out or coordinate the oil deliveries;
3. a domestic political consensus that such deals, including
the potential political strings, are in the national interest, economically sound and afford real security advantages; and

4. the ability to work out the necessary diplomatic and commercial ties with an exporter willing to sell or barter on a government-to-government basis.

It appears that the oil market successes of price and security were quite mixed, often varying with the kind of country, with the poorer LDCs doing slightly better than the industrialized countries. The original hopes of the industrialized consumer governments for lower oil prices have not been rewarded. G-G prices tended to be close to those obtained through straight commercial arrangements. Some countries paid more than market rates, as did France in the mid-1970s. In calm markets the deals have been roughly equivalent.

It does seem that there were some price advantages for the LDC importers, especially among the very poor. This was achieved less through actual lower prices, although some of that did occur, but rather through better terms of payment— longer to pay—which translate into lower prices. OPEC also offered many low interest "loans" to these countries, loans whose repayments have been quite problematic. Some countries like Ghana were even allowed to pay in kind through barter arrangements.

The security issues are harder to measure than price. The fact that a consuming country is dealing with the exporter directly does eliminate the middle man who will always have his own priorities, especially in an emergency, as Japan found out. In theory this was more secure, but in practice the new forms brought as many security uncertainties as they eliminated. This is not only because of the risk of wars or coups or changes of policies in producers, but also because the new market structure is far more fragmented. Consumers cannot automatically fall back on supplies from other sources. There was no longer in the late 1970s and early 1980s that great world pool of uncommitted oil that, in tight periods, could be shifted around to meet unanticipated demand surges in one country or another.

Consumer countries found these contracts more rigid than they would have liked. OPEC governments prohibited reselling or diversion of oil. Also, the use of specific shippers might be proscribed. Some countries such as Saudi Arabia have enforced rules under which purchasers must take a mixture of oil grades including a specific percentage of heavy, sour crudes which may be inappropriate for the home refineries. Related to this and posing serious problems for the late 1980s, and into the 1990s, is that the exporters started (under tight market conditions) to link crude sales to a certain amount of refined product exports. This trend will increase as OPEC members expand their domestic refining capacity. Similar purchase restrictions are generally imposed on sales to the majors, but with large worldwide refinery and sales operations they have more flexibility to meet the OPEC terms and still continue efficient operations. Single government buyers usually lack that flexibility.

Finally, sudden changes in demand at home can occur and turn government contracts into serious price or supply liabilities. In tight markets, a national government committed to a fixed level of imports under government deals very often might continue the imports whether needed or not to maintain the OPEC direct tie. When market conditions changed after 1980 even oil-scarce governments tended to cut back purchases unilaterally. It is not at all clear whether G-G deals are more "sticky" on the down side than straight deals with the majors, but that seems to be the case. This may be because G-G arrangements often involve commercial side deals.

The feverish enthusiasm for G-G transactions after 1978-1979 cooled considerably after the eruption of war between Iraq and Iran, which had been the second- and third-largest OPEC exporters after Saudi Arabia. Governments became chary of latching on to exclusive direct government deals when those governments, through war or revolution, might not be able to deliver what they promised.

Overall, from a market perspective, the new oil structure shifted higher uncertainties and costs, which some estimate at an additional 10 billion dollars, downstream to the consumer government. Also consumer governments now have come to rely on fairly expensive domestic storage facilities to improve security and ensure that the new logistical rigidity does not catch them flat-footed (see Chapter 6). For the 1980s and beyond the best adaptation to the new market system is a diversified mix of private company contracts and government-to-government deals. This volatile cycle of the 1970-1983 oil market revealed the limits of relying not only on any single company for one's supplies, but on any single country as well.

Like the ambiguity of determining net oil market benefits, it is also difficult to determine net commercial benefits. The sale price of airplanes, ships, or insurance services tied to an oil deal are hard enough to uncover. It is especially tough because as the two deals may be negotiated in a package, the buyers and sellers will be willing to shave off on one in order to get a better price on the other.

The officials and businessmen whom we interviewed tended to argue that their initial expectations of tapping into the Arab billions through state deals were not met. Some felt that the commercial deals would have been landed anyway. However, most also felt that there was some positive payoff on the commercial end of "bundled" oil transactions. Japan, Germany, France, and Italy among others have won large contracts for goods and industrial projects in key OPEC countries, as did Brazil and India. Korean firms for example won $15 billion of construction contracts alone in the Middle East between 1973 and 1979. That country also gained a $70 million soft terms loan from the Saudi Fund for Development for harbors and roads. Two years later in 1978 government-to-government negotiations yielded a three year direct deal to buy 50,000 b/d from Saudi Arabia.

While these loans, construction contracts, and oil sales may be directly tied together. Another explanation is that once a country develops a large trade deficit with another, it will be especially aggressive in marketing to that country, and the surplus country will be well disposed to help even out the balance. It may also be the case that governments were most happy when, through a state deal, their construction companies, manufacturers, or consultants were able to shoe-horn their way into what had been regarded as the unofficial commercial preserve of another major country.

Seen from a liberal trade perspective, oil for technology or goods can be unhealthy in principle, allowing less efficient countries to win export sales and distorting trade along sub-optimal lines. But this is part of business as usual for many countries that use export credits and other devices to improve their sales positions on world markets.

As for the political consequences of government-to-government deals producing countries may insist on certain types of goods or services in return for oil which the consumer country may not want to supply for political reasons. Germany, due to its political past, has not wanted to supply heavy military equipment to states who may fight Israel. Producer countries have also sought nuclear technology as a return for oil contracts.

Heavy industrial involvement in industrial projects in OPEC countries can become a burden if war or revolution bring changes that put a project in question in the middle of construction. This is especially the case when the economics of the project were perhaps marginal by themselves, and were only attractive in conjunction with "secure" access to oil in a tight market. In a unique twist to the government-to-government oil deal tied to a commercial contract, the Japanese government was sucked into bailing out a consortium of private Japanese companies led by Mitsui, when the Iranian revolution and war disrupted construction of a huge petrochemical complex the Japanese were constructing in Iran. While not initially a direct government oil package (so far as one can tell), there were very clear government expectations that such a major multi-billion-dollar commitment to Iran would help ensure secure supplies for the future. As the war dragged on, the private firms pressured government to bail them out of their expensive difficulties with a major oil partner, and the government, despite initial resistance, eventually felt obliged to help.

Much of the controversy around these types of arrangements centered on the fear of direct political extortion, a petroleum quid pro quo. Yet curiously, for all the hue and cry by the consumers, and for all the radical claims and innuendos of the producers themselves, over the decade there was surprisingly little change in basic political arrangements that can be attributed to political pressures associated with state oil transactions. This is even true in the area most dear to OPEC hearts—the Middle East. Israel is still by far the most powerful state in the region, while the Arabs were unable to obtain a separate state for the Palestinians. Nor has there been significant movement toward the more general but rhetorically important goals of a New International Economic Order so widely touted by OPEC and other third world groups like UNCTAD.

It is in this area perhaps more than any other where fluctuating markets have eliminated simplistic notions of permanent political or economic advantage. The apparent power of OPEC to win political concessions was quickly washed away (to the extent that it existed) when the oil glut flooded the markets. We argue that to the degree that OPEC itself had political power, and quite clearly it did have some, it was in the area of getting issues before the public. This was a kind of agenda-setting power. But in most cases that we can identify over the 1970s they had surprisingly less power than one would have anticipated to directly determine national outcomes. Importing countries were pressed to listen for example, to Palestinian spokesmen. Some importers even extended diplomatic recognition to the PLO, a clear instance of heavy-handed oil influence. But listening was rarely matched with major material or even diplomatic support. OPEC influence in politics, as in commerce or the oil market itself, was directly tied to the business cycle in the oil market. When the market was tight, the exporters had some symbolic political leverage. Otherwise they had little.

Besides the Arabs, Nigeria and other black African producers have done the same to try to isolate South Africa. And individual producers have used oil supplies, or the withholding of them, to promote their own nationalistic political aims. Such was the case with the selective sales list used by the Ayatollah Khomeini's regime in Iran. Still, the vast political reordering that OPEC craved and the West feared, never materialized.

The consuming nations try to avoid obvious political pitfalls, but at the same time, few miss the chance to make diplomatic gestures of friendship when seeking oil contracts. The most organized political action by consumers has been the creation of the Euro-Arab dialogue by the Common Market members, shortly after the 1973 embargo. The Europeans created a permanent conference arrangement with the Arab League to discuss mutual economic and political interests. Oil was seldom mentioned directly but the Arab side never hesitated to use the dialogue to try to push Europe toward a more pro-Arab stance on the Palestinian issue, among others. Several states with strong policies of fostering government deals have maintained extremely friendly ties with Arab countries. Spain and Italy are major examples. Of course, it is now clear that even the lip-service of the consumer states often hinges on the state of the oil market.

For its part, the U.S. government has also been keenly aware of the possibilities for political interventions into the world oil market, and its own relative insulation by domestic supplies means it could act more freely than Europe or Japan. In 1979, for example, President Carter embargoed oil imports from Iran in direct response to the hostage crisis and in 1981 President Reagan came under increasing pressure from Congress to halt Libyan sales to the United States to reduce revenues for the Qadhafi regime. This interventionist trend in U.S. international energy affairs has also stretched to the nuclear arena where sales of reactors and uranium to countries is decided on a clear political basis, for example balancing Indian and Pakistani interests, and to oil and gas technology where sales to the Soviet Union have been tied to political events in Afghanistan and Poland. In recent cases, government policy has irritated both industry, which sees hard won business gains lost, and allied nations, who often do not share the same enthusiasm to link politics and energy on a punitive basis, although they are politically agreeable when looking for overseas sales.

For the developing countries, the government deals presented more of a political opportunity than a drawback, since with their limited economic leverage they had little to lose. They also tried to build politically on the theme of third world solidarity. The OPEC successes in winning power over industrial countries through oil inspired LDCs to try a broad range of efforts to win political recognition for developing country demands, like reduced trade barriers and more aid. The latent threat of OPEC oil cutbacks also added some muscle to third world leaders in international dealings. The presence of key oil producers such as Saudi Arabia at the Cancun summit in October 1981 did lend some credibility to the developing countries' side. However, the collapse of the world economy reduced whatever limited pressure the primary producers might have had. In addition, the limits of third world unity were revealed once it became clear that OPEC would not press the north to the mat over these issues, nor would total OPEC aid cover total LDC price increases.

GOVERNMENT OVERSEAS EXPLORATION AND DEVELOPMENT

The strategy of government controlled oil acquisition through national oil exploration companies is limited to large industrialized and to advanced developing nations which can afford the expensive, sophisticated operations. Countries approach overseas drilling in two main ways: state sponsorship of small private national exploration companies, or the use of large integrated state-owned national oil companies. The former approach is used most prominently by Japan, whose Japanese National Oil Company guides and supports several foreign drilling efforts. CFP, ENI, Hispanoil, and PetroBras are examples of the latter approach. Elf-Erap was originally a foreign exploration group focused on French North African holdings, but it has grown into an integrated national company with strong exploration efforts worldwide. DEMINEX, the German foreign exploration group, is a separate company with controling ownership held by VEBA, which, in turn, is government controled. These state exploration groups compete in the same arena with private companies, both majors and smaller firms, mainly from the United States and Canada. Frequently the state-controled and private companies will form partnerships to develop overseas high-risk areas, but in many OPEC countries the state groups may receive preferential treatment from the producer governments due to political arrangements.

Since the point of their operations is to develop crude reserves wherever possible, the state-controled companies have also been active in non-OPEC areas including the North Sea, Canada, and the United States. The Japanese have sought entry into the Dome Petroleum exploration effort in the Canadian portion of the Beaufort Sea, and several state-controled European groups have sought toeholds in the oil exploration business in the Western United States and Canada. Ironically, both the Canadians and the Americans have become sensitive about foreign companies' development of their reserves: the Canadians, after a long history of foreign involvement in their oil business, the Americans, reacting to initial moves by foreign groups, and finding the shoe on the other foot for the first time.

The Italians and French pioneered state overseas exploration activity in the 1960s with their large national companies, ENI and Elf-Aquitaine. The French companies started with major concessionary operations in French North Africa which were gradually and at times grudgingly transformed into new-style production-sharing agreements.

The Japanese, lacking a single large national oil company, have instead used a number of small exploration companies which are typically owned by several refiner and consumer companies together with the national government. These companies may be formed for a particular project or concession. The most successful of these companies has been the Arabian Oil Company, founded in 1958, which developed the offshore area of the Neutral Zone between Kuwait and Saudi Arabia. This field resulted in oil exports to Japan which peaked at over 200,000 b/d in the early 1970s. Similar Japanese exploration groups have operated in Abu Dhabi, Indonesia, and Iraq. All together, the exploration groups have brought in generally over 400,000 b/d, slightly under 10 percent of total Japanese imports. The ventures had been supported through the Japanese Development Corporation, which was eventually transformed in 1978 into the Japan National Oil Co. The government has channeled up to $400 million annually to the exploration groups in the form of loans and direct investment and grants, with the biggest expenditures coming after the 1973 crisis. The Japanese government also pursued a vigorous policy of pressuring their domestic refiners to accept the "special interest crude" from such ventures, especially the Neutral Zone output. This was especially necessary before 1979 due to refiner reluctance to break contracts with the majors and the low gravity of the crude. To meet this, the government instituted crude import tariff reductions in 1978, offered refinery conversion subsidies, and made behind-the-scenes threats through MITI to return to a mandatory quota system which would have forced refiners to take a share of the special interest crude (Platt's Oilgram News, September 28, 1978). The Japanese government took the same sort of steps to pressure home refiners to sign up for Chinese crude in the late 1970s in hopes of fostering a major government-to-government import agreement with their neighbors.

West Germany's DEMINEX, founded in 1969 as an overseas exploration company, has undertaken drilling activities in 13 countries, resulting in discoveries providing for 2.3 million tons per year of crude imports to Germany. This, however, is approximately one-tenth of the original optimistic projections for the company. DEMINEX is owned by VEBA and two other private German oil companies. The Bonn government gave it an initial DM575 million in equity and has contributed a yearly DM200 million in the form of project loans which need be repaid only if they result in successful discoveries. The private companies have made a smaller capital contribution. Thanks to its share in the North Sea Thistle field, Deminex began to turn a small profit in the early 1980s and even to repay the government loans, but its ability to open new areas and increase its overall crude production level depends heavily on increases in government aid and German diplomatic muscle. The budget squeeze which hit the federal government in 1981, plus the oil glut, threatened to hold back such expansion (Der Spiegel, June 22, 1981, p. 59).

The exploration and development deals arranged by the importer governments or sponsored by them indirectly are subject to the same geological and technological problems (and financial risks) as efforts by the major companies. Like government import deals, government exploration deals are also liable to political problems. The French national companies for example have had frequent ups and downs in winning agreements from the Algerians because of the chronically hot-and-cold French-Algerian diplomatic relations.

In the third world the Brazilian group BrasPetro (the international arm of the national company) discovered the large Majnoon oil field in Iraq in 1977, but in 1980 the Iraqis decided to take full possession of the crude, though offering a guaranteed amount of crude deliveries in lieu of the usual production-sharing agreement. The Brazilians felt that their third world status and past sympathies should have left them a better arrangement than just a long-term import contract. Still, this exploration deal transformed into a G-G import deal was better than other strict commercial terms offered by the Iraqis.

We see that as OPEC countries build up their own national expertise, they tend to drop exploration by both foreign state groups and private companies, although they may be more inclined toward national companies of third world states like Brazil or India. At the same time, exploration is a tedious, long-term and expensive activity which adds only incrementally to supplies. The oil supplies from such arrangements are thus unlikely to become a very large portion of any importer's total supply. But they can provide a stable base of reserves which may help the national supply picture, and give the national companies some clout in domestic negotiations with the majors.

RELATIONS TO THE MAJORS

The new world supply situation has reduced the role of the majors in several consumer countries; but they still remain central players. At the same time, because of the new instability, consumer governments must relate to them in new activist ways dictated by the Energy Policy Explosion.

Public officials now demand more information than ever before, in an industry where information is power. They seek data on national supply sources, costs, and so on. In a crisis period especially they must know what to expect from them and how national needs will be served. The IEA, which lets governments send in aggregated data in calm periods which does not reveal individual company trading positions, demands highly detailed company-by-company information when a major supply shortage develops. Also by 1984 the IEA had begun in depth reporting on how oil stocks were held in each members country as part of a stockpiling policy review.

The changing political control and ownership of the industry—in effect squeezed between governments upstream and down—combined with market gyrations have led to big changes in corporate structure and operations. The changing economics of upstream oil, plus falling downstream demand and profits, are leading to radical reorganizations. Some companies buy others, while the principle of vertical integration is literally under attack. By early 1984 some interests in the United States sought aggressively to break up companies like Gulf into their constituent parts—to deintegrate them—in order to make the oil reserve-owning company successful while casting off unprofitable refinery operations. This will demand new government responses in the rest of the 1980s and into the 1990s.

Several additional international government-company relations were crucial over the decade. One was how the major private companies would share out oil in an emergency. There were plans, mentioned above, for crisis sharing. But mechanisms did not exist for government-to-government or government-to-company relations during a subcrisis period. In 1979 Canada complained that Exxon and other majors were diverting crude destined for Canada to the short U.S. market. Canadian officials demanded a pledge to maintain supplies and threatened to engage in government-to-government deals to displace private importing. Similar problems have arisen for countries with tight pricing restrictions such as Sweden. When a shortage hits, as in 1979, the majors cut deliveries first to the least profitable markets, that is, those where price restrictions were greatest. The Swedes were eventually forced to seek IEA help to find supplies. There is some new evidence now however that, unlike in 1973-74, the national governments in 1979 were able successfully to exert great pressure on national companies to serve the national market first. Another major subcrisis occurred in 1980 when Turkish national supplies fell below the IEA trigger point, but the other IEA members refused to call a full-scale emergency, and patched together additional supplies from various companies, national and private.

DIVERSIFICATION OF IMPORTS

Importers have had very high hopes of diversifying their imports away from higher to lower risk areas. Mostly this meant out of OPEC, and out of the Middle East. This goal was a staple in national energy plans; countries soon found how very difficult this was to achieve in a tight market, even using G-G transactions as we saw with Korea. Table 4.3 indicates regional and functional sources of oil for major industrialized countries up to 1980. Despite sincere efforts throughout the decade, most countries found it difficult to reduce significantly their reliance on OPEC or even on the narrower group of Arab exporters. Those that did so with even slight success shifted purchases toward Nigeria or Mexico. But with the eased situation after 1982 major diversification took place. By 1984 U.S. dependence on the Persian Gulf was down to 5 percent and Europe below 30 percent.

Another means of diversifying imports was to sponsor national exploration and development in non-OPEC areas. The focus of this activity was in new marginal areas outside the major known oil basins in the North Sea or Canada. The World Bank set up several programs to improve the legal and physical infrastructure necessary to attract foreign firms to oil exploration in so-called marginal areas (West and East Africa, for example). There were also efforts to change tax laws in the industrialized countries to make such overseas operations more attractive to firms. There was considerable success in commer-

TABLE 4.3

OECD (selected) Oil Import Dependence by Region (in percent)

	September 1973	April 1980
United States		
OAPEC	30.7%	52.2
OPEC	68.2	72.3
		July 1980
Japan		
OAPEC	44.7	67.2
OPEC	91.9	86.7
		June 1980
West Germany		
OAPEC	74.8	60.6
OPEC	95.0	78.2
France		
OAPEC	72.5	78.3
OPEC	92.4	89.0
	4th Q. 1973	4th Q. 1979
Italy		
OAPEC	78.2	79.1
OPEC	90.4	85.1

Source: International Energy Statistical Review, September 30, 1980, C.I.A.

cial oil finds in several West African countries, though the size of each field was modest by world standards. Mexico and the North Sea remained the most productive Western sources, although China began to expand its activities in the early and mid-1980s.

During the 1970s, most large oil-consuming countries sought to build up their gas sector as a means to cut down oil consumption. For many countries, including France, Italy, and Germany which have small domestic supplies, the key to expanding gas use has been imports.

In virtually all consumer countries except the United States and Canada, the gas business is run by a state-controlled group or a company, such as Ruhrgas in Germany, with heavy state influence. Thus import strategies contain heavy government involvement. The dramatic French import deals for large amounts of Soviet and Algerian gas in 1982 had a clear political dimension. At the same time gas exporters, including European producers such as Britain, Norway, and the Netherlands, either use state companies to sell gas, or keep tight governmental control over exports. The result is a highly political international gas market, where the major oil companies play a very modest role compared to the producer governments. In addition, the huge front-end costs for pipelines, LNG facilities, ships, and so on, also ensure heavy government involvement, as we will see in Chapter 5.

By the mid-1970s some European producers like the Dutch were cutting back on overseas sales, preferring to keep the gas in the ground as a sort of national emergency reserve. Even Britain and Norway took similar actions, finding domestic uses for the gas produced. The Europeans and Japanese have moved strongly to purchase LNG from OPEC producers to increase import volumes and diversify. The latter had success with several contracts with Indonesia, Alaska, and Middle Eastern sources. The Europeans have had a more disappointing experience since their main supplier, Algeria, took a very hard price line, forcing delays and cancellations, as price negotiations dragged on. They were insisting on price equivalency between gas and oil, though the former is far more expensive to produce and transport. The fall of the Shah killed major Iranian gas projects for both Europe and Japan. Nigeria, another natural supplier for Europe, tried to align itself with Algeria on price demands. Its own huge gas plans were on-again-off-again both due to world market saturation and domestic policy uncertainties. The U.S. LNG industry was also hit hard by Algerian price demands (which made for real political problems in the mid-1980s when the expensive gas was finally delivered to consumers who could now get it cheaper elsewhere). One upshot was dramatic cancellations of Algerian gas contracts by two U.S. pipelines, panhandle and trunkline, in late 1983, which left a permanent scar on U.S.-Algerian energy relations. But even more pain was avoided by U.S. government policy decisions in the late 1970s to turn down two large import proposals. In these cases, the DOE said other gas sources, including Canada, Mexico, and Alaska, should take priority over LNG from OPEC.

Along with the development of LNG in the 1970s, the Europeans led by France and Germany also built up a set of gas deals with the Soviets, major gas producers. The first major deal, involving sales of European pipe and equipment in return for gas, was inspired by Chancellor Brandt's Ostpolitik in 1969-70 and came on stream by coincidence at the same time as the 1973 oil embargo. The Europeans had found the other Soviet deals relatively stable and reasonable, and moved ahead with a giant new agreement in 1981, despite the souring of the détente atmosphere, loud protests, and technology embargo from the Reagan administration. German officials felt the risk of a gas cut-off was small and could be handled by emergency measures, at the same time the trade in pipe and other goods was crucial for the stagnating economies.

But the new supply security could prove expensive. By 1984 France with huge new Algerian and Soviet contracts kicking-in was swimming in unneeded gas. Gas de France was piling up huge losses as it had to sell Algerian gas below cost to meet competition from France's cheap, nuclear based electricity and undertake an expensive storage program to handle in flowing gas volumes. The 1984 Mitterrand budget austerity program hurt, as the French Foreign Ministry ended a subsidy to GdF which had helped cover the extra high price of the Algerian gas which GdF had been originally encouraged to accept for French foreign political reasons. Because gas is a less flexible fuel, with high long-term investment costs attached, France was locked into tough "take or pay" supply contracts and was thus totally boxed in with a diversification policy which was proving more trouble than it was worth.

One final major diversification area is coal. Several consumer countries have realized the price advantages of coal in the late 1970s due to the OPEC II oil price hikes. They sought stable supplies from the United States, Australia, and elsewhere. They began developing transport facilities, and stepped up programs to encourage coal use domestically. The slowdown of the nuclear energy effort in some countries has encouraged this development. The United States has taken a liberal policy toward coal exports, seeing them as a way to pull Europeans away from politically dangerous oil and gas deals with the Soviets and radical OPEC states. The IEA has also been active in this, working in 1979 and 1980 on ways to reduce barriers to coal imports and soliciting pledges of export expansion from members. There are real problems however with quickly building up coal imports that hinge on the lead times necessary for upgrading the ports and rail infrastructures.

Here again we see that one of the principal consequences of the international Energy Policy Explosion was the search to diversify energy supplies. In the same way that the oil exporters sought to diversify both their customers and their economic base through industrialization, so the importer governments sought to diversify the channels through which they obtained their supplies, and the kinds of supplies they imported. Neither the traditional private suppliers nor government-to-government deals for oil from OPEC sources proved sufficient to solve their import problems. Much of the commercial and political logic of the early and mid-1970s was the need to follow, and indeed anticipate, the shift away from the oil majors. By the end of the decade, it was clear that a shift entirely to government-to-government oil deals was as politically undesirable as it was commercially unlikely. And by 1984, with a still feeble world energy demand, governments had more luxury to choose from among the various import channels and steer their economies toward the most reasonable mix, both from an economic and a security viewpoint.

5

ENHANCING
DOMESTIC SUPPLY

INTRODUCTION

Shooting at a Moving Target

As the old international order disintegrated after 1973,
consumer governments sought greater control over energy
imports, as described in Chapter 4, but they also turned more
attention to greater energy autonomy. Expanding domestic
supplies became a high priority. And as with import policy,
production policies were hostages to the fluctuating M-shaped
market of 1973-1983.

The troughs and peaks in the world oil market and international business cycle created real uncertainty on the part of
private energy companies, investors, consumers, and national
governments over how much scarce capital to commit to expensive
energy projects. Uncertainty increased further as real capital
costs increased and growth slowed.

Two principals clashed. On the one hand were the special
investment requirements of the energy industry: huge amounts
of capital, and market stability; on the other hand were the
growing capital costs and extreme volatility in all energy markets
during the 1970s. Energy projects require huge amounts of
capital up front. They have an extremely long planning horizon,
and require making a bet about the best technology at the right
price 20 years down the road. But in the 1970s the requirements for market stability clashed with the realities of market
instability.

Governments and companies continued to commit the capital to expand domestic production, but with each new fluctuation they became more uneasy and project investments became more uncertain.

It appears that the rate of increase in energy projects was affected by the market fluctuations. When prices rose, governments with some lag time committed more resources to domestic energy production, all things being equal. As prices declined, the opposite occurred.

After 1973 the rate of oil exploration to increase domestic production went up as once uneconomic oil and gas resources now became commercially attractive. New investments were greatest in oil but expanded at a slightly lower rate for coal and nuclear power. But when prices fell in real terms between 1975 and 1978, and again after 1980, investments slowed. The reasons for the changes were a mixture both of commercial incentives and changed government attitudes and policies toward domestic energy company operations.

Within this overall picture, however, specific investments and drilling rates varied between geographic areas and political boundaries. U.S. drilling rates went up by 50 percent between 1971 and 1979 (Finance and Development, March 1983, p. 36). Over the same period however the LDC drilling was disappointing and remained flat for the group as a whole. Even the increases after 1979 were smaller than could be expected given the new incentives for oil companies to diversify out of the Middle East/ OPEC areas, and of LDC governments to reduce their oil import burden through increased domestic exploration and production. Thus for every 14,000 wells drilled in the OECD countries in 1979 only 64 were sunk in non-OPEC LDCs.

U.S. oil drilling increased in part because of the political stability of the United States, price control phase out, the ready availability of equipment and skilled labor, and its proximity to large markets; LDC areas were more risky to foreign firms.

But for the world as a whole the pattern held: higher prices, more exploration; when prices fell in real terms between 1975 and 1978, once economic projects were cut back. Some (like synthetic fuels on a large scale after 1982, and nuclear plants more generally after mid-decade) were abandoned or their construction stretched out. The synfuels sector had historically remained close to the margin of profitability and was not considered proven on a large scale when the price gyrations hit. It looked like $40-50 per barrel was the magical threshold point, and when prices fell, so did interest in oil derived from coal and shale.

By 1980 the budget deficits in energy consumer countries crimped funds for new energy projects and long-term research and development. Energy budgets, while still comparatively large, had to be measured against other priorities. In some cases like the United States, they were mercilessly pared down. Finally, the high interest rates that accompanied the deficits made new long term investments in energy production more expensive and this reduced the margin of economic gain and enhanced risks. Finally as energy prices went up forecasts of consumption went down, lessening the need for more production in the medium term.

The financial and administrative burdens of expanding domestic energy supply, and continuing to support oil imports was tremendous. Oil imports alone cost the developing countries about $74 billion in 1980; investments in expanding domestic production have also climbed. It is estimated that LDCs need to double their investments in domestic energy production (up to about 4 percent of their GNP), but many of them lack the money and manpower to do so. The World Bank calculated that all the developing countries (including the exporters as well as importers) will have to spend on the average of $130 billion every year for the next ten years to meet domestic energy requirements, including about $65 billion in foreign exchange.

Governments' understanding of the problem also changed over the decade. They came to appreciate that expanding domestic production was not just a matter of calling in a company to find oil or gas on terms of one's own choosing. Oil companies proved initially reluctant to plunge into uncharted political and geological territories, especially in LDCs. Through trial and much error, government officials found they had to achieve the right balance to make exploration attractive for company profits without giving away the store. As we will see below, this involved a complex calculus of taxation, royalty, managerial control, and even pricing of the domestically produced oil, should any be discovered. Governments also discovered that achieving energy autonomy was very expensive and for most countries, even those like the United States with a large domestic base, was impossible in the medium run.

A crucial factor in countries with some domestic production (for example, the United States, India, and Brazil) was that the world oil market price rises posed major policy questions for the pricing of domestic oil, and hence for other substitute energy forms. The choices were to charge the same price for domestic oil as imported oil, or to price the former below world levels. If world prices as set by OPEC, which consumer governments were denouncing as extortionist, were allowed to pass through and serve as benchmarks applying equally to domestic oil, consumers would suffer and voters would complain. Local producers would enjoy sudden windfall profits from wholly external events. This combination of sudden profits for some and sudden losses for others created a volatile political mixture in countries with domestic reserves.

The United States, Canada, and Australia quickly set up systems to isolate their domestic production from the world market by keeping national prices lower than world prices. However, one unintended consequence of pricing policy to minimize undesirable income effects was to slow incentives on the production side. Only by the end of the 1970s had the negative effects of this policy on production been taken seriously enough to force moves toward world market pricing for domestic oil development in these countries. Still, Canada retains significant controls on prices, keeping them at 70 percent of world levels.

Natural gas was harder to handle because of the complex contract pricing system, and prices lagged behind oil.

In other resource-rich countries like Norway and Great Britain where the state-owned mineral resources were just starting to be developed in the early 1970s, government allowed world prices for domestic production. They did however set high tax and oil-sharing systems which also acted on occasion as a brake on development.

Beyond the oil price question, all consumer countries, including those with relatively straightforward energy production policies, found major obstacles after 1973 in environmental and safety problems which hindered nuclear, coal, and liquified gas projects as well as oil drilling. Virtually all governments were forced to open this issue to public debate. But in some cases, such as nuclear referenda in Austria in 1978 and Sweden in 1980, they had to accept public decisions to put strict limits on energy development. Administrative systems had to be devised to give proper attention to the environmental risks, even in relatively restrictive countries like Brazil where opposition to the military government's nuclear program forced some revisions.

The combination of political and market factors meant that the movement to actually implement domestic supply policies was uneven and in many cases extremely slow. Some governments, especially those with few home resources and confronted with the greatest vulnerability and fewest options, moved directly toward comprehensive policies to enhance domestic production.

In some developing countries where resources were plentiful but underdeveloped, the high cost of oil imports led to quick decisions to step up domestic production, such as Brazil's alcohol programs. But in many other consumer countries, especially those with large natural resources, entrenched industry and social interests, and less dependence on energy imports, the policy decisions were much more complex. In some cases the initial reactions led to policies which discouraged new production, or to long paralyzing public debates that stymied production initiatives by creating additional uncertainty.

Yet, despite the numerous examples of two steps forward and one back, government policies did indeed make a difference for national energy supply, and this intervention was consistent with our picture of the energy policy explosion.

The French government accelerated its nuclear program and the American government slashed nuclear programs like the Clinch Breeder Reactor. Brazil liberalized its oil exploration provisions for foreign investors by the end of the decade and more companies came in, while Canada tightened its provisions and oil companies packed up and left. The Indian government itself developed the Bombay High fields off its western coast, and then began to encourage more private exploration by proving that oil was there. China finally made up its mind about oil exploration policy in 1978 after years of government see-sawing and by 1983, 33 new companies had been granted licenses for 43 parcels. The governments of Kenya and Zimbabwe launched gasahol projects that wouldn't be done purely by private enterprise. Government policies promoted or slowed domestic supply expansion. The key is that governments provided both a set of specific policies and an overall policy framework within which public and private companies could make strategic business choices, while safeguarding other public interests like environmental protection, national security, and human health and safety.

GOVERNMENTAL MEANS TO INFLUENCE DOMESTIC SUPPLY

There were many instruments available to governments to achieve the broad national objective of increased domestic supply. They can be divided into two classes—direct and indirect. The distinction is based largely on whether the government has direct ownership of energy resources and control over the means of energy production (that is, the production companies); or alternatively whether these are held and controled by private companies. In the latter case private managers must be moved to specific actions by government's indirect financial and administrative measures. The requirements and complexities of this arms length policy are quite different from direct ownership and control policies.

Governments also have many responsibilities which conflict with promotion of energy production. These include insuring a fair return to the public on publicly owned resources, determining from a political standpoint the proper scope of state enterprises, protecting national enterprises from foreign influence and providing environmental protection. No oil-importing country was immune from these contradictory imperatives. In some cases oil production policy was nullified or seriously hampered by competing public policy goals.

Finally, despite the morass of tedious technical minutiae of leases, royalties, and buy-back agreements, it was the balance between the bargaining power of the government, and the bargaining power of the oil companies, that shaped the final package of policies governing exploration, production, and distribution.

Direct Policy Instruments

There are two main direct energy production policy instruments.

1. Government Ownership of Energy Resources

In virtually all energy consuming countries it is government, either national or state, that has sovereignty over key mineral resources: uranium, oil, gas, or coal. The United States and Canada are the exceptions. Both retain a legal tradition under which mineral rights belong to private property owners. But even in these countries the national and state governments happen to be owners of vast tracts of the most promising oil, gas, shale, and coal prospecting areas plus the main outer continental shelf zones. They therefore do have decisive influence over exploration and production of a substantial part of the nation's energy resources.

In Europe and most developing countries subsoil rights inherently belong to the government, providing a direct channel of control. Based on their ownership of mineral rights, governments employ a set of key policy instruments to affect production. These include most prominently:

Leasing and Licensing Systems. Leases determine the when, where, by whom, how, and how much of resource exploration and production.

Royalty and Production Sharing Rules. They determine the cut (before business taxes) the government as owner will take of the resources and/or revenue. It is a fee or payment by the company that wants to use the resources to the owner.

By adjusting the severity of these two direct systems government as owner can greatly influence the amount of exploration and production which companies will be willing to do. This is never a purely technical exercise, but a function of hard bargaining between two sides.

The exploration companies, whether state or private, naturally want the rules as loose as possible, and will apply whatever economic and political pressures they can in this direction. Governments, of course, want them as tight as possible. Normally, when exploration and production lag behind what the government feels is a reasonable level, or hoped-for resources are difficult to find, governments relax the rules to encourage the (usually private) companies to step up the domestic production program. When production achieves high levels or new resources are found in abundance, the bargaining balance shifts and governments tighten the screws.

This constant of company-government skirmishing occurs on shifting terrain since other factors are always changing. World market prices rise or fall; energy demand will contract or expand; the resource base will be enlarged through discovery; domestic political coalitions disintegrate, and new technologies become available. All of these factors seriously influence the bargaining and outcomes by affecting the willingness or ability of one of the two sides to impose its preferences on the other.

2. Government Ownership of the Means of Production

This refers to whether the national oil, gas, power, coal, or other energy companies (as distinct from resource ownership) are owned by the government, or by private firms. The degree of government ownership of these firms is a crucial cross-national difference from country to country. It varies widely among consumer countries depending on the dominant ideological forces and historical traditions. The United States, with its free enterprise ideology, has virtually no direct government participation in energy production, especially oil and gas (TVA is the frequently cited exception). In Europe, by contrast, many countries have nationalized coal and electric power systems and also national companies for domestic oil and gas exploitation. Others use a mixture of public and private enterprise. Britain, for example, has strong public traditions in coal, nuclear energy, and gas but, after building up BNOC participation in the North Sea fields, saw a political shift reducing that engagement under a Conservative government. Germany on the other hand relies strongly on private ownership in all sectors but with passive government holdings in several key firms.

Developing countries and those in southern Europe tend toward a heavy government role in energy industries due to both ideologies and the lack of private groups at home which can raise and manage the large investment funds necessary. Even in capitalist-oriented companies like South Korea, public energy enterprises dominate the industrial landscape. The largest public corporation in Korea is the Korea Electric Company (KECO), which is 82 percent owned by government (Department of Energy 1981, p. 252). State enterprises are also active in domestic petroleum exploration and development and KECO dominates the nuclear power industry as well. Korean coal, however, is produced domestically by more than 170 private companies, unlike in India where government dominates (Department of Energy 1981, p. 253). However, government can enforce its policies through state grants and loans. The direct control of production allows for decisive policy implementation as in the case of the French nuclear program and for risky ventures that fulfill government production plans but might not take place under pure free enterprise conditions.

In most cases, because of the danger of tangled administrative lines and the need for a sense of business motivation and autonomy, government-owned energy firms are held separately from the main government bureaucracy. In principle this encourages independence, service, and profits. But in some countries, especially LDCs with weaker and inexperienced bureaucracies, this tradition does not take hold and the ministerial and company roles get hopelessly confused. In Brazil, and even with EDF and Elf/Aquitaine in France and ENI in Italy, the parastatal companies become tremendous power centers in their own right that almost overwhelm governments. This dilutes the direct flow of policy making by cabinet level officials and their deputies. Thus, when the president of PetroBras went on to become president of Brazil there were some who asked whether it was a promotion or a demotion.

Indirect Policy Instruments

The main indirect instruments, that is, one step removed from direct ownership or management, operate on the immediate business environment of the firm through taxation or regulation. These include the following:

1. Power to Set Well-head and Mine-mouth Prices for Oil, Gas, and Coal

These are prices set at the point of production. They are distinct from the final energy price paid by the consumer, although they do constitute an important component. The well-head price for domestically produced energy serves as an important base line (especially if pegged at world level).

Wellhead control of oil and gas prices employed in the United States, Canada, and Australia became a hindrance to new production as well as a nemesis to energy conservation programs. Plans for gradually phasing out well-head controls therefore became a major part of energy production and conservation programs, backed by curious coalitions of big private companies and some conservation groups. Besides the clear conservation problem with keeping well-head prices below world levels, other snags made the policy hard to maintain. Because they created an artificial difference between domestic and imported crude, controlled prices required a means for equalizing costs to refiners of the two types so that some refiners would not get an unfair advantage from receiving more of the low price domestic output. The U.S. answer to this problem, the entitlements system, was cumbersome and justly unpopular. In 1980 the Indian government paid its own ONCC and O.I.L. Rs.305.42 per ton for onshore oil and Rs.434.65 per ton for offshore or about U.S.$5.32 and $7.43 respectively (Petroleum Economist, November 1980, p. 496). This "payment to itself" kept domestic energy costs down.

Governments controlling well-head prices are also forced to use export taxes or other restrictions to discourage sales of their lower cost domestic oil abroad. Here the Canadian export tax system is a prime example. Finally, the domestic consumption of lower cost domestic oil automatically gives the price-controlling countries an industrial cost advantage in international industrial competition.

By the 1980s the United States had dropped controls entirely and Canada and Australia were phasing up toward world prices. But several countries continued to control gas prices based on historical contracts or a fixed relationship with world oil prices.

As with oil, this tended to discourage production. But governments found gas pricing more difficult to adjust due to the
physical structure of the production and distribution and need
for long-term contracts. Also, while post-1973 political demands
for oil price controls were clearly difficult to justify given the
world market oil pricing system, the basis for gas price controls
frequently is well established and can be viewed as a necessity
to protect the public interest.

2. Taxes and Other Fiscal Measures Affecting Energy Production

Traditionally the United States and other oil-producing
consumer countries have used special tax regimes for oil production as a means to favor producers and encourage output. The
U.S. depletion allowance, which was finally ended for large
producers in 1975 as a political reaction to the sudden oil price
surge, was a bonanza for the industry which had resulted from
years of heavy lobbying and the lack of an effective antioil
opposition. It was by no means a "policy" in the post-1973
sense. Some countries like West Germany and India try to promote domestic coal production by taxing oil products or oil
imports. Several other countries maintain major benefits on
their tax codes for oil and gas exploration and development,
using these as an incentive to pull in outside exploration groups.
But also, following the example of OPEC and taking account of
the rise in the value of whatever oil that is found, several countries have introduced tough tax measures which put a heavy
burden on oil revenues over and above any royalty amounts the
government may collect as owner of the oil. Governments usually
use a tax regime that both rewards and penalizes to steer companies toward a desired type of exploration and production.
Canada has both stiff revenue taxes on oil and strong benefits
for drilling in approved areas by approved companies.

3. Control over Foreign Investment in Domestic Energy Projects

Governments exercise this power to insure that nationally
owned oil, gas, coal, and uranium mining firms (state or private)
maintain a sufficient share of national energy development.

In many countries, like Brazil, France, or India, effective
government production monopolies in coal and nuclear power
generation means that foreign investment in many domestic
energy projects is de facto excluded. But detailed control over
foreign investors remains strong in oil and gas. The policy,
with Canada the prime example, is generally aimed at the
American- and European-owned multinationals. It has also

begun to be applied by some countries (including the United
States in an informal fashion) to entry by OPEC and European
state-owned firms in resource rich countries.

Brazil wanted to increase exploration for and production
of uranium while limiting foreign control of that industry, and
did so through a complex uranium export/technology import
deal with West Germany in 1975. Brazil bought a complete
nuclear fuel cycle, and permitted Germany to exploit two uranium
sites totaling 73,000 square miles, restricting their share to an
initial 20 percent of production that could rise afterwards,
while the government's take was 51 percent (De La Court et al.
1982, p. 36).

4. State Loans, Loan Guarantees and Grants for Projects and
   Aid through Research and Development Programs

Governments use direct subsidies, soft loans, and guarantees to support high cost, risky energy production projects.
This is over and above those projects directly owned by the
government and financed through state energy companies and
covers special support schemes for both public and privately
controlled groups. Subsidies have long been used for coal
production to aid against competition from low cost oil. Since
1973 governments have continued such aid, recognizing not only
the economic potential from modernized coal operations but also
the anemic financial state of the coal industry. Also, since
1973 aid in several countries has gone to high technology or
experimental synfuels and solar projects which could not get
sufficient backing through private investment. Oil and gas
ventures, which are of a different nature because of the hide-
and-seek element connected with finding oil, are generally aided
through tax breaks which are better suited to cover the basic
risk of finding or not finding a commercial-sized deposit.
Several countries have set up specific agencies to distribute
loans and guarantees to commercial projects including the
controversial U.S. Synfuels agency and poetically named "French
Agency for the Mastering of Energy." Also many governments
including the German and Japanese have established financing
for the subsidies through direct taxes on imported oil and other
types of energy consumption. A link between the U.S. oil
windfall tax and synfuels funding was proposed but never
established.

The widely touted Brazilian gasohol project was only possible
through a dense network of government-owned research units
and high industry grants and subsidies. At the same time
virtually all countries have governmentally supported energy

research programs paid for directly by citizen taxes through the national budgets. Many research efforts had long concentrated on nuclear energy which was considered a proper field for government work because of the military aspects and high cost of research. As state research budgets grew rapidly in the 1970s because the perceived need to improve nonoil energy sources, coal, synthetic fuels, solar, and other renewables all took a larger share of funds. Much of the work continued to be done in government establishments. But more of the non-nuclear effort was carried on by private industry usually using a grant formula under which the government paid a substantial part of the cost and kept some control over patent rights. This high level of government research aid was cut back in the early 1980s due to the general budget problems affecting most governments. The scarcity of funding forced a period of pruning which was especially tough on large scale, costly projects such as advanced nuclear reactors and large synfuel plants which were already hit by M-shaped market factors.

5. Licensing of Plants and Transportation Systems and Environmental and Safety Measures

States can strongly influence energy production by the degree of toughness of project-licensing rules and general environmental standards which apply to the usually dirty business of digging up resources or producing electrical energy. Equally important is the efficiency and legal standing of the rules and the procedures used to enforce them. As environmental protection groups increased their activities worldwide in the 1970s and new and untested environmental laws were passed, the possibilities for delaying and halting energy projects grew, in many countries out of all proportion to actual problems. Governments were forced to kill some projects to meet their own standards or political needs. Other plans died as industry could not afford the costs of ongoing delays. Some countries instituted programs to cut red tape and simplify procedures to "fast track" important projects. In France and later in West Germany this approach worked for nuclear projects, but in the United States such efforts have been tied up by a fierce partisan debate and the diffuse nature of the legal system. Speed-up measures in the United States virtually remain a case by case legislative matter with the congressional decisions on the Alaska oil pipeline in 1969 and Alaska gas pipeline in 1981 as leading examples. In many countries the environmental issue, especially involving nuclear energy, has transcended the purely energy-related area and taken on a basic social value. Sweden and

Austria have held nuclear referenda and the Netherlands went
through a long term exercise of the same sort. Some of the
United States have also held nuclear votes, but the loss of an
antinuclear proposal in California in 1971 appeared to kill chances
of effective use of this tool in the United States by nuclear
opponents.

General Government Influence

Governments can also influence energy production in more
general ways. One crucial intangible is the amount of political
and social certainty which the government and political system
as a whole can provide about future production policies. National
regimes backed by a clear political consensus that developed
firm plans for enhancing production managed in the 1970s to
attract long-term investments and also gave consumers needed
assurances that a particular fuel would be available. In a case
such as New Zealand's massive switch to gas-based methanol
for autos, this long-term planning was essential because of the
uniqueness of the technology and its application to many separate
consumers rather than a single concentrated one.
This issue of political stability, so often applied to developing countries, set up an interesting and in some ways unexpected
dynamic between the United States and Canada. In each country
individually, where oil and gas pricing and leasing policies were
the subject of fierce political debate for most of the late 1970s
and into the 1980s, private investment held back, waiting to see
what sort of political deal would emerge. Just as the U.S.
energy policy settled down, Canada's was thrown into question
through Trudeau's New Energy Policy, and oil and gas firms
once active in Canada were pushed and pulled out, many taking
up drilling activities south of the border in U.S. fields. This
helped contribute to the economic mini-boom in cities like Denver,
and to the slump in cities like Calgary.
A similar situation faced LDCs anxious to secure control
over national energy resources while also encouraging foreign
firms to explore (Broadman 1983). Over the decade the governments, the companies, and other agencies like the World Bank
wrestled with how to proceed in the face of "political risk."
The evidence suggests that companies are concerned about
instability, but that is defined as much in terms of the rapid
turnover of ministerial staff, changeable drilling regulations,
and uncertainty over taxes and profit repatriation as it is about
fears of outright nationalization or revolution. In India, for

example, between July 1979 and March of 1980 "there were no fewer than seven different men holding the oil ministry portfolio— each with different ideas" (Petroleum Economist, November 1980, p. 496). Turkey, too, has been plagued by frequent turnovers of top energy officials. And political ideology needn't determine "stability." Oil companies have had fewer problems in Marxist Congo or Angola than in topsy-turvey capitalist Nigeria. This is not to deny that political turmoil also can impede exploration and production, as the Indian government discovered during the rioting in the northeast province of Assam. But the insta- bility issue encompasses a broad range of domestic and inter- national factors that affect the local government and the companies themselves in complex ways. Smaller independent exploratory firms, for example, are less able to diversify their risks across several countries than are the majors and may be more conservative in their investments.

The role of "general government influence," as we call it here, in turn hinges on the interaction of the oil market and domestic politics. When the oil market is stable and relatively soft, there will be much less pressure for government to take as active a role as might otherwise be the case. U.S. energy policy under Ronald Reagan has been a nonissue in part because his administration's political philosophy is "the best energy policy is the least energy policy." But this political philosophy has been greatly helped by the decline in prices. The same philoso- phy in a different market would probably produce very different political responses.

Changing Scope and Scale of Energy
Production Operations

A key reason for the sensitivity of potential energy produc- tion schemes to uncertain political conditions is that now more energy production demands larger organizations with larger management and investments capabilities. Energy sector opera- tions have always been big and expensive; they have become more so.

Oil and gas prospecting, while still in some cases possible by traditional small operator, wildcat methods, is more and more frequently a matter of offshore or deep onshore drilling which requires expensive technology, complex testing, and leasing procedures beforehand. Still with no guarantee of success, this demands large up-front capital and expertise which only large companies can manage.

Nuclear and synfuels projects have become enormously expensive undertakings which require vast amounts of preparation and technical input. They can be financially ruinous if brought on stream in an adverse market situation. The situation is worsened because because electric utilities which promote nuclear projects are usually underfinanced. Alternative fuels such as gasohol and solar can be produced on a smaller scale, with less capital risk, but to become important fuel sources they will also require major organizational backing. Coal also is moving away from the small mine to large scale open pit operations which, along with transportation requirements, become giant financial undertakings.

Besides the increase in size and complexity of energy production projects, private companies are tending to diversify into production of several fuel types. Companies in the energy field want to cover all bets, especially as fuel use is becoming more specialized and advances in synfuels have made coal, gas, and liquid products available from a single industrial process. This horizontal integration has been led in the 1970s by the multinational oil companies who have used their large post-1973 oil profits to diversify into coal, synfuels, uranium, and even renewables. This activity has abated somewhat in the early 1980s as the new oil price stability cut profits and forced the oil companies to reduce risky ventures and concentrate on their core business. Also the diversification wave of the 1970s brought a political response which in the United States resulted in proposals limiting oil company holdings especially in coal and solar energy. Diversification does pose real questions about the state's ability to monitor and influence energy developments for the common good. Coal companies have been less able to diversify because of lack of capital, leaving most synfuels activity to the oil companies. In fact, many of the U.S. coal companies became a target for oil company takeovers. This horizontal expansion has been less noticeable among state-owned enterprises. European governments have tended to keep their companies focused on a single energy source and instead create new enterprises to handle developments in new energy sectors, while investment and coordination occurs at the level of the central government. France and Britain have quite distinct, clearly defined groups for oil, gas, coal, and electricity/nuclear energy. In France the main synfuels work has been given to the national coal company Charbonnages de France. The national oil companies ELF and CFP however have gone into solar energy projects. The result is that competition for customers and investment capital among these sectors in a country may be more real (even though it is exercised at the bureaucratic level) than in a supposedly free enterprise system. The French national companies CDF, GDF, and EDF by 1983 had entered into a veritable dog fight to attract customers to competing coal, gas, and electric systems raising charges that the government did not have a real energy plan.

Besides increasing their scope in the energy field, companies both private and state-owned have also increased their geographic scope. Several European-based state oil groups have turned to exploration abroad because of limited prospects at home. Also European coal consuming groups have increasingly sought participation in foreign mines to insure a share of the production will flow to them. The large private multinationals have shown increased selectivity in where they make new production investments, steering away from politically questionable areas.

Finally, there is a pair of policies that governments may employ to expand domestic production, especially of nonoil or new primary fuels, that encompass many of the separate issues raised above. Governments may try to reorganize or rationalize an industry characterized by poor production performance. Governments also can use demand-side pricing policy to encourage more production of a given fuel. These two policies together raise the important issue of coordinating domestic supply policies across industries. When employed in tandem the two policies can complement one another to increase fuel supplies. But they can also work at cross-purposes.

In the years preceding the first oil shock India was faced with the problem of expanding fuel supplies for industry and transport, and turned to the domestic coal industry. It found a sector peppered with many small inefficient mines owned by many separate proprietors unable to step up production because mine modernization was too expensive to pursue individually. Government eventually forced consolidation and improved supply through direct administrative intervention and various new economic incentives that encouraged more rational production techniques.

Governments also encourage greater domestic production by directly promoting demand for a fuel. Sometimes increased exploration, industry rationalization, or other supplyside policies alone are insufficient to revitalize an industry because consumers remain skeptical about supply reliability and are reluctant to switch. Policies may be put in place which encourage final consumers to use a particular fuel. Brazil closed gasoline stations on certain weekend days while permitting

gasohol stations to remain open, and redesigned the tax code
to make it more attractive for taxicab companies to buy gasohol
rather than pure gasoline cars. In the United States a mandatory percentage of synfuels use in fuel was discussed but never
adopted.

Thus, policies to increase domestic production by targeting
the supply side whether directly or indirectly is only one side
of the coin. An integrated national program to increase local
resources cannot proceed without carefully considering the
structure of national energy prices and demand and their
impact on the local supply mix in the country. It is always
the intersection of demand and supply that forms national policy.
Thus the justification for increasing domestic supplies hinged
on the kinds, qualities, and economic locations of the supplies
to be (potentially) produced vis-à-vis the national demand
structure.

This problem of confronting interfuel substitution implications across energy subsectors when promoting local supply
has become a major headache for governments who heretofore
did not have to deal with the issue. For many developing countries the managerial skills necessary to harmonize policies across
a number of products and industries is not available, making
the restructuring of production even more problematic.

In the rest of this chapter we will analyze consumer
government policies to expand or control domestic production
focusing on direct and indirect methods of intervention as
applied in each of the main energy sectors as countries moved
through the decade's M-shaped market: oil, gas, coal, nuclear
energy, and electricity.

OIL

Introduction: Oil Promotion Versus Oil Control

The energy policy explosion forced governments to learn
very quickly how to design new domestic oil policies and instruments to respond to the new international oil market. Some of
these were already in place in 1973; others had to be developed
"on the run" over the course of the decade. The greatest
challenge was to knit together old and new instruments to create
an integrated national petroleum production policy.

We have seen in earlier chapters that the search for domestic
oil became a major economic and political issue. Faced with the
economic challenge of reducing balance of payments problems,

governments pressed hard to expand domestic production rapidly through any means available—which usually meant multinationals. Yet faced with a simultaneous political challenge to national autonomy on the energy front, political leaders had to proceed with caution and maintain as much national governmental control as possible. Sometimes expanding production clashed directly with the desire for political control. This was a more acute problem in oil than in the other primary fuels.

Also, governments had to design policy packages that fit their own unique resource, economic, and political conditions. Officials in both LDCs and industrialized countries had to learn to read the complex and often contradictory commercial and political signals to know when to use each oil policy instrument (leases, taxes, production sharing, etc.).

The problem of domestic oil supply affected different kinds of countries in different ways. For poor developing countries like Tanzania, which by the end of the 1970s was paying 80 percent of its foreign exchange earnings for oil imports, and had only marginal returns on its oil exploration efforts, high oil prices continued to be a great millstone around the neck of national development. Resource-poor NICs like Korea and Taiwan searched for oil but found themselves with among the lowest estimated reserves of all the countries in the Asia Pacific region (Cooper, in Stunkel 1981, p. 367). In the short term, however, their high export earnings made the oil import bill bearable. Those NICs with some actual production like Brazil, Argentina, and India placed great national hopes (and big bucks) on future self-sufficiency. And for former oil importers like Mexico, Britain, and Ivory Coast domestic oil was a symbol of economic salvation by the late 1970s, real or promised, and oil became the lifeblood of the national economy even as it created unforseen economic distortions. In Canada and Australia the accent was put on the key place of oil in the country's large array of national resources and the need for a national policy that reflected that role. In the United States, oil production remained a key element of the national economy and energy system and also a touchstone of the free enterprise ideology, thus a constant source of political debate. Domestic energy production also provided the backbone of economic growth in cities like Anchorage, Denver, Dallas, and Houston.

Yet by the beginning of the 1980s all importers found that the search for domestic production was a process with unforseen costs as well as potential benefits. Countries like Mexico and Nigeria discovered that reliance on this single commodity to earn money abroad provoked severe problems at home when oil prices suddenly plummeted. Development projects were halted, unemployment soared, and foreign debts piled high as oil revenues dried up. The Nigerian coup at the end of 1983 was the final result of this process. If low prices caused problems for domestic producers, high prices also had their domestic costs. Countries like Mexico and Britain found that terrible inflation and exchange rate imbalances threatened the longer-term health of their national economies. The high value of the pound, due to North Sea oil wealth, made traditional British exports much more expensive and uncompetitive (Amuzegar 1982).

Oil MNCs of course were in the center of the search by importer governments for a balance between production and control. Burned by their loss of control and reduced access to OPEC oil, MNCs were more anxious to open up new sources in consumer countries, especially those with seemingly dependable political systems, but they also were ready to use their political weight in consuming countries and their virtual monopoly on production expertise to get the most possible profit from new oil finds, showing a reluctance to invest where economic terms appeared unfavorable. It is this multisided tug of war among the governments, the public (as ultimate resource owners and consumers), private and state-owned companies, and OPEC (as a silent fourth partner) which makes oil policy differ widely from country to country, going far beyond the simple proposition that enhancing domestic production is de facto good policy.

Among the major consuming countries we can make a distinction between (A) those who began the decade with large proven reserves and on-going exploration and production (the United States, Canada, Australia, the United Kingdom, and Norway), and (B) those with some production or oil potential and active domestic exploration programs (Brazil, France, Ireland, India, Argentina, Spain, Turkey, Israel, Greece, Denmark, Austria, West Germany, Italy, and several non-OPEC African countries). A third group of countries with virtually no oil resources and no meaningful production policy includes Belgium, Switzerland, Korea, and Sweden.

In Group B, the newcomers to oil, the policy problem is to encourage new exploration through relatively favorable terms that attract private investment. Typically in Group A, since the companies are already there, questions of high lease revenues, price controls, taxation of profits, national control, well depletion, and pollution caused by drilling and tanker or pipe transport were usually most important, all tending to discourage or control production. But in periods of national economic strain or world oil scarcity, new exploration and expanding production become major issues for both groups.

Paradoxically, from a policymaker's view, the process of looking for oil is relatively simple to manage; finding it in commercial quantities is what creates major conflicts within and beyond government that have no easy resolutions. The transition by one country from group B to group A is often a bumpy ride. And for countries in group B with a singleminded search for oil, the difficulty group A countries have handling oil in a coherent way, especially in those with open decentralized democratic systems that create boisterous political battles, is often hard to grasp. This misunderstanding was at the root of much of the tension between supposedly allied IEA members during the late 1970s.

Oil: Direct Measures

The two direct governmental means to influence oil production, leasing policy and creating a national company to handle at least some domestic exploration and production are by now standard policy fixtures in most industrial and developing countries in both groups. When they are absent it is usually due to national ideological reasons or a historical precedent, not how far along a country is on the way to large scale production. Both instruments are essentially neutral and can be pitched to either promote or restrain production.

Leasing is particularly important as the dominant form by which governments make policy for oil resources. It is usually a government's single most important oil policy tool and as such deserves to be discussed in detail at this point.

An oil lease, as considered here, is a general legal form under which the state (or in some countries the private owner of mineral rights) arranges terms with a specialized company for exploration and production of oil in a specific geographic area. Even if a state intends to exploit some or all of its oil resources itself, it normally uses a lease format to allow a clear definition of the legal situation between the government as resource owner and the government producing agency. This also clarifies what land areas are open to nongovernment companies. Because of the peculiar high-risk, high-reward nature of oil, lease arrangements are complicated, containing a series of benefits to both the owner of the resource and to the explorer-producer.

The essence of the lease agreement is the balance achieved in the benefits to both sides. This is normally reached through negotiation before exploration takes place and may be tilted in one direction or the other depending on several factors, including: the potential richness of the resource base determined by initial testing; the physical difficulty (and hence cost) of exploration and production, especially in offshore and Arctic areas which require high investment; the need of the leasing government for new oil resources given domestic economic and energy situation; and the desire of the production company for new sources of crude given the world market situation and terms of crude access elsewhere, and of course, the balance of demand, supply, and price worldwide. One of the lessons of the 1970s was that these parameters can change dramatically, making leasing arrangements open to frequent renegotiation or unilateral abrogation.

A government with rich potential resources and relatively low pressure to get quick results can take a much tougher bargaining position than one which has poor drilling prospects to offer and needs a quick economic boost from home oil supplies to counter mounting economic problems. Companies have become somewhat more anxious to lease in non-OPEC regions since 1973 because of the vastly tougher conditions demanded by OPEC producers who, in tight markets, can deal from a strong bargaining position. But the companies must balance this against the potential costs of exploration in new areas and their likely profitability.

Adding to the complexity, as activity moves through the cycle from survey to exploration to production, the balance also shifts depending on the amounts and qualities found, and contract terms may be altered midstream. Also, as leases are generally offered in rounds, leasing terms are normally changed from round to round by governments, depending on how the previous round has gone. Britain began its North Sea leasing activities with very generous terms for companies, but under public pressure it introduced increasingly tougher terms as large finds were made. Finally, by 1980 the Conservative government began to loosen lease terms again although the tax aspects remained extremely harsh.

The flexibility to change lease terms and leasing policy is a crucial trump card a government will always try to hold. In virtually all cases government oil leasing is carried out on a discretionary basis. The government retains control over to whom the lease is awarded and certain powers to terminate the lease and change conditions. Only the United States, with its free enterprise ideology, clings to a nondiscretionary lease system. Under this the lease is essentially a blank check to the oil company that bids highest for the lease, allowing it to make full free use of any oil found after the government as owner gets its normal one-eighth royalty. The lease is awarded on a bid/bonus sytem and under law government officials must award the lease to whomever submits the highest bid. The U.S. government in essence gives away much of its power to control leases beforehand, and becomes almost a passive observer once a lease is granted, retaining only power to terminate for flagrant disregard of safety or lack of serious development. What the government does get in exchange is higher front-end revenues driven by bid competition.

Whether discretionary or not, an oil lease contains some or all of the following features which can be adjusted to match conditions and the needs of negotiation. These are:

1. extent—how much acreage is covered. Oil field leases are normally divided into plots of uniform sizes but also can be irregular, especially in difficult onshore terrain.

2. duration—a lease is usually allowed for a fixed period of years, frequently with "due diligence" requirements that demand a certain minimum work or investment commitment within a schedule in that overall period. Frequently duration and extent are connected—a leaseholder must give back unexplored sections of a lease after part of the lease period is up.

3. fees—most lease agreements contain a fixed fee to cover administrative costs but which may also be fixed high to raise revenues.

4. bonus and royalty payments—a lease can require an initial bonus payment which is used in the bidding process to determine award of the lease. The bonus is based on the risk factor in exploration and is in effect a bet by the company that enough oil will be found to cover the bonus plus a profit. At the same time the lessee will normally be obliged to pay a royalty share of the oil produced to the lease owner. In the United States this is one-eighth but can vary. One method employed frequently, including at times in the United States, is a sliding scale royalty system which increases the royalty paid to the lease owner as production increases. This protects the lease owner from losing substantial benefit from a very big find. It also cuts down the size of the bonus and thus eases entry into leasing for smaller operators who can afford less money up front.

5. production sharing—a traditional royalty payment requires the lessee to pay the lease owner a monetary sum equal to the owner's share of oil. This arose from the period when oil companies did the leasing and governments or property owners with no expertise in the oil business were the main

lease owners. But as access and control of upstream oil supplies became more important, and when markets tightened, governments tended to demand a share of the output in kind which they either dispose of themselves or sell to the producing company in a separate business transaction ("buy back oil"). In disposing of the oil itself the government is likely to use its own national oil company or arrange a specific use for a political reason such as the U.S. program to distribute royalty oil from the Gulf of Mexico to small refiners.

6. coproduction—a government may require that any leaseholder form a partnership with a state-owned company or agency to jointly own and manage the exploration and production venture, or to step in after successful exploration to take a share in production activities. This assures the state a strong control in drilling and exploitation and complements a simple production-sharing scheme since the state becomes an equal investor and equal beneficiary of a large find. Frequently the required partnership will be 50-50, but it may be lower to encourage private companies to enter into exploration. There may be a separate agreement setting forth who actually manages production, that is, how much to produce, the rate of extraction, etc.

7. oil disposition—lease holders may also have to accept rules governing sale, export, and refining of their share of oil produced from the lease. This is frequently tied to government policies to limit exports and insure that home refineries and consumers benefit from domestic sources.

LEASING SYSTEMS IN ACTION

Because of the OPEC experience, in which the member states originally offered virtual giveaway deals to the major oil companies and only slowly after 1970 clamped down with harsh terms, the trend for most countries entering the oil exploration race, especially developing countries impressed by the OPEC example, is to start with hard OPEC-like terms and weaken them as needed to increase participation from reluctant firms. Argentina did this in 1976 and was rewarded with a surge of new exploration to complement the efforts of the state company YAP when controls were loosened.

The variability of oil leases responding to government perceptions of oil market fluctuations is vividly illustrated in Brazil and India. In both countries government was for years hostile to foreign exploration, with Brazil's prohibition on MNC exploration going back five decades. In India, government was left

with a bitter taste in its mouth after three companies invited
into India drilled one dry hole each and then left. As a consequence, even their high reliance on imported supplies did not
provoke these two large LDCs to open up their lands completely
to Western companies. At least while oil was relatively cheap
worldwide.

After 1973, the growing pressures of balance of payments
problems coupled to falling onshore domestic production in both
countries, forced these two governments to once again invite
foreign firms to bid for off-shore leases. The governments
accepted the political risk when they weighed the economic
alternative.

The risk contracts first developed by Brazil in 1976 demonstrate two key points about leasing: first, that governments
do now try to control the domestic exploration activities of foreign
firms much more closely; and second, that this control as initially
exercised does not always match market conditions and MNC
preferences and requires successive adjustments. Thus, while
Brazil did open up to foreign companies, its terms were extremely
strict:

1. Foreign contractor pays all exploration, evaluation and
development costs;
2. Government decides when a field is commercial;
3. Petrobras retains exclusive ownership;
4. Petrobras will pay for discoveries with money (rather
than oil which is the more usual procedure);
5. Service area will be reduced 50 percent at the end of
the first third of the exploration period (a negotiated period of
years); 50 percent of the remaining one-half by the end of the
second third. (Department of Energy 1977, pp. 30-31.)

These provisions were extremely detailed, and were an
effort on the part of the government to ensure that companies
not simply obtain a lease and sit on it with little development.
However, the companies didn't bite; bids were few, especially
during this sluggish price period (1977-78), so Brazil successively
loosened its terms as its own oil needs grew rapidly.

In a 1980 review of the Brazilian efforts entitled "Open-
Door Policy to Oil Search," the Petroleum Economist applauded
the government's move and criticized Venezuela and other Latin
American closed door countries "still shackled by nationalistic
and political obstacles that could well see their production suffer
in the next few years." (Petroleum Economist, November 1980,
p. 491). Yet while the Western oil press applaud, domestic

critics frequently pan liberal policies. Government officials, especially in countries like Brazil and India which are highly nationalistic and which harbor a half century of resentment against foreign oil firms, have to take the political factor into account. In December 1980 India's Association of Scientific and Technical Officers of the Oil and Natural Gas Commission (ONGC) argued that if the government had granted the agency the full operational autonomy, it could have done the job necessary to expand production. They also complained that government technology transfer rules were weak and that the multinationals would bid away Indian staff from the ONGC, leaving it stripped of the manpower it needed to develop Indian's oil resources. The Association insisted that "it would have been better for the government to invite the foreign firms to explore areas where Indian technology cannot undertake the task—like offshore areas which lie more than 350 feet under the sea. But the government is giving away areas where Indian expertise is adequate." (Far Eastern Economic Review, December 26, 1980, p. 39.) The government contended that the ONGC already had its hands full and could not be expected to take on any additional work. In Brazil too, the open door policy met with considerable domestic criticism in the press.

This bargaining process is not restricted to LDC. Britain moved gradually to a tough system, amid intense public and party debate and government-company bargaining. Norway, with its social democratic government and initial success in North Sea drilling with the 1969 Ekofisk strike, moved quickly to set up a strong system with heavy government involvement in exploitation. It has also preserved access to the most promising fields for Norwegian companies. Other North Sea countries, with little production to date, have also adopted the tougher form of offshore regimes following the Norwegian-British pattern.

The American leasing system, with its nondiscretionary features gives the government leasing officials much less leeway for softening or hardening conditions. The main areas of flexibility are in introducing new type leasing arrangements such as sliding royalties on an experimental basis, which is allowed and to some extent mandated by the 1979 legislation for Outer Continental Shelf (OCS) leasing; and in how stiffly rules on due diligence and environmental protection are enforced. Any real changes in the leasing system in the United States must come through Congress, but the long legislative process simply does not react fast and frequently leads to a standoff with no major change.

Therefore in the United States since the start of the 1980s the key question in leasing has revolved around the extent of the leasing of federal lands and not the specific provisions in the leases or division of the wealth and responsibilities. This question of how quickly to expand leasing and how to handle potentially rich areas that also have high environmental value occurs in other countries, but in few is it the dominant theme as it is in the United States. The overall push by then Interior Secretary James Watt to open more lands and coastal areas for leasing in fact became the central Reagan administration oil supply policy once oil price decontrol had been effected. Watt was restricted by a series of rules on leasing in offshore and wilderness areas that had been enacted during the environmentalist heyday in the 1970s. His wide ranging battle to circumvent them became a political burden to the administration. In several cases he was pulled back by the White House or censured by congressional action, but his thrust remained to install a policy that all potential oil areas should be leased. In other countries leasing expansion is also controled for reasons which have nothing to do with the environment. Norway kept a ban on oil development off its northern coast for several years, despite indications of good potential, to prevent over-rapid oil development in the north which could totally throw the national economy out of balance. Interference with fishing played a minor role. Also Norway, India, and several other countries have restrained leasing to allow their own companies to get the richest potential areas.

For most countries the question of the regulation of the rate of production from domestic wells is controled through the leases themselves. The state has rights to control the production to prevent over rapid exploitation of resources. In the United States however a different control system had grown up for situations, especially in Texas where oil was produced on private land without government leasing. The object was to prevent uncontroled drilling in the same pool from different properties since this could result in inefficient production that peaked too early and left more oil than necessary in the ground. In this conservation policy which developed in Texas in the 1930s, the Texas Railroad Commission regulated the production from each well to ensure the maximum benefit from each field. The system remains in force but is now virtually meaningless since, with production declining, virtually all wells are granted 100 percent production quotas. It was needed precisely because no coherent government leasing system was present. Now in

America most new oil leasing is done on U.S. or state government land and is thus almost automatically subjected to a coherent production system, but in some areas such as the Appalachians private leasing of new areas remains important.

DIRECT CONTROLS

State or national oil companies (NOCs) are used almost as widely as leasing systems among group A and group B countries as a means for directly influencing domestic oil activities. Only the United States and Germany among the larger countries lack true state oil companies. In many cases the state companies not only play a part in exploration and production of home oil resources, they also seek oil overseas (see Chapter 4) and are active in refining and sale of products to end consumers (see Chapter 6), operating exactly like integrated private companies.

How a state company develops, where its origins lie, and how it does or does not develop into a multifaceted, integrated company depends greatly on the timing of its creation, on the extent of the resource base and the energy needs of the country over a given historical period. Under one model (ENI, CFP), the initial impulse comes from overseas exploration and production, often to compete with the established majors. Later, as in Italy, oil and gas were discovered at home and the state companies moved into the domestic field. In a second model (including the Argentine company YAP, and PetroBras) the state company is set up before the major discoveries are made at home with the purpose of doing the main exploration and controling the production if finds are made. In a third model (Statoil, BNOC, ELF) the company is indeed created after the oil strike occurs as a means for the state to enforce tough oil production-sharing rules written into leases.

In oil supply policy the NOC's three key jobs are:

1. as an exploration spearhead, making sure the preferred drilling areas stay under tight government control and providing a company that will go into difficult or marginal areas as a matter of state policy and not purely on the basis of potential profit or loss. PETROCAN and BNOC have served this function.

2. as a partner to operate the government share of fields under joint production leases and physically handle the government share of oil, and

3. as a "window on the industry" or measuring stick for the government to test operating conditions for all oil companies

active in the country and give the government a first hand sense of the business end of exploration and production.

In most cases the first two jobs somewhat get in the way of the third since the NOC usually has a privileged position as the government representative in getting drilling sites and access to crude, and thus cannot operate as a normal company. But compared to earlier models where the governments were not at all engaged in the oil business and had to accept industry descriptions of conditions on blind faith, the change is clearly helpful.

Except in Britain, where BNOC and the integrated company BRITOIL have been the subject of long partisan debate, NOCs are seldom questioned on their basic oil production activities. Their success is measured generally in how much oil they find and produce, not strictly on profit and loss. A pure profit judgment is frequently seen as irrelevant because starting oil exploration from scratch is so expensive that a new national exploration company cannot expect to show a profit for years and companies created to take over shares of already found oil are in essence getting a giant head start and cannot help being profitable. Finally, companies like PetroBras occupy a premier place in the nationalist pantheon and are said to serve nationalist strategic interests. But finances still count, and even PetroBras, generally viewed as efficient in the oil industry, is criticized for wasting too much of the national treasury on domestic exploration (Smith 1976).

Oil: Indirect Measures

Among the indirect policy instruments affecting oil production the most important by far is tax policy. The reason for this is the large increase in oil prices since 1973 has created a large new pool of wealth flowing to companies. This has forced national taxation systems to adjust to capture what each political system considers a reasonable government share, and since a consensus is rare, and the sums involved are huge, political conflict is frequent.

This natural trend to intensify taxation has also however come at a time when governments are increasingly concerned about encouraging new oil production. The result has been that within generally tougher taxation regimes for oil companies, exceptions are made to favor new exploration and production ventures by companies. These factors have led to major revisions and expansions of the oil and oil company taxation system in most key consuming countries with substantial production (the United States, Britain, Australia, and Canada). The taxation issues frequently involve more debate than leasing and royalties (where the government as owner of the resource has a more clearly perceived right to demand a high portion of the wealth), and many times has had a deeper affect on overall oil production.

Most countries with oil resources have in place what amounts to a three-tier tax system which we designate as primary, secondary, and tertiary. There is a primary oil taxation system in the procedures used for granting leases to exploit government-owned oil resources. This is not a tax in the strict sense, but an economic rent placed on use of the resource in the form of royalties, production sharing, fees, and bonuses. They nevertheless are a major factor in the benefit the oil company gets from production activity and are similar to a tax in effect.

Most countries also have in place a system of normal business taxes which apply to oil companies as well as all other industrial groups. (In the United States this is the 48 percent corporate profits tax.) For our purposes this will be considered secondary oil taxation. Traditionally this type of taxation, when applied to oil drilling, contains several technical differences from the usual business tax system due to the peculiar nature of oil operations. For example, the tax system has to take account especially of the long lead time between initial heavy investment and revenues flowing from production, the inherent chance of investment in a dry hole bringing no revenue, and the application of asset depreciation rules to a resource in the ground.

Finally, in many countries oil profits are considered extraordinary for tax purposes because of the post-1973 sharp price rise which gave the oil companies (when not subject to crude price controls) added profit due to the extraneous OPEC pricing decisions. Thus, we have a tertiary oil taxation level. Some countries such as the United States placed this special oil tax on the part of the oil profits calculated as specifically flowing from price rises above a specified "fair" base—hence, the connotations of unearned or windfall profits. (In many ways this is more like an excise tax.) Some countries, such as Britain and Canada, simply placed a stiff tax on all production, saying they had the right to take a large share of the value of any barrel of oil given the highly improved price situation.

The increase in the secondary and tertiary taxation systems on oil companies has occurred for several reasons:

Long-term Historical Processes

In the United States the large private oil companies, through their Washington lobbying muscle, had built up a highly favorable tax system with percentage depletion allowance as a centerpiece. This system which allowed the annual depreciation of oil assets to be calculated as a hypothetical percentage was a bonanza which far exceeded the legitimate needs of the industry for a liberal cash flow to finance new drilling. After withstanding attacks from reformers for many years, the percentage depletion system was finally ended by Congress for large companies in 1975 because the surge of oil profits made it appear excessive. Another area in which the long-standing system was very favorable to the large companies was credits against U.S. taxes for "taxes" paid on foreign oil operations. For geopolitical reasons royalties paid to certain pro-U.S. governments such as Saudi Arabia for oil have been allowed to be counted as taxes, in effect allowing a foreign state to receive tax revenues at the expense of the U.S. Treasury. While the U.S. system has been tightened up, other countries like Britain have created tough systems to fence off their tax system on North Sea oil from taxes on operations by the companies elsewhere, preventing a similar foreign tax credit advantage.

Political Factors

In several countries tightening oil tax systems was simply good politics for elected politicians responding to a feeling among voters that oil companies were too rich and powerful, and often viewed as foreign exploiters. In the case of the U.S. (and to some extent the German) windfall tax, the political purpose was very precise. President Carter used the promise of the tax to build a bipartisan centrist political block in Congress which would vote to end price controls on crude oil. The trade-off was clear and even the oil companies recognized the political logic and, except for the ideologically motivated small operators, did not mount an all out campaign to kill the tax but instead worked to lessen its impact. Canada's 1981 NEP contained a similar trade-off of higher taxes for loosening of crude price controls.

Budget Deficits

Even extremely pro-business governments like those of Tatcher in Britain and Reagan in the United States have been slow to end oil company taxation because of the need for the

revenues. In Britain under Thatcher the Petroleum Revenue
Tax has been increased with supplementary levies to a level of
almost 90 percent on the marginal barrel and a reduction has
only come up because of a clear deterrence effect on oil companies and independent arguments that the system has become
too much of a hodgepodge with no stability. In the United States
the windfall tax was also attractive and remains so because of
the expected $10 billion annual Treasury revenue which at time
of passage was seen by many as a means to finance synfuels
aid and by others as a way to increase defense spending. With
the U.S. budget deficit soaring in 1982 and 1983, the revenues
seem all the more locked in place and a purely revenue-raising
oil import tax has gained support from conservative politicians.

The key policy question from our point of view is how this
increase in taxation of oil company production operations has
worked against the basic governmental goal of increasing domestic oil production and what governments have done to lessen
the general affect of the taxes.

On the whole governments have taken specific measures
to shield new oil exploration and production ventures from the
tax increases, saying essentially that oil companies in general
will face heavy taxes because of their new wealth, but that
specific use of that wealth to find more oil will be given favorable
treatment. The British Petroleum Revenue Tax (PRT) has
generous deductions for new drilling. Both Canada and Australia
have strong tax advantages for new exploration schemes. In
the United States the windfall tax itself only applies to "old oil"
and does not touch oil found after 1979. It also has major
exemptions for smaller operators who are considered less able
to finance new drilling from normal after-tax profits. What has
been generally rejected is the basic oil company argument that
the real means to encourage new exploration activity is to give
the companies assurance of general freedom from heavy taxation.
Most governments have said in return that this is impossible in
the current situation because of the political perceptions of
fairness and budget demands and that a finely honed tax instrument can both provide sufficient capital for new ventures and
ensure government capture of bonanza-like revenues. The key
is that even in the United States, where so many other policy
attitudes toward oil differ from those elsewhere, political developments have established the right of the government to confiscate
oil wealth if it is perceived excessive. That in the long run
may be the main significance of the windfall tax which unlike
its counterparts elsewhere is scheduled to phase out as production of old oil diminishes. One other argument bolstering the

government position is that whether or not the oil tax systems themselves are efficient policy tools, they clearly are more manageable and acceptable, especially from the prosupply viewpoint, than well-head price controls. Controls are much harder to adjust because of their secondary market effects. Given a choice between the two, all concerned (except consumer groups) prefer taxes.

In some countries the initial harsh oil taxation of the early 1970s has been modified because of political changes and unwelcome supply results. The labor government in Australia in the early 1970s greatly stiffened taxes on oil operations, ending deductions for capital investment in oil schemes and stretching out the capital recovery period to 20 years. By 1975, a conservative government had begun to ease these rules to attract back foreign companies which had started to leave due to the combination of tax, price controls, and preference for domestic operators. But by the 1980s the pendulum had once more moved toward higher taxes. In the United States President Reagan was not politically able to seek total repeal of the windfall tax when he took power although that was his natural ideological position; instead he supported a partial rollback of tax measures in his first tax reform package. In the end the oil tax reduction became a test of lobbying strength between the blocks of small and large oil companies, each seeking to get a larger share of a set amount of tax relief fixed ahead of time by Congress. Canada has made heavy use of tax benefits to encourage exploration in various frontier regions, but in 1981 it went to a system of grants to companies instead of tax breaks. This system was simultaneously used to favor exploration by domestic companies forcing many non-Canadian oil company investors to drop out of new exploration ventures.

The second major indirect policy measure applied to oil, well-head price controls, took on a major importance in several countries in the early 1970s, as a means to dampen inflation. But as the strong supply discouraging impact became clear, they began to be phased out in the late 1970s amid rancorous public debate. Well-head price controls were essentially makeshift measures applied in countries with large existing oil production to protect consumers when the OPEC price rises hit. Britain and Norway, whose state policies centered around the high revenues from the domestic oil discoveries, refused controls, but in the United States, Canada, and Australia the control policies gained wide consumer favor, especially since the governments themselves were busily denouncing the OPEC price rises as highway robbery. It was politically inconsistent to allow domestic production to take part of the same cartel. We have already discussed the international problems the price controls brought and long battles to end them in the United States and reduce them in Canada and Australia. We will discuss them further in Chapter 6. The United States adopted market pricing for oil in 1979, Canada for new oil in 1981. Australia also developed an import parity price system keyed to average prices for Saudi Arabia crude. A major reason for ending the control systems was consumer perception that they offered little long term protection. Controls clearly meant less domestic exploration and production and thus more dependence on the higher-priced imports. Since the eventual cost was going to be the same, it was better to have the production at home. Since governments had instituted windfall taxes to recoup much of the extra price, the additional money paid by the consumer was going neither to OPEC nor to an oil company, but to his own government, which from the voter viewpoint was the least of the three evils.

Taking the tax and price control issues together from the viewpoint of this book—increased government influence in energy— we can say that the OPEC price rise created a powerful force for more government intervention in the domestic oil system. The oil in the ground at home, whether or not discovered, became much more valuable, and the governments had to deal with this wealth issue. Some states tried to take a position to suppress the value of the oil by controls, in the end causing more disruption to the market and delay in long term energy development than it was worth. Sooner or later all governments recognized the legal existence of the new wealth and instead allotted a large part of the excess value to themselves through taxes (not to mention royalties). No government has simply ignored this change and let the increased value accrue to private producers. Only the United States, if the windfall tax is eventually allowed to lapse as scheduled, may after several detours reach this stage.

Restriction of foreign holdings in domestic oil operations is carried out in several countries as a protective policy against the power of the multinational oil companies. It normally takes place in resource-rich countries which have less capital available than needed to develop the large resource base. Canada and Australia are the main examples of countries which virtually force foreign firms to take on domestic partners to operate effectively. Britain and other North Sea countries do not require operating companies to take on local partners, but arrive at the same effect by demanding a 50 percent government share

in exploitation of any successful find. In most developing countries both techniques are used. The state maintains majority
control over operations through leasing rules and forces foreign
companies to take on local partners for any private venture.
This type of policy normally has domestic supply hindering
effects since it reduces the amount of foreign capital that can
be brought to bear in exploration and drilling. But overall,
countries have preferred to steadily increase national presence
in domestic exploration even if it means slower development.

In cases of very poor exploration results or a sudden
need for supply because of economic difficulties, countries may
be tempted to ease up, but even here the first impulse will be
to liberalize lease conditions so that foreign companies can
expect higher return, not to liberalize the amount of possible
foreign ownership. This "nationalist" policy normally has
deep grass roots support. The Mexican elimination of U.S. oil
company holdings in 1938 and Trudeau's moves to lower U.S.
presence in Canada in the late 1970s were both highly political
moves, with wide national implications.

Both Australia and Canada have had long histories of
dependence on foreign investors and companies to open up their
vast natural resources. By the 1970s, when the oil price rise
created a new wave of interest in exploration, it was natural
to extend more controls over foreign participation. Australia,
in 1974, put in place a domestic majority holding rule for all
new oil projects, but weakened this by the early 1980s to encourage new investment. While granting more leeway to foreign
groups, the Australians maintained an important lever of control
through strict rules on exports, which forced projects, especially
on the distant West Coast, to be geared toward the needs of
the domestic economy and not purely to the world market.
Canada, where the influence of the giant American companies
was extremely high, moved more slowly to a goal of 50 percent
comestic ownership of oil operations. By the late 1970s Canada
had developed a sophisticated system of controls on foreign
energy investment focused on the Foreign Investment Review
Agency which had sweeping powers to reject new foreign energy
investments or force inclusion of Canadian partners in them.
The NEP of 1981 went a step further by including heavy discrimination against those foreign-owned groups already existing
in Canada that wished to compete for development of new oil
lands. The state subsidy scheme for such exploration returned
91 percent of drilling investment costs for domestic companies
(including those with minority foreign holding) and only 50
percent for foreign-controled companies. The result was to

force several foreign companies to sell out their holdings, at knock down prices, to Canadians. The Canadians planned to use Petrocan, the national company, to pick up slack, but it appeared that Petrocan lacked the resources to make up the deficit and that the policy would in the end retard Canadian development.

The United States has traditionally maintained an open position toward foreign oil investment. This stems from the heavy surplus of U.S. foreign investment abroad compared to investment by foreigners in the United States which makes such a laissez-faire policy toward capital inflows advisable. But in the late 1970s pressure to change this was rising on two fronts. The Canadian actions against American companies raised demands in Congress for a tougher application of the reciprocity clause in the Minerals Leasing Act to discriminate against Canadian companies. At the same time long-standing fears of OPEC investment in U.S. oil properties were neightened by the Kuwaiti takeover of Santa Fe Minerals in 1981. In the U.S. case the opposition to foreign control had grass roots elements mixed with a tactical element, that is, as a way to get Canada to reverse policy. Up to 1983 the Reagan administration had made no major move to block foreign investments. The American restraint in this area is likely to be severely tested in the 1980s as the liberal rules on oil exploration and development attract more foreign capital from major European and OPEC national oil companies.

Subsidies and grants for oil exploration and drilling are relatively rare for two reasons: First, the technology for oil drilling is not new and there is little justification for heavy research and development outlays. In the United States, for example, oil research funding has centered mainly on enhanced oil recovery techniques and budgets have been miniscule besides nuclear and synfuels spending. Second, many governments already do fund a large amount of domestic drilling through general operating subsidies for their government-owned national companies. Subsidies for private companies are usually done through the tax system. Canada, by shifting to monetary subsidies for development in 1981 broke this pattern, finding that its discrimination in favor of domestic companies was easier through grants than the tax code.

Government environment and transportation policies can play a major role in oil supply development especially as the traditional areas of oil production begin to phase out and exploration spreads out into new areas that are environmentally sensitive or far from established transport routes. America is

particularly important in this regard and, as in most environmental questions, has led the field in controversies. Also in
the United States, pipeline and tanker traffic is seen as an
environmental as well as a pure transport issue creating an
intertwining of problems. In other regions, such as the North
Sea, pipeline transport to shore is a major issue in expansion
of supplies, but it is more a question of government capital
support than environmental hold-ups.

In the United States four key active exploration areas—
the Alaskan coast, California coast, Rocky Mountain wilderness
areas, and New England coastal fishing grounds—are highly
sensitive environmental areas where the amount of leasing itself
is a topic for constant battle between ecological groups and oil
companies. Once leases are granted, the fight shifts to drilling
rules to prevent pollution. In a final stage, pipeline and tanker
routes to move the oil, especially in Alaska and mountain regions
in the lower continental United States, have become controversial.
Starting in 1981, the efforts of the Interior Department, under
James Watt, to open up more drilling areas met widespread
opposition in Congress and the state governments which used
the complexities of the leasing law and requirements for in-depth
environmental reviews to great advantage. Ten years earlier
the oil industry had won a crucial victory in pushing through
the Alaska oil pipeline, which had a major strategic supply effect
in the later 1970s. Future Alaskan supplies were however
potentially affected in the late 1970s by failures, due to local
objections to build an east-west oil pipeline to handle a greater
flow of Alaskan crude. A southern route starting at Long Beach,
California was killed in 1978, sparking attempts for legislation
to streamline environmental rules. A second attempt for a
northern tier route also hit major snags in 1982. The lack of a
cohesive approach to these problems in the United States, which
the federal government so far has been unable to handle because
of the divisions of power between Congress, the departments
and states, has made this policy area a major supply hinderance,
particularly for large-scale complicated projects.

In most other producing countries, oil supply priorities
normally take precedence over environmental concerns, especially
if the national government takes the lead in planning various
leasing and transportation arrangements which are clearly in
the national interest.

NATURAL GAS

Exploration and development of natural gas is very similar
to that of oil from a physical standpoint. Any petroleum drilling

venture has a possibility of finding gas instead of oil or both together. Frequently gas found together (associated) with oil is reinjected into wells to maintain pressure for oil production, or flared (burned off at the well head) if no commercial use is possible. Thus most national oil-leasing systems also cover gas exploration and discoveries, applying the same sort of financial and state participation terms. But because of the physical characteristics of gas, which means that unlike oil it must be carried in a closed pipeline system from the well-head to the end user, there are several major differences between government policies for oil and gas.*

The three key policy differences which affect gas supply are:

1. Gas prices and government policy responses are less volatile than in oil. Because it is sold in a closed system, gas has traditionally been sold under long term contracts which allow the participants in the sale to recover over time the value of the high investment in pipes and other transport equipment. This means that gas prices in general usually remained relatively low despite the oil price rises of the 1970s and efforts by Algeria and others to seek oil-gas price parity. Fixed contract prices remained at pre-1973 levels until expiration, which could be up to 20 years later and governments were under more direct pressure to keep prices lower than oil prices through controls to satisfy consumer demands. This meant that gas prices and drilling activities were less subject to the rapid oil market fluctuations. (We discuss price, fluctuations, and fuel switching in Chapter 6 below.) This lower price characteristic has tended to discourage exploration and production especially in the United States and Britain where the gas-pricing system is a major national political issue.

2. Because of the need for a closed distribution system, it is not feasible to have competing suppliers of gas to end users. Instead, like electricity, a single supplier usually has a geo-

---

*While oil is frequently transported by pipeline too, this is not necessary and when pipelines are used for oil it is because of a cost advantage. Also sea transport of oil is always easier and cheaper than sea transport of gas in the form of liquified natural gas (LNG). But our concern here is production policy. We treat pricing and distribution below.

graphical monopoly over distribution and, also like electricity, the supplier frequently tends to be a government body or a closely regulated utility. This means a generally higher involvement of government at the distribution level which has important influences on pricing options and the entire upstream structure of the industry.

3. Because of the need for expensive pipeline investment and, in the case of LNG imports or exports, further expense for those facilities, government policy to support pipelines both through regulation and financing is also crucial. Often the commercial viability of a gas find will be determined by the government decisions on how transport will be arranged.

Gas has three quite distinct segments or markets and they are usually treated differently by governments—especially regarding pricing policies: gas field prices, prices in the transport system that pipe gas from the fields, and the final distribution or retail market prices.

Overlaying these three considerations is the important role of gas as a substitute for oil in home heating and some transport and, if plentiful, in industrial heating and power. Gas is generally considered a strategic means to lower oil consumption. Thus increasing gas use, either from domestic wells or imports, is usually considered a major policy goal except in a few countries such as the Netherlands and New Zealand, where major reserves have been found and it is considered more important to preserve the resource. Also the relatively clean-burning character of gas makes it more desirable in certain high pollution areas where burning coal or oil is discouraged by clean air rules. However, these are downstream issues distinct from exploration and production.

Even more so than in other energy sectors, there is no coherent gas supply policy in the United States. Instead consumers and producers have fought long battles over pricing and supply issues which are far from resolved. In the confusion, a fragmented market situation has grown up with some gas subject to strict regulation, some not regulated at all, high uncertainty over gas import plans, and in many regions and industrial sectors major doubts about the advisability of gas use at all. The peculiar mixture of no regulation side-by-side with a high degree of regulation, the result of several political compromises and power standoffs in Congress, seems to unite the worst of both worlds and from the outside appears virtually self-defeating.

Almost all consumer countries have an active policy for gas exploration and development which is part of the general oil and gas leasing system. Normally provisions for gas drilling and production are similar to those for oil. In fact, much of the time the actual leasing policy decisions are keyed to oil development and gas follows as a sort of secondary product of oil policy. At the same time however most countries will have an overall gas supply policy which governs the gas use once it is found and can have great effects on actual gas exploration and development. Since in many prospecting areas gas and not oil is the most likely resource that will be found, these policies can also slow or speed drilling itself. The most typical policy patterns are: (1) To restrict gas exports and also limit domestic use to high priority areas such as home heating and transport, thereby allowing national gas reserves to be kept in the ground as an insurance policy against future energy supply problems. The Netherlands, New Zealand, and Britain have adopted this policy to preserve major resources. This also includes rules against flaring imposed by most national governments in their leasing systems. Few large fields have been developed in even the larger LDCs, however, and associated gas is frequently flared. (2) To restrict exports in order to increase domestic use both in high priority and low priority areas and back out unwanted oil imports. This has been the basis of Canadian gas policy for several years and to some extent has discouraged production in the western regions by companies which have aimed at large exports south to the U.S. market. (3) Encouraging exports to spur gas exploration. Australia which maintains price controls domestically has kept up producer activity on gas projects by permitting enough gas exports (at higher world market prices) to insure the economic viability of the projects. (4) Countries with major gas finds that go beyond covering local needs and who have a desire for export incomes tend to encourage export for overall economic development. Trinidad has adopted this policy as has Norway in the Northern European area. Norway has taken a sophisticated approach, using certain gas condensates at home for industrial purposes and exporting the unneeded gas to the continent and Britain where gas demand outstrips home supply. All of these approaches are examples of rational, government-directed policy where a gas reserve is used strategically for overall energy policy goals. They show the increasing attention governments pay to energy policy and the ability to balance use of various resources to get the best results.

In general LDC governments have been less successful in designing effective gas exploration and development systems. There it is likely to be developed by foreign private firms, and the shallow domestic gas markets and higher political risks have not made large-scale gas-gathering systems commercially attractive. At the same time, given the technical complexity, high costs and, after 1981, saturated world market, many LDC governments have not pushed the private companies to develop domestic gas fields. Thailand, Bangladesh, and Pakistan are exceptions, with gas expected to provide half of the additions to commercial energy supply for the latter two countries over the coming decade. According to the World Bank, in about 15 LDCs the current production levels are only 16 percent on average of what they could be, given their proven gas reserves (World Bank, Energy Transition . . . 1983a, p. 53). If governments learn to exert more bargaining leverage with the companies we may see increased LDC gas production in the 30 LDC oil importers with some gas reserves, going mostly into electric power generation, industry, petrochemicals, and fertilizer.

Most countries have state-owned companies which handle gas activities. On the whole these companies tend to act mainly in the transportation and distribution area with a smaller number also having a mandate to find and produce gas. In several major producing states the government company is the sole buyer of gas from private producing companies and has total responsibility for sales to end users. This is the case in Britain with the British Gas Corporation, Gasunie in the Netherlands and Dong in Denmark. Also, the state companies normally are the sole gas importing group and serve as the agency to integrate domestic production and imports into a single policy. The state companies also frequently are the means to control pricing and set in place new price policies. Both BCG and Gasunie have increased domestic gas prices substantially in recent years as part of a specific government policy to discourage waste. The companies are also useful tools to set priority use.

In many cases national companies which started with a mainly domestic role have gone more strongly into importing gas, as demand rises far above home supply, or home supply is purposely restricted. Gasunie, Gaz de France, ENI's gas subsidiary SNAM and BGC have all moved in this direction. Here, more than in oil, political confusion can have negative effects as the Thatcher government decision to change the status of BGC has shown.

In several large producer countries there has been no single state company developed for gas. Besides the United States, Canada, Australia, West Germany, and India's Oil and Natural Gas Commission fit this category. In these cases the predominant gas producers are also oil producers and have not entered the gas shipment business, either because of legal barriers as in the United States or because of the differing conditions and risks. Hence a second line of trunk pipeline and local distribution companies exist which supply end users and local gas utilities. In these cases the government gas policy is enforced through regulatory agencies, and price, and import-export rules.

Of the indirect policy tools, pricing and infrastructure measures are clearly the key ones for gas policy. In almost all countries with domestic gas resources the price for the gas sales to end users is controled. The controls were originally meant to protect consumers against the unavoidable monopoly position of the pipelines but they have frequently served to hold gas below its real replacement value as a substitute for oil and thus hindered supply development. Since there is no world market for gas comparable to that for oil, there is no easily agreed range of prices for gas. Each country thus can set domestic gas prices depending on its own policy needs. While a few countries like the Netherlands have put up gas prices strongly as a conservation measure, most governments do not want to risk the public displeasure and they maintain gas at a compromise price that has as much a political as an economic basis.

The U.S. gas price control system, which was created in the 1930s and reaffirmed in 1954 by the Supreme Court, has been so worked over by political compromises, including the 1978 gas-pricing act, that any market rational is long gone. The 1978 act ended controls for high cost gas discovered after 1979 and provided some upward adjustment for other categories, permitting some of these to be decontroled in 1985.

The U.S. gas price law had several major defects and unwanted side effects, and is a classic case of the difficulties policymakers face in predicting market movements and designing appropriate policies. Written before the 1979 oil price explosion, the law assumed a slow oil price rise through 1985. Instead there was a sudden jump followed by a slow roll back which threw off the calculations of the legislators.

Not only was the end price result far from the mark, but the market actions in between, reacting to short-term calculations, were chaotic. The process proceeded in two phases. In the first, tight-market phase, fears of another massive price jump in 1985, when controls were to be suddenly lifted, elicited demands for accelerated decontrol with prices rising more evenly. Then, in phase two, crashing oil prices made the still-controled gas prices now excessively high in some markets.

At the same time fears that controls would discourage discovery of new supplies led pipeline companies to buy up high priced gas for security, even when lower priced (but seemingly more insecure) supplies were available.

Then the market slumped, and by 1983 companies that killed to get gas supplies through "secure" long term contracts were dying to get out from under the now-burdensome high priced deals. In late 1983 key U.S. importers did break major Algerian contracts. Once again market fluctuations wreaked havoc on government and private company energy strategies. Big industrial users now sought to avoid buying from the pipelines altogether, preferring to make their own direct foreign deals at freely negotiated prices now lower than contract prices and then contracting for their own transport.

A further complication occurred making gas importing difficult since interstate pipeline systems needed approval from government regulators to obtain higher priced foreign supplies. Thus at times American pipelines were prevented from taking specific Algerian, Mexican, and Canadian supplies. In February 1983 President Reagan proposed to clear away the controls, but congressional cooperation seemed doubtful.

Compared with the United States, Canada has maintained a less complicated price control system which allows gas to rise in a fixed relation to oil prices so that the gas price is two-thirds that of oil equivalent. This price system emerged from long, heated negotiations with the producer province of Alberta which sought higher gas prices. Alberta, as part of the deal, agreed to allow use of part of the revenues to help support expansion of the gas distribution network in the eastern provinces. Alberta demands for an opening up of gas exports to the United States through lower prices were not met in the 1981 accord, but by 1983 Ottawa was thinking along those lines. Gas export allowances in early 1983 were up substantially, although the export price was held high.

In both Australia and Britain there are no national gas price controls; instead, the price is determined through the contracts between producers and monopoly gas distributors, usually state-owned utilities. These have tended to think first about their consumers and thus forced low-priced contracts on producers.

The second major indirect policy area affecting gas supply is government decisions on infrastructure and especially pipeline and other transmission facilities. Gas discoveries, especially in remote areas are much more dependent for their commercial viability on expensive transport systems than oil. Oil is generally easier to transport, especially by sea. Government financial and regulatory aid to pipeline building, or actual ownership of pipelines, is normally a key component to putting together international and national gas deals. In the North Sea, Norway has acted effectively to coordinate existing pipelines and plan for new trunk systems which can bring offshore gas to the mainland for liquid extraction for industrial use and reexport to markets in Western Europe. The British have had a totally different experience, with the government being unable to agree with industry on a gas-gathering system. Talks finally collapsed in late 1981 after the production industry, unsure about other aspects of government gas policy, refused to guarantee the needed throughput to make the pipeline viable. Given the ideology of the Thatcher government, the alternative will probably be a series of ad hoc private lines to land gas with no central coordination. In the British case, the gas gathering system was seen as a means to relieve producers from strict gas-flaring rules and also to pick up interest in new gas exploration which was lagging because of low costs and marketing difficulties.

In Canada, gas pipeline policy has been an important supply issue because of the government policy to shift marketing of Canadian gas from exports flowing south to domestic sales flowing east. The Ottawa government has thus been deeply engaged in pipeline support schemes and licensing decisions and the transport issue has been a key feature of the national energy plan.

The U.S. government has strong powers to regulate pipeline construction and operation and tariffs, but does not have a coordinated policy toward extension of the national pipeline system. At most it steps in for special cases, such as the Alaska north slope gas delivery system, to influence the choice between competing systems. But it has no strategic plan, leaving key decisions to the large private pipeline companies.

U.S. uniqueness has been a minor theme of this study. Nowhere is this better illustrated in the gas industry than to contrast the federal government's position on the Alaska gas delivery system with what a European state would probably have done. There the federal government provided enormous indirect support but never demanded in return a partial equity holding in the project, the norm in other more étatist political systems.

Under a special mandate from Congress the administration decided that the economically optimal overland route should follow the Trans-Alaskan Pipeline and then the Alcan Highway.

It included a provision forbidding the private oil and gas companies to precharge consumers in the United States to raise
the necessary capital to finance the line. High gas prices and
high demand seemed to guarantee an adequate return, and
Congress mandated that the free market provide the capital.
But with the gas market reversal and recession the companies
were pinched and did what energy firms typically do under
such circumstances—they turned to government to do a special
deal rather than face the music of the market. Extreme pressure
by Democratic and Republican lobbyists got a new bill through
Congress permitting customer precharging, reversing the earlier
policy. The cost to the consumers, who were to be precharged
whether the line was built or not, is astronomical.

But even with this big boost from Washington the financing
for the project remained elusive and by 1983 the state of Alaska
was looking for other means to market the gas. Significantly,
the Canadian side of the proposed pipeline was much more efficient in arranging permits and financing.

The normal government powers to regulate gas pipelines
and provide support for projects, has been increased in many
countries because of the introduction of LNG transportation
systems which pose particular pricing and safety questions.
LNG tends to be high-cost because of the expensive systems
needed to convert the gas to liquid for transport, keep it at
very low temperatures during the journey and return it to a
normal gas state when it reaches its destination. Also in many
cases it comes from OPEC producers which have sought high
prices linked to oil price developments. Governments have
generally been involved in LNG import decisions because of
potential impacts on the local gas pricing situation. While some
governments like France and Japan have actively intervened to
ensure LNG gas supplies, others like the United States have
turned down some plans presented by private firms because of
the high costs and increased import dependence. Fears over
the safety of LNG transport have also played a role in some
cases, although not as crucial as pricing. Again France,
which pioneered LNG transport, and Japan, have spent less
time debating the potential risks to population. In the United
States the safety issue has not come to a head because several
major projects were already slowed or halted by price and
security considerations. But one plant in New York harbor has
been effectively stopped on safety grounds after an accident
in the construction phase and other projects have come under
close scrutiny.

In tax and national production control policies, government
actions on gas generally tend to be the same as those on oil.

Tax regimes on gas production are similar to those for oil, but since gas prices have remained generally depressed, there has been less of a push for special taxation of gas profits. In the United States there has been mention of a gas windfall tax similar to that for oil in the event of decontrol, but the idea has not gained support because of the much more fragmented political coalitions on the gas price issue.

COAL

Coal differs from oil and gas in several important respects which directly bear on production policies. It is generally easier to find than hide-and-seek oil and gas and its production can be treated much more like a typical industrial enterprise. At the same time its uses are more limited because it is a solid fuel with widely varying qualities and environmental drawbacks. This means that it is generally in lower demand by companies and individuals than oil and gas, and a major part of national coal supply policies is really demand-enhancement policies— that is, convincing consumers to use coal (see Chapter 6). The lower demand has meant lower prices and lower profitability, and in many traditional coal-mining countries supply was only kept up through subsidies and state ownership. It was only after the 1979 oil shock that coal once again began to look like a serious contender as a growth fuel and the price differential between the two fuels stretched to 30 to 50 percent.

There were grounds for the initial government optimism about coal in the wake of the first oil shock. World coal reserves are five times larger than oil reserves and it is a traditional industry (unlike nuclear energy, its big competitor), with a known technology, a strong track record, and natural consumers. Yet despite the rhetoric and some political and financial support, coal production managed to increase by only 3 percent annually between 1973 and 1977.

However, even these figures do not accurately portray the problems and limited successes of repeated government tries to re-start an industry allowed to decline, or to launch a new one. In the first place, most of the expansion occurred in a few countries: India, Korea, Yugoslavia, and North Viet Nam in the LDCs (where the rate of increase was actually 6 percent annually) and in West Germany, Australia, and the United States among OECD countries. Second, coal quality and production costs are very uneven. In many countries domestic coal was still more expensive than imports. Thirdly, there were severe institutional and infrastructure bottlenecks that blocked expansion during the 1970s. Said one report,

> [Coal] can neither expand nor contract rapidly.
> Costs are very difficult to predict. Output cannot
> be planned accurately and changes unpredictably.
> Demand is inelastic in the short run and only
> moderately elastic in the long run, and the period
> of adjustment of demand to new price levels is long.
> (Cook and Surrey 1977, p. 96.)

In most countries coal resources are state owned and treated legally in the same way as oil and gas. But leasing procedures for coal are much less complicated because the amount of resources available on a lease is generally known beforehand and the demand for new coal fields is not as strong. In most countries, instead, the key problem is improving the economics of existing coal production ventures through modernization investments and industrial rationalization. Except in large surface mining countries such as the United States, Canada, and Australia, all potentially viable coal fields in most Western countries have already been exploited and the leasing policy plays no major role. In the United States coal leasing on federal lands is a major factor in new coal development and problems with environmental rules and bureaucratic procedures have hampered coal leasing as much as oil and gas.

In developing countries the move toward exploitation usually depends upon government energy planning, especially to find out what amount of resources actually exist. The prospect of long lead times in starting new mines—it may take 10 to 15 years from initial prospecting to full-scale production—and the inefficiencies of LDC decision-making agencies make coal a slow starter. Even where countries have been driven by poor oil prospects to take some initiative, as in Turkey, Korea, and Brazil, the failure to coordinate potential producers, transporters, and buyers has yielded poor results. Countries with experience in coal production have done better and some like France are hoping to sell this expertise to struggling LDCs. In China, the third-largest coal producer in the world after the USSR and the United States, coal production has been growing at 15 to 25 million tons a year for the past two decades, with government hopes of raising it to the 20 to 30 million ton range over the coming decade with the help of Western partners such as Occidental Petroleum. Korea and to a lesser extent Brazil, too, have moved to upgrade domestic coal production.

The use of state-owned coal-mining companies follows the general pattern in oil and gas but with several major exceptions such as Britain, where coal production has long been a full state 100 percent monopoly. The United States, Canada, and Australia maintain privately owned coal industries in large part because in these three countries the resource situation still permits a reasonable profit from coal operations. But for Britain, France, Spain, Turkey, and most developing countries the pattern of state control dominates. In Germany, the main coal producer is a semiprivate group and the industry is maintained through a strong network of subsidies. While state intervention in the coal industry in most classic coal-mining countries was undertaken as a means to directly control a declining industry and protect social interests, the revival of coal has meant a new accent on profit orientation for state groups such as Britain's National Coal Board. But unlike state oil companies, which can normally count on profits if the resource base is established, such national coal companies remain basically un-profitable, even with climbing world coal prices, because of the usually cheaper import supplies and heavy costs of modern-ization and the social costs of the shrinking labor force. Despite higher world demand, Charbonnages de France had become a critical money loser in 1983 provoking a political battle. There are not the same sort of multinational large scale coal companies comparable to the oil and gas giants. Instead coal tends to be produced by more localized firms, which are frequently part or full subsidiaries of large oil companies or coal consumer com-panies such as utilities or steel producers. This generally weak industrial development is another symptom of the low profitability of the coal industry during the heyday of cheap oil in the 1960s. Even when synfuels returned as a major economic possibility in the late 1970s coal production companies seldom had the financial power to undertake coal enhancement processes and left this to the oil companies who controled strate-gic coal reserves and the market for downstream products.

The fragmentation of the "coal chain" confronted govern-ments with policy headaches. With different sets of owners all along the chain, the links may be imperfectly joined or coordinated (C. Wilson 1980, p. 230). For example, in the United States, Canada, Australia, and South Africa, ownership and manage-ment of the coal mines themselves is often in private hands, while the transportation links connecting mine with consumer are usually mixed, with railroads and ports publicly owned, and shipping fleets for the most part privately owned. The final largest consumers—power plants, steel mills, chemical factories, again may be publicly or privately owned.

Faced with this, governments often step in through state companies to smooth out the industry. In Korea this meant consolidating a number of smaller mines into six larger ones under the provisions of a 1971 coal development law. The Korean Mining Promotion Corporation then provides direct assistance to the mines, often in cooperation with the Korea Coal Mines Association that groups about half of the 172 privately owned mines. In return the companies must meet certain production targets. Indian rationalization policy was quite similar when in the early 1970s it forced the merger of over 200 separate and distinct coal companies operating more than 800 mines (Sankar, in Lindberg 1977, p. 230). The government forced the merger and nationalization of most of these smaller firms into three large ones, leaving only two "captive" private companies associated with iron and steel mills in the private sector. Coal production increased dramatically after this government-mandated rationalization, from 70 million tons in the years 1967-71, to 87.5 million tons by 1974 (Sankar, in Lindberg 1977, p. 230).

The use of a state company to carry out a national coal rationalization and modernization in a developed country is well demonstrated by Britain's National Coal Board. Successive governments have used the NCB to make policy in the face of strong union opposition to major closure actions. Since the initial 1974 coal plan was set out the NCB has moved successfully to maintain production levels and increase productivity. It has not been able to carry the initial closure program due to political pressure, but has nevertheless slowly oriented production toward more economic areas. It also has not been able to reach a profitable operating level and must get on an average 5 percent of its income in the form of direct state aid. The appointment of Ian MacGregor to run the NCB in March 1983 was a new sign of the businesslike orientation in coal policy. MacGregor had previously worked vigorously to rationalize the British steel industry and with American coal experience was expected to fit Britain's coal industry more firmly into the international coal picture. The union leaders immediately identified MacGregor as a natural enemy and by Spring 1984 had ordered a nationwide strike. Their power was on the wane in part because of a decentralized NCB pay system, based on bonuses, which was beginning to erode miner solidarity. The government has also used the NCB in two other key areas: promoting coal demand and research in coal use. The NCB itself has established an arrangement with its main customer, the Central Electric Generating Board, under which it delivers a guaranteed amount

of coal under fixed pricing arrangements which recognize the
CEGB's right to import coal to supplement domestic supplies in
areas where this is economically sensible. The NCB is taking
a long term view that maintaining coal use has top priority in
the short term so that markets will still be there when British
coal supplies can be provided at more competitive prices. This
has become all the more necessary as North Sea gas has emerged
as a direct alternative to coal for industry users. The NCB's
coal research work has been intensive in both direct use and
synfuels, combining the best features of government and private
initiative.

Elsewhere in Europe the French national coal company
Charbonages de France plays a smaller role because of France's
limited resources and because the weight of supply policy has
shifted to a separate coal-importing agency. Turkey also has
a national coal company (TKI) to carry out its ambitious production plans. But other key producing countries, Germany and
Spain, have kept their coal industries in semi-private hands
and preferred to exercise government control indirectly through
subsidies, forced demand, and import restriction policies.

There are several indirect policy measures to initiate and
expand domestic coal production. Most were of course driven
by the number one priority of encouraging fuel switching from
imported oil to domestic coal. Some indirect measures aimed at
the production end of the chain, others at the demand end,
and others still at the infrastructure in between. Most governments employed a mixture of demand and supply-side measures.
Grants and subsidies to the industry have been quite substantial,
and have been channeled through a number of tax, grant, and
aid instruments. Table 5.1 gives an idea of the amounts and
the supply/demand composition of British government grants
in 1979/80.

Other grants to the industry include social costs (£20.9),
and contributions to increased pensions (£41.1). These indirect
and direct subsidies yield a combined total of £251.1. The
average direct aid figures, in million pounds, for other European
countries during that time included: 208 for Belgium, 334 for
France, and 1,386 for Germany. That works out to approximately 34 pounds per ton for Belgium in 1979, 18 per ton in
France; and 16 pounds per ton for Germany. For Britain,
despite its infamous strikes and subsidies, the direct aid to
the coal industry amounted to about two pounds per ton in 1979.

These policies have both nationalist and regional political
roots and remain important in several cases because the political
heat to cut back coal would be severe. In Germany, the main

TABLE 5.1

British Government Grants to Coal Industry, 1979/80

	Million £
Coke stocking aid	12.9
Coking coal subsidy	8.5
Promotion of sales of coal to electricity generating boards	8.4
Deficit grant	159.3
Total direct aid	189.1

Source: Adapted from The Economist, February 28, 1981, p. 54.

support system is a guarantee from the electric power industry to purchase a fixed amount of domestic coal production annually. The price difference between the high cost local coal and the cheaper imports is made up by an extra charge to electricity consumers, the Kohlenpfennig or coal penny. The government also gives a direct subsidy to coal production through stockpile aids and its quota system for coal imports. Because of the power of the voting block, especially in the Ruhr region, dependent on coal, neither SPD or conservative leaders have questioned this system even though major moves to cut subsidies to other industries have been undertaken. German industry, especially in metal and chemical production, which is losing competitiveness because of the high power costs, has been able to get piecemeal concessions which allow use of imported coal for power supply to plants that otherwise would have to close. But overall, maintaining coal support system threatens Germany's power-intensive industrial production.

Spain, while not nationalizing the coal industry, has a major program of industrial aid to companies that modernize production. Britain as we have described, subsidizes through its state-owned coal company as does France. In Brazil, first, the Ministry of Mines and Energy agreed to equalize fuel price differences for cement makers through subsidies during the transition to coal use. The Ministry of Mines and Energy agreed to build coal depots in five cities and the Ministry of

Transport would upgrade eight ports, improve navigability
of several rivers in the southern coal province of Rio Grande
do Sul, and also improve rail and road transportation between
the mines and the cement-producing areas. The mining
industry agreed, for its part, to increase production if the
other parts of the program were implemented.

An especially critical indirect policy area for coal supply
in the late 1970s was transportation infrastructure. While
coal does not need a sophisticated transport system like gas,
it still needs heavy investment in railroad, and dockside
equipment and harbor expansion. In many cases this capacity
had been allowed to deteriorate as coal took on a diminished
role in the 1960s. In the United States, for example, coal
and railroad companies had little capital to make improvements.
In other countries such as Japan, Italy, Canada, and France,
the high volume of coal imports or exports was new and thus
transport capacity had to be built from scratch to meet new
government coal policy goals. The Italian government has
developed a plan to build three major coal ports plus inland
transport systems, hoping to carve out an entrepôt role which
it already has created in oil. The Japanese also have a major
port development plan, plus a strong state program to reduce
environmental complaints about coal. Canada is moving to
develop major coal export centers at Roberts Bank on the
Pacific coast and Sydney, Nova Scotia on the Atlantic side.
A joint Canadian industry-state group is also developing a
plan for rail transport improvement, especially in the west.
In the United States coal infrastructure development has been
less smooth, especially because of budget restraints and political complaints that such a program would be a giveaway to
the ports and rail lobbies. The current fight in the United
States over proposed coal slurry pipelines that would cheaply
move powdered coal through long-distance pipelines but also
threaten the railroad industry with the loss of one of its main
cargoes, is yet another example of the political tug-of-war
over all major energy projects in the United States.

Neither taxation nor price controls play a major role in
coal policy. Coal provides too little profit to tax and the
problem with prices is they are too low, not too high.

SYNTHETIC FUELS

This fuel source is the classic case of an energy technology held hostage by the M-shaped market. Besides subsidies

for mining operations, almost all major coal-producing countries have financed research programs for production of liquid or gas synthetic fuels from coal. Some have also begun programs to begin commercialization of such technologies but until now the roller coaster character of oil prices, which is the key competitor for processed coal products, has prevented a serious commercial breakthrough. Only repressive South Africa, which moved early to coal liquifaction with government funding and forced low mining wages as a means of creating national energy independence, has a successful synfuels production program. Both Britain and Germany, with strong coal reserves, had done extensive research work, but have had no economically sound reason to move to commercial production and as of 1983 no immediate action was expected and no government program was envisaged beyond the demonstration stage. German industry in fact seemed much more likely to profit from its long years of research and practical experience during World War II by selling synfuels processes abroad. South Africa depends heavily on German equipment and in 1983 the Soviet Union showed strong interest in German coal technology for development of remote coal resources. In the Russian case synfuels made sense as a means to get around heavy transport costs of raw coal over thousands of miles to consumption centers. In 1983 CDF bought into U.S. synfuels technology expressly to move into equipment export business.

In the United States research into coal-based synthetics has been underway for several decades together with shale oil technology. In the 1979 oil crisis, a major push developed in Congress to provide special commercialization aid to synthetics projects through a Synfuels Corporation. The policy was motivated by fears of recurring oil import cut-offs and was based on the assumption that oil prices would remain high enough to permit economical synfuels production once the government had primed the pump. But several things went wrong. First the market fell and after Carter launched the plan the incoming Reagan administration took a minimalist position, making the synfuels aid available only in extreme cases and cutting off separate funding for semicommercial projects. In the most spectacular failure, a Gulf Oil Company attempt to build a coal liquefaction plant in West Virginia using solvent refined coal technology collapsed due to equivocal administration support which forced German and Japanese participants to cancel plans. The Synfuels Corporation, which offered loans and price guarantees to projects, remained in business but because of questionable political backing it made little headway.

In Australia, the government has moved to aid coal and shale research but has not provided direct aid to commercialization. Nevertheless several commercial projects are under study with the most advanced the Rundel Oil Shale project. Canada has used state enterprises as a partner to private firms to support synfuels projects, especially oil sands development in Alberta. But as in the United States, changing oil prices and technical problems often frustrated efforts.

On the whole, governments have grasped the long term benefits of synfuels production as a means to cut oil and gas import dependence. But they have not made heavy commitments to commercial production, except in repressive and security-minded South Africa. This is in part due to the nature of synfuels production which demands a great amount of upfront capital before any production can take place. Most government, like industry, cannot invest one or more billion dollars in a plant which may or may not turn out to be profitable, especially since competing fuels remain easily available. Significantly no state synfuels production companies have been created in industrialized countries except for South Africa. At the same time the highly expensive synfuels production is beyond the means of most developing countries. Brazil has successfully pushed use of alcohol fuel, which is relatively simple to produce and does not pose the high capital cost problem, and has launched a gasification project in São Jeronimo (Rio Grande do Sul) for coal gas for industrial use.

NUCLEAR POWER

Even more than coal and synthetic fuels, importer governments worldwide placed great hopes on the nuclear power industry as the number one alternative to expensive imported oil. And even more than coal and synthetic fuels, government nuclear ambitions were beaten back by market volatility and political opposition. Despite the closest imaginable direct government ownership and controls and despite massive indirect influence through research and development, pricing, and safety regulations, the nuclear power dream was not fulfilled. Even the étatist and pronuclear French had to scale back their reactor construction program by one-third in 1983, prompted by Electricité de France's $13 billion debt to pay for the 24 reactors built and the 14 already under construction. The Brazilians too, equally étatist and pronuclear, were forced by market volatility to stretch out their own investment program over more years.

As an energy source nuclear (and hydro) research advances have virtually no application aside from power generation: it can only boil water to turn turbines to generate electrical power. But to boil that water requires tremendous government involvement over each phase of the nuclear fuel cycle, and the industry is perhaps the most government intensive of any. And, as we will see in Chapter 7, because any country in the world with money and willpower can generate energy domestically with nuclear technology, the industry has become central to the energy policy debates and the energy policy explosion of the decade.

Like gas or coal, nuclear power has a complicated sequence often with a patchwork of different public and private agencies responsible, and there have been long standing policy headaches all along the chain, at the "front end"—that is, in plant construction, and in the provision and preparation (milling) of the uranium so that it can be enriched to generate electricity; at the generation phase (as occurred at Three Mile Island in 1979 in the United States); and especially at the "back-end" of the cycle—the transportation, storage, and reprocessing of spent fuel from the power plant's reactors.

Back-end waste disposal problems, for example, plagued West Germany where courts upheld a legislative ban on further nuclear development until they were satisfactorily resolved. The California State Supreme Court in the United States did the same in 1983. Japan and France (in Brittany) have themselves run into front-end problems of original plant sitings and the former has resorted to expensive payoffs to local communities (6.3 billion yen for each 1 million kilowatts of generating capacity). However, neither all the political payments nor all the research and development could put the economy together again. When interest rates zoomed, and electricity demand slowed (from 7 percent annually to 1 percent in the United States) mostly due to international developments, governments were left holding a great deal of expensive domestic spare capacity.

Yet since the first commercial nuclear power plants were built in the late 1950s national governments have normally supported expansion of nuclear power production, first because of its supposed cheapness and later, when environmental problems and costs wiped this out, because of supposed independence from foreign energy sources. Also its potential military security applications required governmental involvement. Large industrial countries with little home oil and gas resources, such as France, Germany, and Japan found nuclear power indispensible and even those with major reserves such as the United States and Britain promoted major programs based on the longer-term perspectives for nuclear compared with nonrenewable resources.

Nuclear power was affected by the fluctuations of the world oil market and the international macroeconomy plus policy twists and turns that reflected changing public attitudes to nuclear development. As public doubts about nuclear power arose, especially after the American Three Mile Island disaster in 1979, some governments tempered their support based on these political trends and reinforced by deteriorating economic conditions. In smaller countries, such as Austria and Sweden, relatively modest nuclear programs were subjected to referenda. In 1978 Austrian voters blocked further development and in 1980 Swedish voters approved a limited nuclear program. No such national referendum has taken place in a large country. On the whole Western governments have supported nuclear power programs with the assumption that they are economically viable systems that can compete with classical power production under normal circumstances. While almost all governments have publicly funded nuclear research efforts, only those with existing traditions of public power ownership have also directly financed commercial plants as part of the ongoing state power company program.

In reviewing the catalogue of direct and indirect government measures to support nuclear power, we find heavier weight on the indirect side. Because of the relatively limited spread of uranium mining areas, because the cost of the raw ore is a relatively small share of total costs, and because the supply sources seem secure, government direct ownership and leasing policy to encourage domestic uranium production is not as important as in oil, gas, or even coal. And as we have seen, the direct ownership of nuclear power production facilities tends to depend more on traditional patterns of state holding in electric power industries. Nor has there been any clear tendency for power-generating systems to be nationalized because of increased dependence on nuclear power.

On the indirect side, the amount of government involvement is strikingly high in several areas: research, regulation, infrastructure aid, and, more so than in other fuels, attempts to provide a general political consensus to allow use of the controversial energy source. Virtually every industrial country and several developing countries have an atomic energy research and development program and several have government participation or ownership in reactor building and supply companies. Also, virtually every country has a government agency to regulate nuclear power, grant permits for construction of plants and assure safety of the public in case of emergency. In most countries the government also has some role providing for disposal of nuclear waste, a factor which is becoming a major issue in determining future nuclear power development.

As the economics of nuclear power has become doubtful due to growing safety and waste disposal costs, governments have changed certification rules and procedures to cut costs for operators. This type of development has shown the limit of how far governments will go to maintain nuclear supply options, stating in effect that some capacity is desirable but that long-term expansion is not absolutely needed if the overall costs are too high. This attitude has been mirrored in the funding of the research efforts for advanced breeder reactors. Governments in the United States, Germany, and elsewhere have had second thoughts as costs of major research projects have gone far above original estimates. In the United States the breeder program was carried through mainly through heavy lobbying from regional politicians and industry, while in Germany the conservative Kohl government has forced industry to increase its cost share to keep the breeder program alive.

Nuclear research is a natural focus for governmental attention not only because of the high costs but also because of the military implications. The main supplies of enriched uranium in the West through the 1970s came from U.S. and French enrichment facilities based on military needs. Certainly defense has played an important part too in the efforts of India, Pakistan, Brazil, and Argentina to develop a robust domestic nuclear industry. Most Western countries have total energy research budgets heavily tilted toward nuclear development with fossil fuels and renewables usually struggling for leftovers after nuclear gets the lion's share. Only in the 1980s funds for nuclear research have come increasingly under question, especially as environmental opposition to the breeder reactor has spread and other new energy sources have won favor.

But by far the most troublesome aspect of government involvement in nuclear energy has been in safety and design regulation, and licensing where agencies such as the Nuclear Regulatory Commission in the United States, the National Commission for Atomic Energy (CNEA) in Brazil, TUV in Germany, and similar boards elsewhere have been caught between industry needs for efficient licensing procedures and public demands for strict safety. The high degree of control is necessary because of the potentially catastrophic consequences of a nuclear accident and this has frequently overrideen government supply policy considerations. While as industry claims some regulatory red tape has been clearly excessive, the safety stakes have been too high to allow a genuine relaxation of the standards themselves. Governments have normally taken a very cautious line on this, creating improved procedures such as the German "convoy system" unveiled in 1981, based on a single reactor design for the entire industry. Governments have also been forced to reevaluate and make more precise their judicial review systems to prevent endless legal suits against projects. The ambiguity of government policy has been nowhere more evident than in nuclear plant siting which has become a political football and decisions are based strongly on regional and local situations. As the landscape in several countries has become filled with projects, the ability to find places for yet another plant has frequently depended on finding willing local officials who for one reason or another see a nuclear plant as a local boon and have the sway to put the decision across. In West Germany siting of a potential nuclear waste site has bounced around in this way with state governments and local government decisions playing the decisive role. Even under Brazil's military government, opposition developed to some coastal sitings south of Rio de Janeiro.

Governments like Germany and the United States also had to address the health and security concerns in nuclear power when it promoted or licensed export of nuclear fuel or technology overseas, especially to the LDCs. Western concern over nuclear nonproliferation grew rapidly in the 1970s fed by an Indian atomic device explosion in 1974 and subsequent developments in countries like South Africa, Iraq, Israel, and Brazil that had not signed the Nuclear Non-Proliferation Treaty of 1968. Although not directly related to domestic energy production, governments realized that popular domestic hostility to nuclear power exports would also sour national energy programs. While private companies and some government agencies did promote overseas sales, other powerful political groups feared the military uses of diverted nuclear fuels in overseas regional wars. Western governments responded with bilateral (or unilateral) actions, such as the tightened Carter administration rules in 1978, or the multilateral London Suppliers' Group that sought to regulate overseas sales by industrial powers (including the USSR, which participated in the Group).

The other side of the same coin is the effort by LDCs to avoid the debilitating debt and economic effects of oil imports by promoting nuclear power in their own countries. For Taiwan, Korea and other energy poor countries this was a serious consideration. Our interviews showed that for other countries

energy savings were perhaps significant but were only contribu-
tory to national decisions to proceed with domestic nuclear
development along side military and technical "status" arguments.
Thus, all of the biggest themes of energy policy in the 1970s
come together over nuclear power: market volatility, environmental trade-offs, political opposition, U.S. uniqueness, and
the uncertain role of technology all collide like splitting atoms
in nuclear power fuel promotion. We will return to these themes
again in Chapter 7.

CONCLUSION

Our survey of domestic energy supply policies shows that
over the decade governments came to rely on an ever more
sophisticated arsenal of direct and indirect policy tools to reduce
their dependence on the volatile international supply system.
Whether oil, gas, coal, or nuclear energy, public officials used
more state involvement than before. This included more direct
state ownership of energy resources and firms to allow the
government itself to produce more local energy, and as a means
of greater leverage over private firms. In this way the government came to rely less on the private firms, and the character
of their reliance shifted.

The energy supply market (actually a complex network of
brokers, drillers, equipment companies, consultants, etc.)
was, of course, never eliminated. Rather, governments were
pressed by domestic supply inadequacies and high priced imports
to devote greater detailed attention to domestic supply through
indirect means like taxation, price setting, loans and grants,
industry rationalization, and even supply expansion through
coordinated demand management.

We also argued that while all energy industries have similar
sequences from exploration through distribution, they differ
according to which stage will tend to attract the most official
attention. Most governments are now involved in oil leasing
and promoting exploration at the upstream stages, but fewer
are directly in transportation or retailing oil. Coal however
does require a great deal of downstream intervention to improve
transport links and encourage final demand. Nuclear development requires close government controls at every stage. Government officials had to learn the special requirements of each.

Consumer government supply enhancement strategies have
achieved a qualified success in many countries. For the IEA
alone in the period up to 1980 the depletion of existing oil

reserves was covered by new oil production leaving a substantial gain, but for gas the depletion of old wells outstripped new finds creating a slight loss. Coal production gained steadily through the late 1970s as new projects slowly came onto line. Nuclear power also began to rise sharply after 1973, but more because of investment decisions taken before the crisis. The rate of increase slowed markedly by 1980 as environmental and technical problems slowed projects. Hydroelectric power and other new fuels also made modest gains but like coal were not susceptible to quick progress because of long lead times.

On balance the question remains however—how much of this generally positive domestic energy supply development has been due to government policy and how much a response to purely macroeconomic or fuel-specific market incentives? Also, how much potential supply was hindered over the decade by government policies restraining production because of environmental reasons or by imposing strict leasing arrangements? There is no simple answer to this. Even a complex answer would probably only be approximate, since one would have to calculate such a wide range of international and domestic energy, and macroeconomic, factors.

Many of the changes were intangible ones, but important ones nonetheless. Legitimacy for government energy interventions was increased. Government supply policies even in "normal" times are now considered a legitimate means to give continuity and allow decision making on long term projects with some minimum guarantee against the dangers of sudden market changes. This is especially true for the Anglo-Saxon laissez-faire countries with little past experience in emergency situations where all publics now expect their governments to help national companies seek out secure supplies, especially in a system where oil and nuclear prices are unstable.

Government officials, too, have come to see national policy as something which could be used in a pinch to replace parts of the market system in an unreliable world. This was seen in the planning and decision making in the 1979-80 period when fears of a severe cut in oil supplies because of Middle East tensions were rampant and governments were forced to consider extreme supply measures. One example of this was the U.S. crash program to develop a synfuels industry, which later was derailed by a new market price situation and political wrangling once the danger had passed.

While government awareness and use of supply promotion policies has increased through the 1970s, there has also been a major turnaround in attitudes toward policies that hinder supply. Governments have found oil and gas price controls counterproductive and also have eased up in general on very hard leasing regimes which drove away potential projects. In some countries, such as the United States under the Reagan administration, environmental rules blocking production have been eased and in virtually all countries moves have been made to clear away needless red tape and permit efficient project decision making. The government supply role should sustain its new importance. The tighter markets that most anticipate for the late 1980s can only confirm this trend.

6

ENERGY
DEMAND POLICIES

I

INTRODUCTION

In many ways the most important part of the Energy Policy
Explosion was the radical change on the demand side. Though
governments were slowed by institutional roadblocks and inex-
perience, by the end of the decade there were more dramatic
adjustments in energy conservation and demand than in supply.
Yet also by decade's end the fluctuating market once again
raised questions about energy policy backsliding and the
permanence of recent conservation efforts.

Even so, national demand policies had dramatically changed
in conception and effectiveness. Prior to 1973 there was no
consistent demand policy as such; over the decade of the 1970s,
this changed as public officials in all importing countries slowly
learned they could adjust to the OPEC supply revolution by
cutting back domestic demand.

Besides a more dependable means of energy supply, they
also needed to control energy demand. Up to 1973 demand
considerations played almost no role in official thinking and
there was no governmental, political, or economic force to
question the supply-side reliance on cheap oil. In fact, many
countries, as we saw, responded to the trauma of the first oil
shock by trying to keep prices low, with crude and product
price controls to maintain social equity policies and fight off a
new inflationary surge. By doing so, however, they also took
the cutting edge off the demand, dampening power of the OPEC

price rises and thus made their own still-to-be-developed long term demand control efforts more difficult. Many countries slacked off conservation in the middle years, only to be rudely reminded of energy vulnerability and the need to conserve after 1978-1979. But once again, after 1981 prices were more stable and some countries threatened to return to earlier ways.

How Demand and Supply Policies Are Different

The politics of domestic energy supply and energy demand are different in important ways that bore on policy making in the 1970s. Whereas supply policies enjoyed a long history with public officials, corporate managers and end users, demand management policies were new on the scene. This had several consequences over the decade. First, no strong private market existed for conservation, and government initially had to take a large role. Markets for energy supplies were plentiful. Second, government had fewer policy tools on the shelf to use to promote conservation and demand management. Third, there was far less experience in dampening and redirecting demand, and governments had much less certainty in the early and mid-1970s about what programs would work and what wouldn't. This also meant that demand management goals and priorities were less clear than on the supply side. Finally, but as importantly, there was a lot of direct institutional and even political opposition to the very idea of conservation. Most skepticism was from economists, technicians, and officials in supply industries who saw any decoupling of energy growth from economic growth as a dangerous heresy—cut back energy and you cut back economic growth, they reasoned. Utilities, oil companies, and other energy supply interests saw in conservation a great threat to their market positions and frequently opposed it.

Another relevant difference between demand and supply policies are the links to the macroeconomy. Where the impacts of supply were more specifically tied to one area of economic activity and hence more insulated from the rest, the impact of demand management (government price-setting policies for example) had more direct and widespread effects. These included impacts on inflation, cost-of-living indexes, manufacturing and export costs, and on international competitiveness.

The political impacts of these wider distributional effects is why government-mandated fuel price adjustments in Sweden are sometimes postponed until after the regular national labor negotiations. The state thereby hopes to prevent energy price hikes from raising the consumer price index and hence union demands. And European textile manufacturers complained bitterly for years that American price controls on oil unfairly advanced U.S. manufacturers' sales by subsidizing a key input for man-made fibers.

Changing Attitudes Toward Demand Policy

Government demand-side policy before the 1970s was designed for very specific purposes that had little to do with what came later to be called "conservation" or "energy efficiency" (that is, getting the same amount of output with less energy input). Rather it was to gain government tax revenues and to cross-subsidize different fuels for different classes of consumers. In some Asian countries, for example, the government took in approximately 10 percent of its annual receipts from taxes on petroleum. And in many other LDCs like Kenya middle-class car owners paid more for their gasoline so rural and urban poor could be charged less for their kerosene. Also fuel oil was taxed in Germany and Britain to subsidize and protect uncompetitive coal mines. But these were less demand management than social or regional employment policies. No thought was given to higher prices as a means to force greater fuel efficiency, although governments were quite willing to save foreign exchange through reduced fuel imports that resulted from higher domestic prices. Pricing policies were in place by the time of OPEC I— but not for conservation reasons.

The upshot of all these different social and political objectives was that taxes levied by European governments in the late 1970s accounted for a full 43 percent of the price the consumer paid for oil, while OPEC's share was only about 30 percent (the rest went to transportation, refining, and marketing margins) (al-Chalabi 1980, p. 152). For the United States the government take was only 10 percent, accounting in part for the lower prices (controls accounted for the rest). The European figure had dropped only moderately over the decade, down from about 54 percent in 1970 (al-Chalabi 1980, p. 152). The figures in aggregate value terms are also rather interesting. For example, in the 1960s governments of the consuming countries "collected nearly four times as much revenue per barrel as did the oil-producing governments." (World Bank 1981a, p. 46.) By the start of the oil glut in the early 1980s governments were still imposing taxes but now for very different, demand management reasons.

Potential energy savings could come through several means. Different forms of demand management had different time horizons, different up-front money requirements, different political implications, and different repayment periods. Table 6.1 indicates the pay-back period of various conservation measures.

Actual policy implementation and successful savings came more slowly, partly because of political heat and also because some measures simply took more time to implement. The most effective demand control measure, total pass through to consumers of higher world prices, ran against the emotional and political tide of the moment. Politicians in consumer countries were busy denouncing OPEC price rises and found it difficult at the same time to convince their constituents that immediate domestic price hikes were necessary for full adjustment to the new world conditions. Officials eventually found that price increases were salutory for long-term economic health but also realized they might not be in office in the long term if they raised prices quickly.

Therefore the key demand control trends in the 1973-1983 period were gradual and begrudging recognition of the value of pegging domestic prices more closely to international levels leading to a slow phase out of long-standing or newly imposed price controls; a popular and expert consensus that government-promoted investment in energy efficiency was as powerful an energy tool as supply management, followed by a first round of government measures, both short term and long, that slowly reduced consumption.

The second OPEC shock of 1978-80 was a watershed in these developments. It convinced officials and the public that higher prices were here to stay and had to be accommodated in domestic policy. Also new price relations, programs, and regulations were in place to which the public had become accustomed. In addition the results of higher prices and government programs were clear. In the industrial countries oil use fell by 5.6 percent between 1973 and 1975, then increased by 4.1 percent annually between 1975 and 1978, but fell by almost 8 percent when the OPEC II effects hit between 1979 and 1980. It dropped an additional 5.7 percent the following year (IEA 1981, pp. 11, 13). Oil imports into Europe fell from 60.2 percent of total primary energy in 1973 to 48.1 percent in 1978 (IEA, 1980, p. 23). Thus, in 1979-80 almost nowhere were new price controls slapped into place. Also, governments with a better policy arsenal and more experience under their belts acted more quickly than in 1973. They filled in the gaps in the patterns of previous policies and also toughened existing measures, such as taxes on oil products. Finally, and perhaps most importantly, the private sector of importing countries responded decisively to increase efficiency. Using a range of techniques, industry top management mandated existing plants to cut back on energy waste by improving insulation and industrial processes, they purchased new computerized energy-monitoring and control systems, and they insisted on more energy-efficient equipment and plant when they replaced their older ones.

Another more slippery side of the 1979 watershed was that it tipped Western governments into the uncertain and dangerous territory of trying to dampen energy demand via higher prices while also slamming on the macroeconomic brakes to fight inflation. Oil prices were allowed to rise, but consumer and commercial credit was reined in, government spending held in check. The resulting 1980-83 government-encouraged recession, stronger than the 1974-75 slump, helped cut energy demand but did almost as much social damage as the price increases themselves.

Thereafter (1982 and beyond), the energy question has been whether the subsequent fall in energy demand (and hence slack prices) was provoked more by the ferocity of the recession or the successes of conservation. If lower demand rose from conservation, the changes are more permanent and once growth revives, the world could hope for an inflation-resistant recovery. But if it instead was caused mainly by recession, recovery would again boost energy demand and prices, pushing the world back to the knife-edge balance that it knew in the late 1970s. Theories abound—the IEA wisely said it was a 50-50 split. Only the impending recovery will prove one theory or the other correct. Meanwhile, billions are bet by companies selling both energy supplies and energy conservation services.

By the spring of 1983 the fluctuating market was sending mixed signals. Prices were higher than in 1973, six and one-half times higher in real terms, but there was still a price slump compared to 1981 (Russell 1983, p. 6). In the face of falling prices European officials spoke anxiously about the consequences. According to Étienne Davignon, energy commissioner for the EEC, they were not out of the woods yet. "The decline in the "world] price of oil does nothing about Europe's oil problem. We use too much from foreign sources." (Business Week, March 14, 1983, p. 25.) Many governments slapped on new product taxes to keep prices more stable, like Ireland imposing a 17-cent-a-gallon tax hike on gasoline and France upping oil product taxes at the start of 1984 by 2 to 5 percent.

In the United States and even Europe by 1982, bigger, more fuel-hungry cars sold better than before interest rates

TABLE 6.1

Payback Periods of Various Conservation Measures

Less than one year
  Good housekeeping measures
  Installation of thermostats (United Kingdom)
  Insulating heat piping (United Kingdom)
  Heat recovery installation (Germany, Netherlands)
  Better maintenance of heating (United Kingdom)
One to three years
  Waste heat recovery (United Kingdom)
  Heat pump for industrial use (Germany)
Three to five years
  Insulation of industrial buildings (United Kingdom)
  Regulation, control of process (Sweden)
Five to ten years
  Heat recovery (Sweden)
  Industrial process (Denmark)
  Insulation of industrial building (Netherlands)
  Solar collector industry (Germany)
  Combined heat and power production (Netherlands, Sweden)
More than ten years
  Insulation of industrial buildings (Sweden)

Note: There is considerable difference in the calculated figure of the pay-back period of a particular measure in various countries. This seems to be due mainly to different energy price levels prevailing in these countries and to the different types and amounts of investments.

Source: International Energy Agency. 1979. Energy Conservation in Industry, p. 50. Paris.

weakened the thrust of government sponsored aids for energy efficiency spending, and there was a general relaxation of public worries about pricing as headlines concentrated on OPEC's internal divisions.

One indication of the new attitude occurred, when in July 1983, the German government took a preliminary decision to switch to lead-free autos starting in 1986 because of a perceived environmental crisis threatening forest lands. This move, which appeared likely to bring all of Europe into the lead-free camp by 1990, was in part made possible by this relaxed attitude toward conservation which made an increase of 10 percent fuel use in the transport sector acceptable as a trade-off to get the environmental benefit. The plan threatened to short-circuit a French government research project to develop a super fuel-efficient car based on leaded fuel. Also by 1983 the tone of IEA statements took on an increasingly strident note of warning—some editorials said hysteria—against relaxation of conservation efforts. They stressed instead that the apparent surplus conditions were due mainly to the recession and that a strong economic pick-up would send us off again. In this chapter we will identify, as in Chapter 5, the new policies devised, this time to achieve new demand control since 1973. We will see how they filled out the existing framework of pre-1973 policies, and the pre-1973 economic and political conditions which indirectly affected demand. We will also show how they competed with the deeply imbedded political notion of equity in most countries. Equity became a major issue due to the social impact of energy price increases after 1973. We will explain that underlying political conditions in countries led to the choice of one instrument over another, and finally gauge what measures will remain important in the 1980s and beyond.

II

POLICIES AND INSTRUMENTS

Governments rely on a variety of instruments to meet demand management objectives. At a very general level, most countries rely mainly on broad market forces of demand and supply to set price levels and guide consumer behavior. Interventions by governments therefore usually occur at the margin of energy markets, but they are important nonetheless. While governments may choose direct fiat, physical controls, or arms-length regulation to bring about conservation, shaping price signals through markets remains central.

Government pricing measures constitute the main tool for influencing energy demand. Retail prices are the signals to which consumers respond most directly, and governments find them relatively easy to influence by various indirect measures like taxation. Price policies can be applied across the board (i.e. "raise all fuel prices 10 percent"), and they can be narrowly targeted for equity or efficiency reasons ("raise gasoline prices 10 percent but reduce heating oil prices 10 percent").

Countries have different formulae for setting energy product prices (Krappels 1982). Complex formulae govern which fuels and which companies, are affected, the timing of the price adjustments, and how the increases (or decreases) are calculated. In France, Italy, Austria, Sweden, and Japan government ministries take a hands-on discretionary approach and rely less on automatic rules than the play of economic and political forces at a particular time. Special politically sensitive fuels are pinpointed for greater or lesser controls. This depends on the fuel's economic centrality and its political visibility. For example, in Japan today kerosene is widely used for heating purposes and in Africa for lighting and cooking. This popular fuel is politically sensitive and is price controled below market clearing levels. The U.S. and Brazilian love affair with the automobile means that gasoline prices were especially subject to price controls. In Japan and the United States, under the old system, adjustments were made irregularly after commercial and political heat built up, while in France they were monthly.

The Energy Policy Explosion forced governments to make their decisions about energy pricing much more explicit. Higher free market prices in Germany and lower controled ones in France did not mean one set was closely monitored and the other wasn't. It meant that having reviewed the situation those two govern- ments reached different conclusions about how, how much, and for what purposes to let world price levels influence domestic price levels.

LDCs faced a special set of demand management problems. For example, iron and steel, cement and glass making are industries dominant in the early stages of industrialization and are extremely energy intensive. Second, transportation looms large in the energy balance accounting for up to 40 percent of total commercial demand. A large part of this is imported oil for road transport for which fuel-switching possibilities are limited. But while a rail line and rolling stock may be the most energy-efficient solution to imported oil, it would be much more expensive for government than a single paved road used by privately owned buses, trucks, and cars. Third, government power to control energy prices and efficiency in rural areas is limited by staff and distance. Fully 50 percent of national energy may be rural households' use of fuelwood. Since tradi- tional cooking fires are only 5 to 10 percent efficient, most of the useful energy literally goes up in smoke.

However, the notion that since the less developed countries are less industrialized they have no effective scope for energy savings and therefore conservation policies are irrelevant or even harmful misses the mark. While true that energy-use patterns are different between LDCs and developed countries, there is ample scope for energy savings in the former. For example, Desai estimates that India in the post-1973 period had reduced its oil use by 30 percent through a series of demand management measures that included some price pass-throughs by government, direct physical allocation requirements, and the creation of a state fuel efficiency advisory service (cited in Dunkerly and Knapp 1981, p. 69).

The main kinds of demand management policies follow:

Measures to Reduce Demand for All Energy Forms Across the Board

These are policies which governments hope will reduce their overall national energy demand and its accompanying cost to the economy, while creating breathing room to allow them to better manage the energy sources they do have available. In contrast to the two measures below, these are less targeted to one specific fuel. The emphasis instead is on reducing all energy use and building a new mass psychology which actively supports public goals while convincing individuals themselves to use energy more efficiently. This group of measures is the most widely used and makes up the core of the Energy Policy Explosion on the demand side. This category of policies includes:

Pricing Measures Aimed at Giving the Fullest Possible Play to the Existing World Market Price Dynamic. This includes both decisions to forego price controls as well as to lift controls in place or at least to pull up artificially low prices while maintaining the system of control in theory. Also included are measures to remove socially inspired price subsidies on fuels. These policies must of course be frequently balanced against long-standing equity policies, and the new goal of protecting the poorest in society from sudden increases in a key consumer item. This group depends for its effectiveness on increasing energy prices or a continuing level of high prices which stay in place long enough to influence basic long-term investment decisions as well as day-to-day energy consumption decisions. They quickly lose their force in periods of stagnant or decreasing prices especially when consumers expect a long-term downward trend. One extreme version of these policies was proposed by Henry Kissinger early in the decade—to impose an energy price floor in times of dropping prices to avoid the harmful effects on conservation planning.

Nonprice Measures to Encourage Conservation Via Tax Incentives, Government Subsidy Payments, and Straight Regulation of Investment, Consumption, and Product Design. These measures complement the market pricing mechanism and are particularly important when because of market rigidities, equity, or other considerations market pricing is not fully operative, or when market pricing exists but prices are falling. These measures cover a wide field and, as we discussed above, may be short or long term. Direct physical allocation, for example, was tried in India after the first oil shock to push fuel switching and general conservation. Initially, oil users were given quotas equal to their 1973 consumption; then cuts were imposed based on a judgment regarding substitution possibilities. A firm could get its allocation increased if it proved that it needed more oil for export production, for import substitution, or to cater to defense demand" (Dunkerly and Knapp 1981, p. 58).

The first set of policies involving prices generally apply to a specific type of fuel, and thus affect all consumers of that fuel. Controls on crude oil prices of course have a very wide effect while product price controls may have a more specific effect (such as gasoline in the transport sector) but also can be scattershot (middle distillate for example covers both heating oil and diesel transport). The nonprice policies are by nature more narrow in application and are normally aimed at a specific group of consumers. Usually a given measure will apply only to transport, industry, residential, or government sectors. While a single concept such as tax breaks for conservation investments is workable in several sectors, the program for each sector usually is proposed and administered separately.

Measures to Switch Use of Fuel Toward Sources That Are More Desirable from a National Supply Security Point of View

In the perspective of the supply security and foreign exchange problems connected with oil and gas imports and especially the high oil dependence in several consumption categories, the main thrust of this policy has been to shift consumption from imported oil and toward coal and nuclear energy. In many cases governments have also seen shifting from oil to gas as a desirable policy goal because gas sources are more spread out. Fuel switching is a more complicated concept than straight conservation and less susceptible to public awareness campaigns. It is however a key issue among large industrial users. It is thus mainly aimed at such sectors and power generating where moves to coal and nuclear fuel can bring large scale results. The key objective in the residential sector has been shifts out of direct oil heating to either gas or electric power. In transportation the possibilities of shifting away from oil are small compared to other sectors because of the easy-to-transport character of the liquid gasoline and diesel fuels. This is especially problematic in LDC importers where most of the imported oil may go to this sector. In fuel switching, market fluctuations have to be carefully considered and policies continually updated. Oil price decontrol is a major aid, and a weakening oil market a major problem. (Now, however, nuclear cost overruns and coal transport problems also play major parts.) In this area the four main policy tools are:

Direct Legal Bans on the Use of Oil or Gas Especially in Power Plants and Industrial Boilers. This is an extreme step used mainly in cases where governments have no other means of effectively influencing decision making. Often used in LDCs, such measures may affect new plants and may include orders to phase out existing oil and gas by shifting plants to burn coal.

Fuel Switching Via Direct Government Investment Planning in Cases Where Utilities and Industries Are State-Owned and Government Jawboning (or some regulation) in Cases of Private or Semi-private Ownership. In this case governments with strong national economic control policies, such as in southern Europe and developing countries, have an advantage. Its purpose is to guide investments toward equipment that uses the preferred fuel, such as coal or gas.

Government Encouragement of Intermodal Substitution in Areas Like Transportation. A major energy-using sector, here freight or passenger hauling is shifted from trucking to trains or toward cheaper river transport. This may include shifts away from private cars toward motor bikes or public transportation.

Government Aids Such as Loans and Tax Breaks to Aid Consumers Bear the Cost of Switching. They may cover investments in new fuel-burning equipment, subsidizing the price of desirable fuels and even slanting price controls to give an advantage to the favored fuel. This category leaves the greatest freedom to the individual consumer on the final choice of fuels and is used in all sectors.

Measures to Meet Short Term Emergencies

When the initial oil production cut-backs occurred in late 1973 governments suddenly found that they had to put immediate measures in place to curb demand and distribute existing supplies on the smoothest possible basis. The initial solutions such as weekend gas station closings to discourage pleasure driving and prohibitions on unneeded commercial lighting were crude and had a doubtful real effect. Some governments already had experience with fuel rationing during wartime, but the type of quick-hitting shortages caused by unpredictable political events, or natural disasters which could end in a matter of weeks, were a new experience. After the first shock passed governments began some planning for future disruptions but were slow in implementation. The first aim was to improve sharing of existing oil supplies among consumer nations. In the 1973 case the governments had to rely solely on jaw-boning and ad hoc measures by oil companies. The quick agreement on an IEA scheme not only solved that problem (on paper) but also provided strong incentive for domestic planning to distribute scarce or extremely expensive energy in emergencies. In order to ensure fairness, IEA rules required such planning. The measures in this category exist aside from normal pricing mechanisms since they are based on scenarios in which drastic supply cuts have occurred and normal pricing criteria have gone out the window. In fact, a major problem with such systems is normally that they must include a means for installing temporary fair price mechanisms to allow shifting of fuel among companies and consumers in crisis periods. This group of policies includes:

Hastily Planned Short Term Controls Applied at Energy Consumption Pressure Points During the Shortages Such as 1973 and 1978-79. These cover gasoline, but extend to industrial fuel oil, power and fuel for heating, and fuel for farms. In some countries gas supplies are also controled at short notice, but this usually is connected to severe winter conditions.

On-going Stock Building Measures, Especially in the Oil and Gas Field, to Ensure Reserve Supplies Are on Hand for Future Emergencies. The key here is the concept of strategic petroleum reserves owned by the government or mandated to be developed by industry.

Long-term On-the-Shelf Planning for Future Emergencies. This includes actions to give the government more power to allocate fuel supplies under certain shortage scenarios as well as the actual drawing up of rationing and other crisis plans on the domestic and international level.

We began this chapter by identifying the differences between supply and demand policies, and suggesting similarities
in demand policies from country to country. At the same time
there are important crossnational differences, due to many of
the same factors that influenced energy supply policies: the
size of the domestic energy base, the characteristics of the
political system, the level of economic development, and a host
of other geographic differences. For example, evidence suggests
that a large domestic energy base makes it harder to convince
the population to conserve what appears to be abundant, and
governments are reluctant to raise prices. National transport
costs will be higher in huge land mass countries like Brazil and
Canada, lower in compact nations like the Netherlands and
Japan. France has more industrial demand than India, and
heating costs are higher in northern European countries like
Sweden and lower in tropical ones like Kenya.

Table 6.2 and Table 6.3 illustrate some of these cross-
national similarities and differences in conservation policies.

III

PRE-1973 INDIRECT POLICIES:
ENCOURAGING CONSERVATION

Most countries had begun policies in the pre-1973 era
involving key energy supplies that unintentionally had major
conservation effects. The most striking example of this is the
traditionally high gasoline taxes in European and developing
countries which were introduced in the early postwar period as
a revenue-raising luxury tax. In Thailand, for example,
petroleum taxes equalled about 9 percent of total government
revenues. In Europe when imported oil prices dropped during
the 1960s governments found they could increase the gasoline
tax and produce even more revenues with little public outcry.
Since the tax was de facto progressive it was not particularly
unpopular. At the same time, European governments maintained
a strong public transportation policy partly as a social policy
(not an energy policy).

The main unintended consequence was the widespread use
of fuel-efficient cars there long before the real international
price made it necessary, and the maintenance of good public
transport systems during a period when in the United States
the auto was rapidly replacing the train and bus as the dominant
surface mode. The result was that by 1973 the per capita con-

TABLE 6.2

Implementation of Energy Conservation Measures in Industry*

	Financial/Fiscal Incentives			Reporting/Auditing			Information, Advice/Assistance			Other Measures	
	Grant/Subsidy	Loan	Tax Incentive	Target Setting	Reporting	Auditing	Information/Publication	Meeting/Seminar	Advice for Small & Medium-sized Firms	CHP	Waste/Waste Heat
Australia	–	–	x	–	–	x	x	x	x	x	x
Austria	x	x	x	–	x	x	x	x	x	x	x
Belgium	–	–	–	–	–	–	x	–	x	–	–
Canada	x	–	x	x	x	x	x	x	x	x	x
Denmark	x	x	x	–	–	–	x	x	x	x	x
Germany	x	x	x	x	–	x	x	x	x	x	x
Greece	P	x	–	P	P	x	x	x	x	P	P
Ireland	x	P	–	x	P	–	x	x	x	x	x
Italy	P	P	–	–	x	–	x	x	x	xP	xP
Japan	x	x	x	x	x	x	x	x	x	–	x
Luxembourg	–	–	–	–	–	–	x	–	–	–	–
Netherlands	x	–	x	–	–	x	x	x	x	x	x
New Zealand	x	x	x	P	–	x	x	x	x	x	x
Norway	x	x	x	–	x	–	x	–	P	x	x
Portugal	x	–	–	–	–	x	x	–	x	P	–
Spain	x	x	x	x	x	x	x	x	x	P	P
Sweden	x	x	–	–	–	x	x	x	x	–	x
Switzerland	–	=–	x	–	–	–	x	–	x	–	x
Turkey	–	–	–	–	–	–	x	–	P	P	P
United Kingdom	x	–	x	x	–	x	x	x	x	x	x
United States	x	x	x	x	x	x	x	x	x	x	x

x = exists.
P = in preparation.
– = does not exist.
*They are described in more detail in the country chapters of the annual publication Energy Policies and Programmes of IEA Member Countries.

Source: Country Submissions for IEA 1977, 1978, 1979 and 1980 Reviews of National Energy Policies. Quoted in International Energy Agency. 1981 Energy Conservation: The Role of Demand Management in the 1980's, p. 23.

TABLE 6.3

Implementation of Energy Conservation Measures in the Residential and Commercial Sector*

| | Fiscal/Financial Incentives | | | Building Codes | | | | Prohibition of Bulk Metering | Efficiency Labelling of Appliances | | Information Advice |
| | Discount on Taxable Income | Subsidy Grant | Loan | New Buildings | | Existing Buildings | | | | | |
				Manda-tory	Volun-tary	Manda-tory	Volun-tary		Manda-tory	Volun-tary	
Austria	–	–	–	–	–	–	–	–	–	P	x
Austria	x	x	–	P	x	–	–	–	P	x	x
Belgium	–	x	–	P	–	P	–	–	P	–	x
Canada	–	x	x	x	–	x	–	x	x	–	x
Denmark	x	x	–	x	–	x	–	–	P	–	x
Germany	x	x	x	x	–	x	–	P	P	x	x
Greece	x	–	P	x	–	P	–	–	P	–	x
Ireland	x	x	–	x	–	–	x	–	P	–	x
Italy	P	–	–	x	–	x	–	x	x	x	x
Japan	–	P	x	x	–	P	–	x	P	–	x
Luxembourg	–	x	–	x	–	x	–	–	P	–	x
Netherlands	x	x	–	x	–	x	–	–	P	–	x
New Zealand	–	x	x	x	–	x	–	–	P	–	x
Norway	–	–	x	x	–	x	–	–	P	–	x
Portugal	–	–	x	P	–	P	–	–	P	–	x
Spain	x	x	x	x	–	x	–	x	P	–	x
Sweden	–	x	x	x	–	x	–	P	x	–	x
Switzerland	x	–	x	x	–	x	–	–	–	–	x
Turkey	P	P	–	P	–	P	–	–	P	–	x
United Kingdom	x	x	–	x	–	–	–	x	P	–	x
United States	x	x	x	P	–	–	–	P	x	–	x

x = exists.
P = in preparation.
– = does not exist.

*They are described in more detail in the country chapters of the annual publication Energy Policies and Programmes of IEA Member Countries.

Source: Country Submissions for IEA 1977, 1978, 1979 and 1980 Reviews of National Energy Policies. Quoted in International Energy Agency. 1981. Energy Conservation: The Role of Demand Management in the 1980's, p. 31.

sumption of gasoline in Europe was half that of the United States and Canada. This gap became a real international political problem once the consuming countries banded together to meet the OPEC challenge, as there was less fat to cut in Europe, but consumers were already used to higher prices. Although the new burdens would be painful, the public was used to the punishment.

The United States was at the opposite end of the scale on this issue when the 1973 crisis hit. The federal gasoline tax had remained at a miniscule four cents a gallon and state taxes brought this up to an average under ten cents a gallon. This, of course, was less than a 50 percent tax compared to the 100 percent and higher European rates. The result in the United States was not only that the amount of energy use in road transport was much higher than in Europe, but also that consumers were not used to making cut-backs in the auto transport field. When the crisis hit Americans, imbued with a strong feeling that cheap oil was theirs by right and the fact of large domestic reserves, decided they were already being fleeced by the companies and fiercely opposed any new gasoline tax, despite several efforts by President Carter. The first post-1973 change did not come until 1982 when the Reagan administration pushed through a small five-cents-a-gallon increase which was not tied to energy policy at all but instead was a measure to raise funds to repair the decrepit federal highway system. Still, U.S. per capita gasoline consumption remained far above European levels into the 1980s and for European public opinion, the Americans, with their refusal to take painful measures on gasoline taxation, appeared to be insincere allies in the common front against OPEC.

Beyond gasoline taxes there have been several other types of government policies with indirect energy conservation effects which skewed long term consumption patterns. European governments tended to tax fuel oil before the 1973 crisis hit, but because of social reasons they were not nearly as high as gasoline taxes. Especially important have been programs such as that in Germany to force power consumers to subsidize the domestic coal industry through a surcharge on electric rates. This began as a purely industrial-social policy to maintain miners' jobs, but was reinforced after 1973 when keeping coal mines open also became a key energy supply policy goal. This expensive power policy in Germany has long forced German companies in power-intensive sectors to be energy conscious to remain competitive. Like the industrialized countries, the LDCs reduced energy consumption by taxes on motor fuel levied for other social purposes.

PRE-1973 INDIRECT POLICIES: DISCOURAGING
CONSERVATION

The tendency of governments to control energy prices at
low levels in order to protect their consumers became in the
years after the 1973 crisis a key obstacle to strong conservation
efforts. Improved energy efficiency was only one goal in a
complex hierarchy, and could run counter to other, often more
long-standing political commitments. Much of statecraft in the
decade was balancing these conflicting imperatives. Each country's historical background and "social contract" assured that
the motivations and tools used to do so would differ greatly
(cf. Jean Saint-Geours, in Yergin and Hillenbrand 1982). In
some countries like the United States equity and energy had
long historical roots dating back to the trust-busting early
days of oil. In others, access to cheap kerosene and electric
power became an economic entitlement defined as a sine qua non
for achieving rapid and just development. For others, the notion
of energy equity did not carry such force. And, of course, in
each country different social groups defined equity in their
own interests and mobilized themselves accordingly.

Elaborate systems of oil price controls were in effect in
several European countries especially France, Italy, and Spain,
as well as under an indirect system in Japan long before the
1973 oil shock. These had a clear distributional aspect, but
they were used basically as instruments of government economic
policy to help guide and adjust national economies and enforce
market stability. Countries such as Germany and Britain, whose
economies were more laissez-faire and more market regulating
did not have a tradition of strong government oil price controls.
Also these countries had either strong oil companies of their
own (Britain) or a healthy market structure (Germany) plus
functioning anti-monopoly rules to afford protection to their
publics.

When the first shock hit, the existing patterns remained
almost intact. Those European countries with a tradition of
controls, continued them, using them mainly to provide as much
economic stability as possible in a tumultuous situation and some
selected consumer protection. While Britain with a Labour
Government in power did go to a mild price control system at
the start of the crisis, this was lifted in 1974 in favor of a price
commission which merely observed markets for irregularities.
The Germans never imposed controls at all.

What is important in the European and Japanese cases is
that the notion of equity for consumers was only one of many

considerations and not at all the key one. For several reasons
the European public was less attuned to seeing all fuel prices
as a direct give and take battle between themselves and the oil
companies. And where they did they were less inclined to believe
that they were being unjustly handled when prices went up.
These reasons, encompassing several of the fundamental differences between European and American attitudes toward energy
policy include:

The Politics of Choice. Because so little oil is produced in
Europe and Japan, the public could not get too choosey about
price: they paid what the world market asked, and then some.
The companies were seen as intermediaries, not producers.
Europeans got used to getting oil through foreign suppliers
who were simply importing a product. The connection between
the actual production cost and sales prices was always fuzzy to
the average consumer. In addition, refinery margins were un-
clear and hard to separate from crude prices. When OPEC
stepped in and began to raise prices in a way clearly visible
to the average consumer, Europeans were inclined to feel that
the OPEC owners of the oil were in their rights to seek higher
prices, even as they opposed the increase itself. In this case
a more natural awareness of the give and take of international
trade prevalent among Europeans played a role in their adaptation and their interpretation of the equity issue.

Different Governmental Styles and Responsibilities. For those
countries with traditional dirigiste economic policies the public
generally considers the government as the setter of fuel and
many other key prices in the economy, based only loosely on
purely economic considerations. This position holds too in the
developing countries. The price of gasoline or heating oil is
basically what the government says it is and can be influenced
by political pressure either through the ballot or informal lobbying and string pulling. Because of this the role of the oil
industry as such is much less visible.

Thus, in Europe energy pricing as a national equity issue
was not well developed in the broad public. Even if intellectual
and left circles denounced the power of the multinational oil
companies, the average consumer did not act as though he or
she personally was being cheated or could do anything about it
anyway.

In the United States on the other hand, and to a certain
extent in other major oil producer states such as Canada and
Australia, the equity issue has played a much more dominant

role, especially in the history of price controls. The average American had been suspicious of the oil industry since John D. Rockefeller's Standard Oil monopoly and welcomed the efforts of the trustbusters to control oil company practices. However, because of the power of the oil lobby and the strong American tradition against economic controls, prices were never controled in the United States except during wartime. At the same time gas prices did come under controls, a reflection of strong public pressure to impose "political" controls. When the 1973 crisis hit, the Republican Nixon administration moved rapidly to control fuel prices as a desperate antiinflation measure. But this provided the break that consumer groups had long been seeking. As OPEC pushed its own prices up it became politically more and more difficult to lift the "temporary" controls since this would create a clear profit for the oil companies on their domestic reserves. Thus the cumbersome control system was retained in 1975 legislation and survived until the end of the Carter administration and the windfall tax designed to substitute a tax equity system for price controls. In the United States the essential political fight was over the very existence of price controls. There was no peacetime tradition of activist government domination and the price controls stayed in place only as long as the balance of political forces allowed. Canadian and Australian price control had the same equity content and as in the United States, in Canada the equity fight was sharpened by the perception that the main profit from the domestic oil price rise would accrue to American oil companies which were exploiting Canadian resources.

The reasons for these attitudes on equity in the United States sprang from sources which were the mirror image of the European experience:

The Politics of Choice. The production of oil in large quantities at home by a domestic industry with a long record of anticonsumer practices helped raise equity issues. If American oil producers were making money producing crude at $3 per barrel, much of the public felt there could be no justification for them to suddenly charge $12. The OPEC producers were considered simply a particularly rapacious band of oil producers and the domestic oil companies were immediately suspected of doing all possible to ally themselves with OPEC and win similar price hikes.

The Administration and Congress Were Seen Mainly As a Battlefield in Which the Industry and Consumer Interests Would Clash. The government itself had no a priori rights to control oil and fuel prices. In practical political terms what was missing else-

where was the intense ideological fervor always introduced into
the American debates. Nor were there as serious ideological
debates in the developing countries. Equity-oriented pricing
was widely used for many fuels which de facto discouraged
energy savings. Countries like Sudan or Egypt faced sharp
political pressures to control prices from unruly urban poor
and middle classes balking at price hikes on visible consumer
goods and services like kerosene and electricity. When subsidies were removed, riots and demonstrations occurred. But
the accumulation of pre-1973 price controls made a fertile ground
for new interventions later. This posed political problems in
LDCs as elsewhere when it became expensive after 1973 to
continue what had once been cheap. For example, the Indonesia
oil product subsidies jumped to fully 9 percent of government
tax revenues or about $10 per barrel of domestic consumption
(Dunkerly and Knapp 1981, p. 72). These subsidies undoubtedly
helped the poor make more purchases than they would have
been able to afford otherwise. But in the aggregate only 20
percent of the subsidized kerosene went to the poorest 40 percent
of the population. Of course, commercial fuels like oil and electricity are mostly consumed by middle- and upper-income groups.
The very poor mainly use noncommercial fuels and many people
use some mix of the two.

Although most LDCs did heavily subsidize kerosene for
low-income consumers, there was considerable variety from
country to country. The kerosene-to-gasoline price ratios in
Bolivia, Sri Lanka, and Jamaica were .35, .24, and .39 respectively. At the other end Colombia, Thailand, and Philippines
were all similarly priced at around .90. Jamaica, at .39 in 1973,
dramatically increased the differential under an increasingly
populist regime to reach .19 by 1977.

NON-OIL DEMAND MANAGEMENT ISSUES

In the case of natural gas and electric power pricing, the
American and non-American experiences are also different.
The general results of the several policies were similar however—
discouraging fuel saving—only to be gradually phased down in
the late 1970s as conservation gained higher priority.

In most countries of Europe and in Japan gas and power
prices have been strongly controled by governments. Most of
the time this stemmed from direct government ownership of
utilities or at least a decisive role in rate making which generally
went beyond the regulatory powers of American utility boards.
Since lighting and home heating, the main private uses of gas

and electric power, were considered necessities, they were the
natural object of pricing systems which amounted to subsidies
for special consumer groups. This tilt was maintained in many
countries after the oil crisis began, with both French and
Italian consumers, for example, enjoying cheap power and gas
far into the 1970s. Only at the decade's end did these prices
begin to come in line with world market conditions. The EEC,
a strong advocate of market pricing for all energy, took the
position that pricing subsidies should be eliminated and replaced
by straight government transfer payments to target groups.
In LDCs rural electrification schemes are heavily subsidized by
governments and run persistent and costly deficits. Government may pay for the capital construction costs, but leaves the
company (usually public) to somehow cover the operating costs.
This is usually impossible since government also holds the rural
rates very low, often below marginal replacement costs. This
forces the companies to run down their system and service
since they lack the necessary revenues to reinvest and keep
themselves going.

In the United States, traditional equity principles were
able to triumph in the 1930s and the gas issue has been highly
political ever since, especially since different parts of the
industry are owned by different firms. In Congress the industry
and the Reagan administration were unable through the early
1980s to win a clean break in the political deadlock over gas
price decontrol. On the electric power side, American price
regulators (usually at the state level) tended to approve rates
which kept pace more or less with rising generation costs,
however, they also tended to use the straight economic argument
that larger power users should get discounts. The conservationists' counter-proposal of ending block rate discounts for
industry was only put into effect slowly as part of the general
push toward more explicit demand management and conservation
policies.

Normally, conservation and environmental thinking go hand
in hand. The less energy required means the less need for new
energy production from off-shore drilling, nuclear plants, and
other environmentally harmful operations. But at the same time
some environmental rules have been put into place in consuming
countries which can mean higher energy use. The clearest
example of this is the drive to clean up auto emissions from
gasoline fueled cars. The most complete system for this is the
catalytic converter which must operate on lead-free fuel. But
by removing the lead, which is itself a dangerous pollutant,
more highly processed gasoline, and thus more crude oil, is

needed to get the same power. Environmental demands on
governments pose an even greater problem for fuel switching
since the premium fuels oil and gas are relatively clean burning
while the most favored objects of switching, coal and nuclear,
have major pollution drawbacks. Since in most cases price is
the critical factor in successful fuel switching, the high extra
costs for clean coal burning through scrubbers and other equipment can reverse the initial advantage of low coal market prices.
The rising costs of nuclear power generation have proven harder
to control or even estimate.

IV

POST 1973 DEMAND POLICIES

We now look more closely at the main post-1973 demand
policy target areas—transport, residential, commercial, and
industry—and the ways governments have acted in each. Our
objective is to see where consumer governments have followed
similar policies and what internal domestic reasons caused
divergence. Finally, we also identify the policies most likely
to remain important in the late 1980s and beyond. It will be
at that point that the initial conservation push from surging
oil prices fades, governments have fewer funds for structural
aids, and consumers find investments harder to finance.

GENERAL ENERGY SAVINGS MEASURES

The politics of energy conservation has been particularly
important since the first months of the Energy Policy Explosion
in 1973. Governments were confronted with a demand side
challenge that offered positive ways of encouraging savings,
but also political pitfalls. Politicians had to stress equality of
hardship for all members of society for the common good. Most
tried immediately to achieve this through public campaigns and
other means to build enthusiasm for conservation. Virtually
every industrial country and many of the larger LDCs mounted
information campaigns, stressing the dollars and cents gains
of serious conservation. Governments also tried to convey a
sense of fighting a common enemy. Conservation became a way
to stand up to OPEC and foreign (and some not so foreign)
multinationals. This feeling was often potent, as seen in the
driverless Sundays ordered in the Netherlands in 1973 when

the Dutch joined the United States on the Arab's special boycott list. The empty Dutch highways became festive bicycle paths as the whole nation enjoyed its small but memorable defiance of OPEC.

Governments had also to watch the natural divisions among different interest groups affected by demand management measures beginning with the split between industry and private uses. Industry groups, farmers, and other commercial groups with powerful political lobbies may be better able to protect themselves against potentially harsh measures, and government cannot be seen as bending to the particular will of one sector while sticking with the rules on others. They then lose their ability to push through tough measures elsewhere. Some governments sought a way around this by seeking cooperation on a voluntary basis, coopting business groups into setting standards for themselves. In many countries the phase-out of heavy oil-burning boilers by industry in favor of coal was handled in this way. In the United States the bitter conservatism of Detroit auto makers, which opposed introduction of small cars until the success of the Japanese competition based on oil crisis economics forced their hand, made mandating fuel consumption regulations necessary.

Besides conservation campaigns to build public enthusiasm and win business support, another means government frequently used was imposing conservation measures in their own ranks. Government buildings are usually put on tough temperature controls as a symbolic gesture for the entire country. Both state office buildings and government car pools (post office vans, city busses, army service vehicles) are used for energy pilot projects. The actual savings from such projects is negligible, but the need to set a good example, especially in delicate policy areas, is far more important. One final means of building public interest and compliance in demand management policies is international cooperation, especially through the IEA programs. Governments can show how conservation programs have worked in other countries and use statistical comparisons to show where their own countries lag. For example, U.S.-Swedish comparisons were an important means to convince many Americans of the value of demand management.

Now we turn sector-by-sector to the specific policy instruments most widely employed in the post-1973 decade.

Transportation

Conservation of energy in transportation is almost totally an oil-savings proposition, and therefore quite desirable where possible. In almost all countries, even those with extensive electrified rail systems, well over 90 percent of all energy used in transport is oil and over 85 percent of that is road use of oil. Not surprisingly, consumption of gasoline by private autos is a prime government target for reduction. Because fuel is such a highly visible cost factor in any transport business, it is assumed by governments that commercial operations such as airlines and trucking companies will already be doing much to conserve fuel. It is the private car driver who tends to be less aware of his conservation options and even the impact on his pocketbook. Almost all countries made new efforts after the energy crisis broke to further control auto fuel consumption. Some sought to improve the energy intensity of each unit (that is, more miles per gallon), others to alter the structure of the transport sector. In the United States a near saturation of second cars and superhighways, had been reached; in Europe (and certainly LDCs) the fleet was still growing. In North America the volume of oil consumption in transport was expected to grow from 440 millions of tons of oil equivalent (mtoe) in 1973 to 462 mtoe in 1990, a scant 4 percent. In Europe during the same period oil use in transport was expected to jump 43 percent from 133 mtoe to 201 mtoe.

In LDCs even higher rates are anticipated. The exact national rates will vary of course. For example, Brazil's government very actively and directly promoted auto manufacturing and use, while the Korean government had different priorities. Thus transport conservation must be for Brazil a key sector (admittedly, it is a larger country physically than Korea) and one better understands the Brazilian fuel alcohol program.

TABLE 6.4

Car Ownership Relative to Gross Domestic Product, 1975 (cars per million 1975 $GDP)

Industrial	
United States	69
France	45
Japan	34
Developing	
Brazil	40
India	9
Korea	4

Source: Dunkerly, Ramsay, Gordon, Cecelski 1981. Energy Strategies for Developing Nations. Published for Resources for the Future by Johns Hopkins University Press. Reprinted with permission.

The main conservation measures used in this sector are:

Fuel Taxation. The old standby of gasoline taxation has never lost its popularity among governments as either a revenue-raising measure or conservation measure or both. Use of a gasoline tax hike for conservation usually is acceptable in a crisis situation and almost all Western countries used it in 1980-81. But in quieter times the main urge comes from the revenue side with the conservation argument thrown in for effect. These taxes can be used to pay for subsidies on other fuels and then are called "cross-subsidies." The clear drawback of the policy is its direct inflationary effect, especially since it touches all driving, including necessary commuting and hauling goods. It only has a mild economic effect if it forces drivers to reduce discretionary driving, that is, for pleasure or errands that can be accomplished without a car. It also runs the risk of igniting public anger. One variant of this approach has been to give more favorable tax treatment to diesel fuel over gasoline on the basis that diesel motors are more efficient, but that is not widespread because of other problems with diesel fuel including poor public acceptance because of lower performance.

Rules to Force Production of More Fuel-Efficient Autos. Almost all countries with substantial auto manufacturing industries have programs to either force or cajole companies to reduce fuel consumption in their new cars through motor design changes and/or downsizing. Governments have also taken advantage of the natural desire of the consumer to buy a fuel-efficient vehicle by programs requiring testing of new models for average mileage and publication of results at points of sale. The most radical program has been in the United States, which starting in 1978 mandated an increase in fleet averages from 18 miles per gallon (mpg) in that year to 27.5 mpg by 1985. The tough law was backed by strong testing systems and has survived several attempts by the auto industry to relax rules in the name of pumping up dangerously depressed profitability. Defenders of the system in Congress have pointed out that since 1978 it has given mossback Detroit executives the goad they needed to meet Japanese small-car competition more effectively. Japan also has a mandatory fuel efficiency system and Canada was moving in 1983 to stiffen its voluntary system with new testing and labeling rules. Australia, Germany, Italy, Sweden, and Britain all have voluntary programs. All the existing programs aim at bringing mileage standards up to between 25 and 30 mpg by 1985, goals, which are technically feasible.

Penalty Taxes on Large Cars and Motors. In most European
countries car operation taxes are gauged by car weight and/or
motor size. Also, in some countries such as Italy, road tolls
are set by car size. This approach has been customary in
Europe, while the United States has no such differentiated tax
system. The "freedom to choose" argument overcame several
proposals put forth, especially under Carter, and the Congress
rejected them. In Canada where car taxation is a provincial
government responsibility, the movement by some provinces
toward the European system was set back in 1982 when Ontario,
the most populous province, decided to stay with a flat system.

Speed Limits. Posting of mandatory speed limits at relatively
low levels, geared to maximum efficiency of fuel consumption,
was one of the first measures many consuming countries took
in the mid-1970s. At present all IEA countries have some sort
of posted limits connected to energy savings effort with Germany
being the only one to merely recommend and not enforce the
desired speed. The limits widely vary, with the U.S. 88 kph
(55 mph) at the low end along with Japan, New Zealand, Ireland,
and Norway. Most other European countries have highway limits
of between 100 and 130 kph range. The IEA recommends 90 to
110 as the peak efficiency levels.

Pooling and Public Transport Subsidies. Virtually all industrialized governments developed policies to promote more efficient
use of private transport and greater use of public systems.
Companies have been offered tax breaks on vehicles used for
commuting by employees to eliminate use of inefficient single-
person autos. Car and van-pooling information campaigns have
also been widespread. Governments have also tried to increase
support for public transport since 1973 although these steps
have rarely been decisive. Countries with dense transport nets
have maintained them and made some praiseworthy advances
like the French TGV fast train system, which has mainly cut
into airline traffic, while those with poor ones have normally
done little more than prevent new erosion. The biggest success
of the U.S. federal railway system, AMTRAK, has come on
specialized routes in heavy population zones such as the Boston-
New York-Washington corridor. A revival of true cross-country
trains in the United States has not taken place. Public spending
on transport is highly sensitive to government budget cutting
however. Oil price cuts also impact as cheaper gasoline prices
reduce the incentive to leave the car at home in favor of the
bus or subway.

The transportation of electric power is an additional problem area for some developing country where extremely high and expensive transmission losses are not uncommon. Over 20 of 76 countries surveyed by the World Bank suffered from losses in the 21 to 30 percent range, a very high figure. Reductions of these losses through greater efficiency and better maintenance could save even a middle-sized country $4 to $5 million annually in fuel costs.

Residential Conservation

Home energy use especially for space heating has become the second major target for government conservation programs. The situation was even more extreme than in auto transport because governments had traditionally treated home heating as a necessity and thus did not tax that sector as heavily. Virtually every government where climate conditions made home heating necessary developed a program after 1973 of tax incentives, loans, and grants to encourage home owners and renters to insulate and replace old, inefficient heating systems. The Canadian system, for example, provided up to $1,000 in grants for residential energy savings, the exact amount depending on the income level. Canada has found the average $350 grant has brought normally a 29 percent saving, paying for itself within five years. Frequently these efforts have been part of a national program which also encouraged fuel switching. Denmark and the Netherlands have such comprehensive programs. Less common are government benefits for passive residential energy-saving features such as south-facing windows and special heat-retaining construction.

Beyond the basic loan, grant, or tax break mechanisms other residential conservation measures include:

Energy Audits. Several governments provide programs under which the cost of experts to check homes for ways to improve efficiency are provided free, or at cost, to consumers. Some of these services may be mandated by state governments. Government also provides training grants for auditors.

Improved House Construction Codes. This type of change has come about slowly, but since 1973 almost every IEA country has upgraded codes. Also, improved codes for electric appliances and strict labeling to help consumers choose the most efficient appliances are now widespread.

<u>Individual Metering for Energy Use in Apartment Blocks</u>. This
measure is not always feasible but has been adopted by many
countries to force consumer attention to wastage.

<u>Temperature Control</u>. Governments have normally tried to
avoid strict rules on temperature in residences because it
smacks of violating the "my home is my castle" maxim. Here
the main approach has been through advertising campaigns and
setting examples with public building regulations.

On the whole residential savings programs have been well
received by the public. Governments have stepped in to help
consumers save money individually, promoting greater national
energy security in the process. Here is a classic case of policy
working through market incentives. The impact of the huge
jump in home heating bills since 1973 has been reinforced as a
conservation goal by two other factors, the relatively low cost
at the start because of the lack of high taxes (which made the
percentage cost increase greater than gasoline) and the fact
that home heating bills come bunched up in the cold months
and thus hit harder. The do-it-yourself nature of the needed
improvements is also appealing. Statistics show substantial
reductions in energy consumption per dwelling in most industrialized countries between 1973 and 1980, including Canada
(7.3%), Germany (6.4%), Sweden 19.3%), Great Britain (3.7%)
and the United States (17.3%). On the whole, less dramatic
savings were made in warmer countries. In most cases government incentive programs in all countries were restricted to a
certain period, usually two or three years long, designed to
hurry up consumers into making decisions on insulation as fast
as possible. On the other hand the improvements once made
are permanent and not subject to reversal as fuel prices slide
downward. It is unlikely consumers will rush up to the attic
and rip out the fiberglass when the oil barrel price drops.

Industrial and Commercial Conservation

Energy costs naturally became a major new headache for
the largest consumers—the industrial and business operations.
They had strong incentives to save on their own, and governments everywhere set up programs to prod them even further
in the right direction. Besides tax breaks and loans, energy-
auditing assistance was provided and proved to be quite successful. In several countries, special industry branches with high
energy consumption have been targeted. Frequently industry
associations have acted as the liaison between government and
industry in providing information and in some cases, such as

Canada, setting voluntary savings targets. The Canadian industry had set a 12 percent goal for savings between its 1972 base year and 1980 and, helped by the new price increases, were able to reach 15 percent. They have since set a new 23 percent savings goal for 1985. The Australian government in 1980 produced a comprehensive national industrial energy management scheme which provided small and medium firms with audit grants, seminars for senior management and plant person- nel and a series of awards for energy conservation achievement. IEA statistics show in 1980 industry energy use for the member countries was 6.6 percent lower than in 1973 even though pro- duction in that year was 112 percent of 1973 levels. Thus the energy use per unit of industrial output of the OECD dropped sharply through the late 1970s and into the 1980s.

Only the most advanced LDCs like Brazil have shown the capacity to mount a centralized energy audit campaign. There the Instituto de Pesquisas Tecnologicas in São Paulo did a major series of energy audits for industry (the National Productivity Council in India launched an analogous program even before the crises). It also issued conservation manuals. Our inter- views in Rio and Brazilia, though, showed that the responsibility still lay largely with the enterprise itself to seize the opportunity (although some sectors were pinpointed for special attention). This too is a problem for countries where many of the largest and most energy-intensive enterprises (like steel or cement) sell in price-controled markets, and where factor market prices for inputs are also tightly controled. With so little discretion managers have little incentive to be more energy efficient. Yet some LDC factories may be 30 to 40 percent less energy efficient than in OECD countries. We also observed this during energy interviews in the Soviet Union, with eventually the state simply mandating a certain percentage energy savings from each factory.

Power generation has only a limited potential for energy conservation because generating stations are normally geared for maximum efficiency. But there is a sector where conservation comes into play: recapturing waste heat for use in nearby homes and industry. Some European governments, especially Germany and Sweden, have promoted district heating plans with tax breaks and regulatory assistance. Because of the high up-front money involved this sort of aid is frequently crucial for new develop- ment. Governments have also encouraged more efficient use of privately generated power by establishing the right for such producers to sell excess power to public utilities or other con- sumers, breaking through formerly restrictive power distribution rules that the utilities in the United States, for example, fought

to retain. Once again, the political opposition to making regulations or laws more proconservation should never be underestimated. Many of the big utilities initially threw their influence
into combatting the idea of conservation, seeing it as a threat
to their business. Many executives remained quite hostile until
their accountants showed them it was usually cheaper to invest
in a "barrel of conserved oil" than build a new plant.

FUEL-SWITCHING MEASURES

Fuel-switching measures pose distinctly different problems
for government decision makers from purely conservation policies
for several reasons. Most importantly, they are driven by a
combination of national policy considerations with price only
one factor. In some cases the price relationship between oil
and more desirable alternatives may work in favor of the government policy, but the driving force in fuel switching (especially
in industrialized countries) still remains the hypothetical insecurity of oil or gas supplies. In many cases the pre- and
post-switch fuels had equivalent costs. This always gives
fuel-switching policies a more <u>dirigiste</u>, abstract tone which
makes raising public enthusiasm tougher. Added to this, the
less desirable fuels are frequently more convenient to handle
and cleaner to burn. Gasoline remains the first choice of most
drivers; diesel, methane, alcohol, or other alternatives are
considered second-best. Because of these characteristics, the
scope for fuel switching is usually very narrow, with power
generation and use in some industrial heating operations the
prime target. Also fuel switching demands strong planning
capabilities in both industry and government but does not bring
the same political rewards as pure conservation. A drop in oil
use through substitution may earn a government some political
points, but it does less to save final consumers money than
does conservation. In some countries, such as New Zealand
with its gasoline-to-gas switching or Brazil with its alcohol fuel
program, a fuel-switching campaign may help raise national
pride. But for most uses the general positive political impact
is more obscure. The public may be as skeptical about coal or
nuclear as they are about oil and gas. In the United States
the main impetus for the switch to coal has come from the self-
interested coal industry and miners' unions, not from the public
at large and the large subsidies proposed for the power industry
to make the switch to coal were at times viewed as yet another
give-away to the "greedy utilities."

Primarily, fuel switching has been less influenced by past policies than pure conservation. Gasoline taxes have not shifted auto fuel to other sources, and up to 1973 most plans for coal and nuclear installations were as additions to overall capacity and not as replacements for oil and gas. Because fuel switching only saves a company or consumer money when oil and gas prices are high, the incentive to switch diminished greatly in the early 1980s when oil prices stabilized. With conservation there is some economic advantage no matter what the fuel price but not with fuel switching. Thus by 1983 the IEA was deeply concerned that the efforts would bog down in the mid-1980s. Here more than in conservation a heavy, directed government involvement would be needed to maintain momentum.

The main targets for government fuel-switching policies are:

Power Generation and Industrial Fuel Use

Large utility and industrial boilers are the main target for government fuel-switching programs because they are readily convertible to coal use and can be easily regulated. In virtually all developed countries and many developing ones some type of tax break is allowed for conversion away from oil use, in many cases accompanied by a statutory ban on new facilities using oil and gas as well as a phase-out schedule for existing plants. The official thinking was that while a new oil plant might make microeconomic sense from the profit position of a single company, in the aggregate the nation as a whole would be too vulnerable to future supply disruptions or price rises if many individual plants took the same decision. Much of this rule making was laid down in the late 1970s and has thus not yet been affected by the easing of the oil market in the early 1980s. Electric generating facilities were even easier to control than other industrial applications and IEA forecasts expect a dramatic decrease in oil use by the power sector through 1990 to 106 mtoe (5.7% of total consumption) from 184 mtoe (15.5% of total power consumptio) in 1980.

On the industrial side, the main targets of fuel switching have been heavy industries such as iron and steel, cement, and pulp and paper. Some countries such as Australia, in an effort to promote coal use in industry, have lowered environmental rules as well as offered tax incentives. But in several European countries the threat of acid rain has forced new restrictions at a time when investment in fuel switching was already weakening. In developing countries, or threshold countries where industry buildups are still in the initial stage, planning away from oil and gas use toward coal and hydro is frequently highly effective. Turkey has developed a strong program based on domestic lignite and water resources. While annual oil use in Turkish power generation is expected to grow from 1.2 mtoe to 2.1 mtoe between 1981 and 1995, solid fuel use and hydro may both rise from below three mtoe to over 18 mtoe in the same period. However, much will depend on the managerial skills and political commitment to bring these more difficult forms on stream. The Brazilian authorities coordinated a switch-to-coal project for large consumers like cement. There is little evidence of switching in the smaller LDCs, although there too it will depend on what fuels are domestically available. Where there are domestic resources, there is far greater incentive to change over than simply to substitute one imported fuel for another.

Fuel Switching in Residential Uses

Some governments seek to switch homes from oil heat to gas or electric based on overall planning schemes. But in most cases this sort of choice is left to the individual based on market considerations plus a certain incentive. Some households will switch from oil to other forms of energy because of fears of a cut-off during a supply shortage. Gas and electricity seem more dependable than a delivery to the home of a truck load of oil. But bulky, dirty coal is out of the question in industrialized states (though widely used in some countries like Korea).

One of the key areas for government activity is promoting use of solar energy in residences as a means to cut oil and gas use. Virtually all governments offer some aid for solar equipment, especially for water and space heating. Solar power systems are less advanced and as yet hardly form a substitute for normal electricity use in houses. Here too the M-shaped market has acted as a spoiler, since the spread of such solar applications was slowed by the drop in oil prices, as by higher interest rates in the 1980s. The demand one would anticipate for solar-powered electricity in LDC houses is limited by the still-high costs.

Many LDC governments are ambivalent about domestic fuel switching. Since most households rely entirely or in part on noncommercial fuels like wood or dung, any switch would probably be toward oil, worsening balance of trade problems. A switch the other way "back" toward wood may threaten forests and scarce agricultural land. Faced with this ambivalence or limited capacity to affect residential fuel choices, most poor governments do little.

Fuel Switching in Transportation

Switching transport away from oil use is extremely difficult and on the strategic level is unlikely to bring any substantial results during this century. In most countries efforts to promote cars running on electricity, methane, and other nonpetroleum sources have been restricted to pilot projects with no real impact. Only in a few countries where the government has organized a large scale effort, and backed it up with disincentives to gasoline use, has any progress been made. In most cases such efforts are based on use of a home-produced fuel which gives the effort a more nationalist flavor. The key examples are the Brazilian alcohol fuel program which forced the use of a mixture of alcohol and gasoline, and the New Zealand compressed natural gas program.

The New Zealand program aimed at the conversion of 200,000 vehicles by 1990, relying on a series of grants for conversion of cars to gas and loans for creation of gas fuel stations as well as government advertising and fleet conversion. It converted 27,000 vehicles between 1979 and 1982, far behind the target, with the key stumbling block continued preference for the more familiar fuel. The New Zealand government is also actively promoting auto use of LPG but here resistance from the public centers around safety factors.

In the United States the use of alcohol fuels as a gasoline additive had a vogue during the late 1970s, promoted heavily by farm interests as a means to exploit corn supluses. A modest federal alcohol production aid program was set up, but it made little progress as oil prices came down and the public finding alcohol less efficient or at least less familiar, stuck with gasoline. In this case the government was unwilling to take the needed step of ordering a percentage alcohol use and also not ready to aid the consumer. Like many other energy programs in the United States, gasohol was the hobby horse of one interest group and was never fully accepted as a national energy priority.

One area considered by LDC officials, but not yet fully acted upon over the decade, was to reorient the national development strategy away from very energy-intensive industries and end uses, and toward less energy-intensive ones. Here, for example, the state could invest more in rural agriculture than in heavy industry or urban infrastructure. This possibility led one Brazilian Central Bank official to suggest after OPEC II that it had "rendered our economic model completely unviable," necessitating "a redefinition of governmental priorities and restructuring the economy." (From O Estado de São Paulo, July 7, 1979, p. 24, quoted in K. Erickson, in Stunkel 1981,

p. 2.) As of now, no country has radically redefined their
development strategy because of a desire to use less energy.
Yet at the same time energy conservation now figures much more
prominently than before in all development plans in the third
world, making some investment projects less and others more
attractive than before 1973.

EMERGENCY PLANNING MEASURES

The ability to handle supply-and-demand problems in an
energy crisis situation became a key priority for all consumer
country governments. The experiences of 1973 and again in
1979 during mild scarcity situations was not encouraging. Actions
to cut demand on an extremely short-term basis were not effective and when some customers' supplies ran out at critical points,
especially retail gasoline distribution, measures to reduce frustration and assure fair apportionment were only partially effective.

During the two periods of apparent or short-term scarcity
in the 1970s the main government actions were aimed at gasoline
use. They included driverless Sundays, closure of gas stations
on weekends, allowing purchase only on odd or even days
depending on license plate digits, speed limit restrictions (which
often became permanent), and regulations against hoarding and
topping off. Gas stations themselves also imposed limits on
amounts sold per customer. In other sectors less was possible
with restrictions on commercial lighting and rules on building
temperature the most universal.

A key problem facing governments was that the most effective ways to enforce savings and fair distribution of supplies
were politically or administratively unacceptable—either through
pure market systems where the price would skyrocket, or through
a total rationing system which was extremely difficult to manage
and not worth the effort.

Governments also realized that it was advantageous to set
up stockpiles against shortages which would give them some
breathing room in a crisis and delay the need for rationing.
But stockpiles presented their own problems, requiring rules
on when they could be used, who could gain access, and how
much would be charged for the released oil. They also faced
high costs for purchasing and storing the oil, especially if
government was to do it on its own account instead of simply
requiring certain levels of private stocks.

By the early 1980s almost all consuming countries had
developed stockpiling rules and emergency plans. After the

U.S. objections were raised in 1982 about high West European dependence on Soviet gas supplies, gas stockpiling, and emergency plans also began to be discussed. Gas storage is a much more difficult proposition because of the natural properties of gas and the main suggestion was for greater shut-in of secure gas supplies, such as in the Netherlands, as a European reserve.

The key options facing a government in setting up an oil stockpiling plan are to buy and store the oil themselves, require industry to do it, or create a mixed system. Ironically only the United States has taken the first option, creating its Strategic Petroleum Reserve in 1975 as a totally government-owned and controlled operation. The refusal to depend on industry for storage was rooted in the strict ideological separation in the United States between government and industry. It was virtually impossible to conceive an acdeptable rule under which the government commanded companies what to do with private property, that is, oil stocks. Thus it was necessary that the emergency stocks be government property. The history of the SPR has been a running comedy of errors and political battles, with Congress and succeeding administrations fighting over fill-rates, budget amounts, and purchasing policy. Because of the large initial stockpile target of 1 billion barrels of oil the SPR budget allocation became a giant item in the Department of Energy budget and a target of Department critics and White House budget balancers. A key problem with the reserve was the rule forcing buying of oil on the spot market through normal military purchasing. In 1979, when the potential need for the stockpiles was higher than ever, the soaring spot prices overshot acceptable levels under the rules and the government was forced to stop filling the reserve. As a result of the ensuing political battle, the government quietly began using government-to-government contracts with Mexico to get a steady supply at reasonable prices. France and Italy used the opposite system from the Americans, relying completely on government rules forcing all oil companies to hold 90-day supplies—amounts safely in excess of normal operating reserves. The French had put down such a requirement in 1958 in the wake of the first Suez crisis and it became the model for the EEC-wide system adopted once the energy crisis hit in earnest in the 1970s. This sort of approach is possible because of the high degree of government control over oil movements and operations in both countries—given the leverage the state has, it would be difficult for a company to refuse.

Germany, Japan, and the Netherlands (a giant oil depot country) have mixed systems. In all three countries industry

naturally holds a certain level of operating reserves. Beyond
that, however, a further amount of company oil must be held
as a strategic reserve. In Germany this oil is held by a special
association set up by the oil companies with government financial
help which allows the companies to own the oil without carrying
the dead assets and cost of storage on their normal balance
sheets. Both Japan and Germany also have relatively small
government-owned reserves which are earmarked specifically
for emergency purposes, acting as a first buffer before industry
supplies would be called in. Like the Germans, the Japanese
have provided subsidies to oil companies for the extra storage
costs.

The differing national methods of creating reserves has
led to a vague IEA policy on what constitute emergency reserves.
The IEA merely requires all members to have on hand supplies
which would allow 60 days normal consumption without net
imports. The rule does not make clear whether these reserves
should be government or industry held and whether they should
be partially industry working stocks, which is the case in most
countries. If the United States ever reached its 1 billion barrel
SPR target, it would have the required 60 days supply totally
under government control, but most countries would consider
maintaining such a large supply of oil in storage segregated from
commercial activities out of the question. The IEA rules, while
quite specific on sharing of oil supplies, also leave each government to define for itself how oil from the national reserves would
be used domestically in an emergency. The IEA merely requires
that an emergency plan exists. But besides stock draw down,
this policy can also include rationing, increase of production
of domestic substitute fuels such as coal and other short term
conservation measures. Because IEA member countries are
obliged to share their own domestic stocks with another members
should that country find itself in a dire emergency, watching
one another's stock levels has become an important concern.
In early 1984, when the United States made clear it would use
its giant SPR as a "first resort" measure to squelch a crisis,
a major struggle began inside the IEA to align other member
stock policies to this position.

While most Western governments have given a great deal
of thought to crisis planning and potential actions, these have
seldom been raised to the level of public debate. They have
had more the status of civil defense measures and in most
European countries there has been little questioning from
industry or the public over the planning. In the United States,
however, it has become a major political issue, related to the

general fight about the proper amount of energy policy, of
government intervention into energy markets, and even the
need for a Department of Energy. Because of the demise in
1981 of earlier energy emergency planning authorization, the
incoming Reagan administration was able to follow through on
its laissez-faire line that little specific crisis planning was
needed and that it was better to wait until a crisis hit to decide
on concrete measures. Democrats in Congress tried to force
through legislation providing for more preliminary planning,
but could not muster agreement among several factions seeking
particular rules for farmers, industry and other groups. The
Reagan administration also ignored IEA calls for more emergency
planning as the new period of plentiful oil supplies opened up
in 1982-1983.

Only an embarrassing set of errors by U.S. officials during
a simulated test of the IEA sharing system in the Spring of 1983
broke this serenity. The DOE planning division was shaken up
and congressional critics gained a new toehold on the issue.
The incident also forced a thorough review of the IEA sharing
system and how it would stand up in a real crisis given widely
diverging views of the United States and other members on oil
controls. The way these tensions are resolved is through the
working of politics, and it is to the politics and administration
of energy that we now turn.

7

THE POLITICS
AND ADMINISTRATION
OF ENERGY

I

INTRODUCTION

The Politics of Energy and the M-Shaped Market

The volatility of world energy markets in the 1970s buffeted interest groups, political parties, and the average citizen as much as it did government officials in oil-importing countries. Developments in oil markets were key, but sudden changes in nuclear markets, and even the slower developments in coal, solar, and other fuels, sparked and sustained citizen and consumer concern. Fluctuations in each forced continuous shifts in political attitudes and behavior, and these in turn affected public policy.

In most consumer countries the public perceived that the 1973 oil shock was motivated in part by political changes in the Middle East and the fact that governments had to consider politics in their responses. Energy adjustment after 1973 became a highly politicized process, and political leaders had to pay close attention to consumer and voter opinions.

Thus public attitudes and government policy came to be more closely attuned than in the past, although in imperfect and unpredictable ways. While energy policy making in most countries was historically apart from the rough and tumble of national politics (especially those without a large resource base), the energy shock knocked the topic into the political arena and out of the almost exclusive control of the technocrats. Public popular attitudes and political pressures came to shape policy much more directly than in the past as to what could realistically be proposed and what the public or other political actors like state or national legislatures would accept. Public attitudes were also shaped by the effectiveness—or ineffectiveness—of energy policies.

There is a striking correlation between world oil price movements and public attitudes toward energy, especially toward nuclear power, solar energy, and conservation. One could trace public attitudes toward energy over the decade, and demonstrate how the "energy attitude cycle" followed the energy price cycle.

The changes in the international oil market system imposed costs and conferred benefits on different categories of domestic consumers and they often responded politically. Some were relative losers, others winners. Sometimes the winners and losers were obvious. When prices rose the owners of energy resources gained more rents, royalties, and profits. Users paid higher prices and received, all other things being equal, a lower standard of living. These differences between relative winners and losers were the stuff of national energy politics.

Sometimes energy winners and losers were less obvious, and this uncertainty itself created conflicts and slowed the adjustment process. For example, who won and who lost when government handsomely supported solar energy with subsidized credit? Solar energy equipment makers probably won in the short term, but did the nation as a whole?

If we change the time parameters of the question, some short-term losers can become long-term winners, and vice versa. Initial government support for synthetic fuels or breeder reactors artificially nurtured industries and provided high incentives to invest in such technologies when prices were high. When government support dissolved as world oil prices fell, companies who were short-term winners appeared now as medium-term losers. Whether they will be long-term winners remains to be proven. Some argue that consumers are short-run winners under energy price controls, but long-term losers. By letting prices rise in the short term (after 1973, for example), consuming countries could better protect themselves from even more severe shocks and disruptions further down the road, as occurred in 1978-80.

In retrospect, we can see that the key political problem was how to parcel out the negatives and positives of national energy adjustment to various categories of citizens. That distribution in turn reflected national patterns of political and economic influence. Typically, any change from the status quo left some people feeling worse off than before and trying to protect themselves through political channels. Since government was extensively involved in energy distribution already, this further guaranteed that politics would be important.

Energy and Politics: A Two-way Street

The intersection of energy and politics worked in both directions. Energy influenced political events, and political events influenced energy. In 1971 President Nixon, looking ahead to the next year's election, imposed wage and price controls to dampen inflation. Oil prices were included, creating a terrible political roadblock to raising domestic prices to world level after 1973. Henry Kissinger feels Nixon's preoccupation with the Watergate crisis led him to neglect the oil crisis.

The outbreak of the 1973 Middle East War in the middle of sensitive oil negotiations is perhaps the example par excellence of politics influencing energy production and prices. Another is the radical regionalist politics of India's Assam region that by 1980 led to riots, slowing on-shore oil production and forcing higher levels of imports. The Swedish Center Party's search for a hot campaign issue which it found in nuclear power and conservation is another case, one that led eventually to the fall of the Social Democratic government of Olaf Palme. And it was only the national configuration of social, economic, and political power that after the mid-1970s launched the much-vaunted ethanol program in Brazil that benefited the powerful sugar-growing elements and the urban middle class auto owners.

Energy also influenced politics. Politicians, parties, and governments could and did rise and fall on energy. The Conservative government of Joe Clark in Canada was pushed from office in part when he tried to impose a 50-cent gas tax. The Green party in West Germany, organized around opposition to nuclear power and support for a clean and green environment, was an important factor hurting the Social Democrats and in bringing the Christian Democrat party to power in 1982. U.S. President Jimmy Carter used up a great deal of his all-too-scarce political capital trying to resolve extremely difficult domestic and international energy issues. The image of Carter as indecisive internationally and confused domestically was in part due to his handling of energy issues; was there a surplus of gas bubbling through the U.S. system or was the country really running out? Were Americans really faced with the moral equivalent of war (with its acronym MEOW) or was Carter simply crying wolf?

Not only governments but also nongovernmental groups were pressed by rising costs to seriously pursue energy politics in new ways. A wide range of long-standing traditional groups got involved in the politics of energy, from the Catholic Church in Brazil, to the French Communist party, to civic charities worldwide.

Yet far more important than the traditional groups were the entirely new groups spawned during the decade specifically to deal with energy, such as the Green party in Germany. Energy was first pushed onto the public agenda by higher prices and insecure supply, and thereby pulled out of the daily control of small cadres of technocrats and financial experts. But this process did not occur automatically. Nor did it occur by markets alone with consumers and producers responding like Homo Economicus. Nor did it occur through the careful rational direction of the national political leadership acting through established institutions. Most often the reordering process was yanked and prodded along by individuals and groups marginal to the national power systems. Energy adjustment was preeminently a political process (Yergin, Hillenbrand 1982). Price shocks and energy insecurity mobilized new political constituencies. It was these little groups that over the decade had the biggest impact on reshaping energy policies and administration in oil-importing countries.

The New Politics and the Permanent Government

Governments responded to direct domestic political pressures in several ways. On the institutional side, they created new agencies with special energy responsibilities. The ways that energy was handled by legislatures, executive departments, courts, and regulatory agencies changed dramatically as did the relations among them. In the United States the staff of the executive agency responsible for energy increased dramatically over the decade, and then fell slightly as President Reagan tried to eliminate the Department of Energy. Power struggles erupted in the Congress over the choicest energy jurisdictions. Budgetary allocations for energy skyrocketed worldwide. The World Bank estimates that LDC spending will have to increase from 2 to 3 percent of GDP in the late 1970s to 4 percent, necessitating further administrative expansion.

Official responses varied from very technocratic tactics that husbanded political authority in the hands of a small group

of specialists (as in France and Brazil), to allowing greater
access to policy making (as in the Scandinavian countries and
the United States). Nowhere, however, did the pressures result
in a revolutionary overhauling of the national energy policy
apparatus. National political leaders, in other words, responded
in ways that were not untypical of their responses to other
policy problems. This was to be somewhat expected, given
the considerable constraints exercised by the resource base,
the economy, and the structure of the political system.

Persisting through the sharp swings in energy prices and
public attention was the "permanent government" that characterized energy policy making in all importing countries. Energy
policies had traditionally been in the hands of a small cadre of
technically oriented public and private officials well insulated
from public sight and pressures. Whether Brazil, Botswana,
or Belgium, decisions about energy prices, production levels,
and fuel mixes were usually taken in bureaus tucked away in
ministries of industry or in government-owned energy companies.
But whether the operating company was government or privately
held made less difference than that energy officials in government and energy managers in firms were in close and frequent
contact and shared an engineering and financial supply side
perspective on energy issues.

The positive side of this arrangement was that when stability
and low prices reigned outside this tight system, then national
policy was frequently well guided. But in periods of economic
and political turmoil it faltered. The insular community of
experts was assaulted by new international conditions in energy
markets, and by domestic demands for information, performance,
and quick responses. When innovative changes were not forth-
coming in the early 1970s some accused the energy establishment
of being an "Iron triangle" blocking necessary reform including
the drive for wider participation and new views. National
adjustment was delayed during the 1970s by bureaucratic inertia
and entrenched interests as much as by uncertainty or lack of
information.

Several commentators have described this characteristic
way of making energy policy, among them Leon Lindberg who
termed it an "energy syndrome" (Lindberg 1977, p. xi). Critics
saw energy policy built on three premises: it was fuel-specific
and hence fragmented, presenting no view of energy as a whole;
it was elitist, technocratic, and closed to outside views; and
it was heavily supply oriented and overlooked the potentials
for demand management as a response to higher prices or limited
supply. For these critics the consequence was that when the

oil shocks occurred, the iron triangles of energy policy making in the LDCs, in Europe, and the United States responded in predictable ways: Problems were to be met by increasing supply, they ignored demand management, they overlooked the possibilities and limits of interfuel substitution and coordination, and they resisted the introduction of new evidence, solutions, and participants in the process. These three attributes of the old "energy syndrome" helped foment the political dissatisfaction and tactics of newly mobilized groups who lay outside the system.

II

THE POLITICS OF ENERGY

Our argument here is that energy politics in oil-importing countries resulted from the interaction of three factors: the mix of energy supply options; the mechanisms available for selecting among competing options; and the kinds of groups vying to make and influence public energy policy. All three national factors operated within and were further influenced by the fluctuating world oil market.

Basic cleavages in the political system were most likely to be activated when the following conditions were found:

1. Where several primary energy resources are available domestically, and

SUPPLY OPTIONS
    a. different resources are located in different regions or geographical areas;

    b. energy resources are in one region, and the major consumption centers in another;

2. Where traditions of government ownership of natural resources are weak;

CHOICE
MECHANISMS
3. Where traditions of government intervention in markets are weak;

4. Where the political system is federal and decentralized, and where courts may legitimately get involved in policy making or implementation;

5. Where a parliamentary/legislative control is held by a coalition which

has only a very narrow electoral
majority;

GROUP   6. Where interest groups are active,
CHARACTERISTICS   well organized, and well financed.

Lines of Conflict

Over the decade political conflicts and coalitions tended
to form along several well-defined fault lines in all consumer
countries. These splits were most explicit in domestic politics,
but did occur at times between domestic and foreign interests.
The main lines divided the following groups: (1) consumers
from producers; (2) proponents of one fuel option (i.e., nuclear
industry) from proponents of another fuel option (i.e., solar
or coal industry); (3) demand-side enthusiasts vs. supply-side
supporters; (4) within the same subsector or industry, whether
policy benefits (or costs) should go to the production stage,
the transportation stage, or the distribution stage. This intra-
industry politics especially afflicted gas and electrical power.

Producer-Consumer Politics

The principal political cleavage over the decade was between
energy consumers who wanted to keep prices low versus producers who wanted to raise them.

Governments in consuming countries found themselves
sandwiched between these two large groups that, given energy's
ubiquitous nature, included all citizens of a country. However,
this very fact also gave a curious twist to energy policies. Although all consumers had an interest in trying to keep prices
low, since energy historically constituted but a small proportion
of total domestic or individual expenditures (in the 9% to 14%
range for households in the United States, or higher for some
industries), most consumers were not moved to engage in politics
to keep prices low. They might vote for politicians or support
parties that pledge to keep prices down, but normally they went
no further.

By contrast, the large energy-producing firms (public
utilities, oil, or coal companies), though fewer in number, had
much more self-interested incentive to get politically involved.
This is a classic case where the costs to one large group are
highly dispersed and somewhat marginal, while the costs (and
potential benefits) to a smaller group are considerable. It is

the latter group that typically got active in energy policy. And this dimension too had a regional dimension when one region in the country produces energy and another consumes it.

However, the political sensitivities of the environmental movement did merge with consumer interests to create, in some industrialized countries, a coherent antiproducer political force.

Conflicts over Inter-Fuel Options

The more options the more politics. The presence of several alternative primary energy sources opened possibilities for more secure domestic economic development, but also more possibilities for political squabbling and conflict.

In countries with domestic energy reserves the first policy question then is, "Which resource should be developed first?" As we saw in Chapter 5, in large countries richly endowed with coal, oil, gas, and hydropower like Canada, Australia, or the United States this issue quickly became politicized. Conflicts arise because developing one resource before or more than another will help or harm some interests, some of them quite powerful, more than others—whether those interests are owners/producers or consumers/users, states or provinces, or industries and banks. Typically, potential winners and losers in political competition were politicians and businessmen speaking on behalf of regions, states, or provinces, and the specific fuel industry spokesmen themselves (i.e., owners, workers, related services). Producers and resource owners typically press to have "their" fuel developed, brought to market, and, if possible, subsidized ahead of other fuels.

The content of the politics is harder to predict beforehand than the likelihood that some political conflicts will develop along standard lines. For example, regional political leaders may push central government to help develop and sell their local resources, as occurs in the state of Texas or in Canada's Alberta Province; but local leaders and citizens may also oppose energy developments as occurs today in the American West and Southwest where residents in the Dakotas and Colorado worry over the environmental and water degradation from coal. In Japan and France by contrast, two resource poor countries, there is little choice among domestic fuels. For the near term they must import oil, gas, and coal and develop nuclear energy.

The politics of energy choice between fuels was also quite active at the national governmental level. Even among relatively disinterested analysts there was honest disagreement over which fuels should be promoted, in which order, and at what levels. Genuine uncertainties existed about the economic and environmental consequences of promoting nuclear energy over gas or coal. Here the politics of expertise comes into play as competing agencies and their experts vye for the attention and favor of the final decision-making authorities (Greenberger 1983).

Politics of inter-fuel options was also prompted by the companies and firms that exploited and sold the fuels. In countries with strong private sector traditions both the resources and the energy firms may be privately owned, and in such countries inter-fuel politics can be quite intense since the stakes involved for managers' careers and investors' returns are quite high. But even in countries where the resources and the energy companies are publicly owned there is considerable pressure and maneuvering to get government through its investment and pricing policies, to favor one fuel over another. For example, nuclear and hydro officials have skirmished in Brazil, as have the Gaz de France and Electricité de France staffs in France.

The Politics of Energy Demand

Immediate self-interest merged with appeals to the public interest in another category of energy politics that pitted the advocates of demand-led, renewable energy strategies against the proponents of a traditional supply-led approach to energy policy. The "soft-path" advocates and the latter "hard-path" people engaged in furious political debates (Nash 1979). The soft-path supporters were more likely to be members of public interest groups than on the payroll of one company or in the employ of one region or another, but they were just as involved politically as well paid lobbyists of giant oil or coal firms.

The examples given above were drawn mostly from the supply side, that is, political disputes over which primary fuel should be selected to expand energy supply. A new kind of politics grew up around whether demand should be pressed as strongly as supply as a means of improving national energy security. Environmental groups like the Friends of the Earth argued that the solution could not only be found in supply but had to include demand management policies that would press for greater energy efficiency, whether prodded by government setting higher prices or other institutional means. This form of inter-fuel substitution politics was expressed in national lobbying and political campaigns. And, in an interesting twist of the politics of persuasion, the Harvard Business School's energy study Energy Future came out for demand management (i.e., conservation) as the best new "fuel to mine" for America (Stobaugh and Yergin 1979). This establishment group expressed their demand-side policy preferences in classic supply-side terms to make them more politically palatable to a generation of energy analysts raised on expanding production as the solution to our energy problems.

Intra-Industry Politics

There are also politics involved in energy choices within the same fuel. These political conflicts arise when governments must decide where precisely to intervene in the industrial process of production and distribution, through what instruments, and how much. It is not enough to say, "Government wants to promote the national coal (or oil or nuclear) industry." Financial, equity, and political consequences vary according to the points of intervention. If the minister asks his energy advisors, "How can I expand my coal industry?", they may give him several alternatives. He will select the final policy using political as well as technical and financial considerations.

For example, a direct government subsidy to coal companies, a burden to taxpayers, would please the coal interests, who might be displeased should government try to force mergers or capacity reductions which always involve twisting arms. Downstream, the minister could raise prices for coal which would have the same bottom line consequence but would anger the consumers, large industry groups using coal, and all electricity users even as it delighted stockholders.

It is clear then that different producers and consumers within the same industry will press government for different instruments and points of intervention.

These political issues between fuels or within them are particularly acute when foreign interests are involved as owners or as processors. In such cases the absence of a domestic resource will not necessarily stop conflict, as has occurred in Brazil and India when there were domestic groups that opposed, and some that supported foreign oil company exploration and production in the countries.

POLITICAL PARTIES, IDEOLOGY,
AND ENERGY POLICY

Behind official government positions on energy matters
lies the constant pull and tug of party politics and electoral
competition. Consumers as voters were concerned about energy
prices and security and they made known their feelings to
government. Even in those developing countries without
regular elections governments had to play to their constituencies,
and everyone's constituencies were in some way concerned about
energy issues. This was especially the case for the countries
in our sample, all of whom had some form of partisan party
politics.

No major party in the OECD countries, or in India, Korea,
or Brazil has been able to take unambiguous energy positions
free from internal debate and dissension on the key issues.
Energy uncertainties ran rife through all of these societies and
they were exacerbated in the 1970s by the uncertainties of a
stagnant world economy. Political parties wavered between
several positions and were not able to agree on single permanent
energy truths. This reflected no doubt their own uncertainties,
as well as the conflicting preferences of the publics they served.
For these and other reasons, by decade's end it became very
difficult to know in advance what beliefs were typical of the left
or the right, although several distinct trends did emerge.

It is perhaps curious that the mainspring for popular
agitation and concern over energy issues, especially in large
Western European countries and the United States was not the
traditional established parties, but rather smaller splinter groups
or parties or loosely organized social movements. It was not
the Parti Communist Français or the British Labor party that
led the movement against nuclear power in France of Britain,
or elsewhere in Europe, but smaller groupings like the French
Unified Socialists, the Italian Proletarian Democrats, the Scots
Nationalists, or the strangely centrist Green party in Germany.

Hans Landsberg has pointed out how much public position
on energy policy is itself driven by broader societal values.
"The energy problem provided a tailor-made arena for ideological
and value conflict: It was a convenient opportunity or pretext
for the propagation and pursuit of a much more deeply held
Weltanschauung" (Landsberg 1980). Some of the critiques of
mainstream energy policies were linked to such broader concerns
as the rise of the environmental movement, disenchantment with
modern technology, and the small-is-beautiful trend (especially
in the United States). Also important was the growth of con-

sumer protection movements aimed at keeping prices low for basic goods and services. On the other side, the defense of long-standing ways of making energy decisions by power companies and oil multinationals, including their sovereignty to make pricing and other decisions, were trumpeted with equal vigor and conviction by a worldview formed by values of continuous and unlimited growth and large-is-beautiful. In LDCs, to these similar values one could add concerns about national sovereignty and nationalism.

Because these are deep-seated and powerfully felt values, and because energy itself is so vital to all aspects of modern life it is not surprising that pronouncements on nuclear power, conservation, and other energy issues became more ideological during the decade of the 1970s. Ideology guided thinking about energy just as it guided thinking about abortion or nationalization of industry.

Nelson and Pollack in their study of antinuclear groups in Europe suggest that "[a]s the nuclear debate has developed it has moved from an initial concern with specific technical questions . . . to become a symbol for political concerns about the desirability of technological progress, the credibility of the government regulatory apparatus, and the viability of democracy in an expertise-based society" (Nelkin and Pollack 1977, p. 334).

As we indicated above in our discussion of supply policies the principle of the fuels with the greatest choice having the greatest politics surrounding them meant that nuclear power and conservation, both potentially available to any country with the financial means and the political will to develop them, were surrounded with political conflict. These two fuels were also attached to important other values of land use, centralized, or decentralized government, and so forth.

These were important social issues that the main political parties could not afford to ignore. However, precisely because they were so deeply felt most parties did what they typically do on difficult issues, they waffled and temporized whenever possible. This led many who felt most deeply about the issue toward other political groupings that did articulate energy and environment issues more forthrightly. By the end of the decade, however, all parties and governments were forced into taking more explicit stands. Their constituencies became more informed and sophisticated about the issues, and the emergencies, such as Three Mile Island and Iran, brought the costs of current policies closer home.

What positions then did left wing, right wing, and centrist parties take on these issues?

Left Positions on Energy Policy

Like other important questions on the political spectrum there is no single left position as such, but rather a cluster of ideas typically embraced by socialist and communist parties, and by consumer and countercultural groups. In fact, a striking feature of the politicization of energy is its origins in movements on the fringes of the established leftist institutions. Individuals active in the antinuclear, proenvironmentalist movement pressed their positions in splinter parties, and in the youth wing of the established older left parties. The Social Democrats of Germany and Mitterrand's Parti Socialist in France were consistently pushed by their youth wings, and by the positions taken by smaller leftist parties. In the United States the left position was most often and clearly articulated by nonparty interest groups like Citizens/Labor Energy Coalition or Friends of the Earth, and then pressed within the centrist Democratic party where it was watered down.

The left groups can be subdivided into those that favored some development of nuclear power and those that wanted a conservationist, soft path without nuclear. The European communist parties took an ambivalent position that leaned finally toward nuclear development, while the splinter socialist parties preferred more conservation and an end to nuclear power. The large socialist and labor parties stood somewhere in between.

These parties and their affiliated unions and constituencies were naturally concerned with energy's impact on jobs and employment. What forms of energy would keep people employed in existing jobs, and which would create new jobs in the future? Would an oil shortage reduce economic growth? Would nuclear power sustain it?

The French communist party, for example, argued that electric power is needed for economic growth, and that a strong nuclear industry would also create new construction and operating jobs. (The counter argument that soft path options seem to be more energy intensive has not been widely accepted by unions—it was tough to argue what might be, in fact of a strong existing industry with existing jobs.) The Parti Communist Français supported the nuclear option in principal, but criticized its implementation under the center-right governments of Giscard d'Estaing and Pompidou, which they accused of being antidemocratic and antinationalist. They said the Gaullist government of 1974 was selling out to the Americans by buying foreign technology instead of technology produced by French workers and that it didn't take local populations opinion into account

(Bupp and Derian 1978, p. 112). The Italian CP was also pronuclear.

European socialist parties have also been ambivalent when
faced with complex nuclear questions. The Parti Socialist
Français (the PS of Mitterrand) favored a rather substantial
slowdown of plant construction and a far greater emphasis on
conservation. Before the fall 1977 elections, it called for a
two-year moratorium on new nuclear construction, but only
after a vigorous internal debate between progrowth and proenvironmentalist forces; while the party refused to back a
complete moratorium, it did promise to slow development if
elected. What it did in office we will discuss below.

The German and Swedish Social Democratic parties were
the ruling parties early in the decade and faced a different
set of political dynamics. They lacked the advantage of attack
of their out-of-office French counterparts, and carried the
burden of defending state policies, a problem also faced by the
Austrians. In both countries the government was challenged
by centrist parties. Sweden had already held a nationwide
debate on nuclear power in the early 1970s prior to the first
oil shock, and the centrist party had seized the issue of clean
environment and clean fuel as its own. The government had
decided to proceed with its nuclear construction program, going
beyond its current plans. When OPEC I occurred the Centrist
party was already positioned to maintain political momentum.
The tradition for clean environment and the participatory style
of Swedish life seemed challenged by pollution and the technocratic character of the issue.

A similar challenge process occurred in Germany, Austria,
and the Netherlands where nuclear power plans were slowed
due to national referenda and discussions. Like Sweden, the
ruling left party in the latter two states was holding narrow
electoral margins. In Austria, an antinuclear petition drive
collected 60,000 signatures, which "corresponded to two seats
in the parliament, exactly the margin of the Socialist majority
(93 out of 183 seats)" (Nelson and Pollack 1977, p. 353).

Center Positions on Energy Policy

Clearly, there was considerable pressure on governments
from the centrist and environmental parties. In some respects
these parties took positions hard to place on the traditional
political spectrum, especially with the Green party in Germany
but also with the Swedish Center party.

The Center party in Sweden forced the nuclear safety issue that eventually helped topple the Social Democratic party. Long a party with a rural base among farmers and other non-urban constituents, it gave itself a new lease on life when it pressed the soft path approach that appealed to the Swedish electorate. All of this was couched in terms of participatory democracy and a decentralized framework.

The Green party in Germany is probably the best known party of this kind. The Greens, as their name suggests, are a proenvironmentalist group whose leader quit the right-of-center Christian Democrat party in opposition to their pronuclear position. Situating the Greens on a left-right continuum is not simple because they hold some ideas that seem left-leaning and grass-roots, but are also more pronationalist than other left parties.

By 1983 the Greens had crossed the 5 percent hurdle in five West German states and the federal elections of that year, giving them an important parliamentary role.

Right Positions on Energy Policy

Of the three positions the parties on the right tended to show more consistency of perspective and policy preferences. The Christian Democrats in Germany, the Gaullists (PRP) in France, the Conservatives in Britain and Sweden, and others tended over the decade to support the continued expansion of nuclear power plant construction and were skeptical of conservationist claims. They could count business and industrial interests among their constituency, and they reflected this fact. They tended to view the antinuclear groups as extremists and harmful to national economic growth. Like the Republican party in the United States these groups favored very limited public intervention in private markets, energy markets included.

PUBLIC OPINION AND OIL-IMPORTING COUNTRIES

The policy positions these parties took in the 1970s reflected popular attitudes and opinions on energy. If these positions have changed over the decade, this expresses public opinion toward energy. After all, politicians pay attention to polls and public opinion as a matter of selfish survival, and public opinion acts as one of the constraints on energy policy making.

The M-shaped market to which public and private managers had to respond and adapt also affected citizen perceptions. In fact, we argue that an important gauge of the effects that the twists and turns the market had on domestic society is expressed in the changeability of public opinion on energy.

In spite of the changing attitudes fluctuating closely with oil price movements, the basic issues remained constant. In other words, the key questions persisted if the answers to them changed. Was there really an energy crisis? If so, what caused it? Who really was to blame? What should governments do? What fuel is really the best? The constancy of the questions posed over the ten years indicates the base line stability of the Energy Policy Explosion, despite the fluctuations. By mid-decade energy was definitely on the national agenda. Still attitudes toward the two key bellwether issues—nuclear development and conservation—rose and fell in step with the price movements on the world market. Let us look at these changes in one country, West Germany. Table 7.1, compiled from a number of separate polls, indicates this fact graphically. Different survey wording makes comparisons imperfect, but they do illustrate the magnitudes and directions involved.

Positive evaluations of nuclear power were highest at the two peaks of the price cycle, and lowest at the bottom of the price trough in between. At the two peaks the memories of OPEC I and OPEC II were fresh and worries of insecurity high. When prices fell the concern for the energy autonomy nuclear power was reputed to bring was far less. During these middle years (see November 1978) antinuclear, pronuclear, and neutral views just about balanced. As the prices fell, so did support for the pronuclear position.

Equally interesting is the decrease in percentages of indifferent respondents. Many apparently became opponents as they learned more about the subject. This suggests that the Energy Policy Explosion of sustained high-level policy attention to energy was accompanied by some seemingly long-lasting changes in public attitudes.

The author of the study just cited concludes that by 1980 values had changed from the earlier periods. The German population had not returned to a naive or disinterested acceptance. "There had come to be," Renn writes, "an increasingly critical evaluation of the safety of nuclear facilities and their engineering maturing [reactions to the Three Mile Island accident] and the increasingly positive evaluation of their economic necessity" (Renn, p. 225).

Attitudes, like policies, also differed from one country to the next, as well as through time as the resource base, the political heritage, and the shape of the economy produced differ-

TABLE 7.1

Nuclear Energy Attitudes in the Federal Republic of Germany (summary of various polls)

Positions	(1) 1975	(2) Jan. '76	(3) Dec. '76	(4) Mid '77	(5) End of '77	(6) May '78	(7) Nov. '78
Adherents	60	39	57	59	51	39	32
Opponents	16	20	41	40	27	18	36
Indifferent	24	30	3	1	22	43	32

	(8) Dec. '78	(9) Apr. '79 Hesse	(10) July '79 Hesse	(11) July '79	(12) Aug. '79	(13) Jan. '80	(14) June '80
Adherents	40	50	61	52	37	56	67
Opponents	39	33	22	30	48	42	32
Indifferent	21	12	17	18	15	2	2

1. Quoted from D. Goerke (Goerke 1975, 131, p. I112).
2. Infas Study, FRG, No. 1315, 1976.
3. Sample Institut, Hamburg, source: letter to "Deutsches Atomforum," April 2, 1977.
4. Intermarket poll, source: Kernzeitung, New Information kreis Kernenergie, only edition, Bonn 1977.
5. Spiegel poll: Do We Need Nuclear Power? (Brauchen wir Atomkaft?), No. 8, Hamburg 1977, p. 163.
6. DIGOE Marketing Service, Vechta, May 1978 (Goerke 1978 ..., p. 133).
7. Infra-Test, FRG, November 1978.
8. Stern, July 17, 1979.
9. Frankfurter Rundschau, August 16, 1979, Infas-Hessen.
10. Same as note 9.
11. Same as note 8.
12. Frankfurter Allgemeine Zeitung, August 8, 1979, Forschungsgruppe Wahlen, Mannheim.
13. Der Spiegel, No. 19/1980, p. 44.
14. Emnid 1980.
Source: Compiled by O. Renn 1981.

ent approaches to the same energy issues. Polls on nuclear
energy taken in Western Europe just before and after the
second OPEC shock bear this out as Table 7.2 indicates. The
support runs from a high of 75 percent in the United Kingdom
to 38 percent in the northern European countries of Denmark
and the Netherlands. The Nordic countries, as we have already
seen, consistently press for a more "soft path" approach to
energy policy. Germany and France typically find the hard
path more desirable. Some of the differences may lie in resource
base or geography, but much of it has to do with traditional
attitudes toward environment and the role of government.

Value differences within each country have proved important for energy policy in oil-importing countries. These subnational differences—age, education, sex, employment, and
others—do influence attitudes toward nuclear power and conservation. The young are more critical of nuclear power than the old,
women more than men, with businessmen, white collar employees,
and professionals tending to support nuclear development more
than other groups. Also, rank and file workers and union members may be more critical of nuclear development than their
leaders (Nelkin and Pollak 1980, p. 108-109).

Recent surveys in the United States found that ordinary
nonexpert laymen were more critical of the main institutions
involved—government and companies—than were elite respondents.
Apparently the inability of the so-called experts to agree on a
clear-cut analysis, much less clear-cut policies, aggravated
public mistrust of the energy leadership (Greenberger 1983,
p. 339-40).

New Governments in Power—Do They Make a Difference?

Constrained and guided by political attitudes, new grass
roots movements, and established political parties, and confronted
with domestic resource scarcity, and intense international
insecurity, how much leeway did political leaders have once
they took political office? What can one national government
do in the face of the major domestic and international constraints?

In point of fact there have been critical occasions where
new governments have made a demonstrable difference in either
the overall direction of national energy policy, in policies toward
one subsector or another, and/or in the changes of emphasis
within policy areas.

•The Swedish election of 1976 that brought Terbjorn Falldin
to power with a coalition government that replaced that of Olaf

TABLE 7.2

Support for Developing Nuclear Energy Among West European
Publics: Spring, 1979 and Fall 1981
("Nuclear energy should be developed to meet future energy
needs." Percentage among those expressing an opinion)

	"Agree"	
	April 1979	October 1981
United Kingdom	75	72
United States	(N.A.)	71
Germany	62	69
France	60	67
Italy	51	65
Greece	(N.A.)	56
Belgium	53	49
[Luxembourg]	[57]	[47]
Ireland	46	43
Netherlands	38	43
Denmark	38	36
European Community	60	65

Source: Ronald Inglehart, "Public Attitudes Toward Nuclear
Power," Public Opinion, Feb./March 1984. American data are
from September 1980 Consumer Outlook Survey carried out by
Survey Research Center, ISR University of Michigan; they are
listed under the 1981 column.

Palme, led to a marked slowdown in the nuclear program in
direct response to pressures from within his own party and
from a national referendum.
    ●President Jimmy Carter's defeat by Ronald Reagan led to
a significant reduction and also reallocation of federal monies
among energy programs. Money was bled out of conservation,
solar energy, R&D, there were reductions of federal funds for
synfuels, and legislation was introduced and executive actions
taken to eliminate the entire Department of Energy. Some changes
might have occurred even if Carter had been reelected as oil
prices fell making other alternatives less attractive, but they
certainly would have been less drastic.
    ●A new Conservative government in Britain under Thatcher
kept its preelection pledge to privatize much of the nationalized

oil industry, gutting BNOC of much of its gas operations and considerably reducing the power of the government to influence private operators in the North Sea.

●Canada's reelection of Pierre Trudeau in 1980 was based in part on his campaign pledge to develop a more nationalist energy program than the incumbent. His NEP was indeed quite a radical departure from the previous policies and dramatically reshaped the contours and the permanence of the oil industry in Canada.

●Aside from modulations in nuclear policy the changes of power toward the left in France in 1981 and to the right in Germany in 1982 did not lead to major new energy policies but instead surprising continuity.

ENERGY ADMINISTRATION

Not only did the changed structure of the world market provoke a new kind of politics, it also called forth new forms of administration to manage government policy. Organization of the public energy agencies could be as important as the content of the policy. Indeed, at key points the two merged. The extreme fragmentation of the United States energy set-up made coordinated and effective programs very difficult. Similar problems afflicted the LDCs and thwarted some of their best intentions. France's effective conservation program could be implemented through a government apparatus that Britain, for example, lacked.

The new challenges raised by the world oil market required a formal structure and effective process. The administrative activities that governments came to be expected to perform over the decade included the following.

1. Obtain the information necessary for government officials to make the best decisions to promote and protect national interests. This meant obtaining up-to-the-minute information, as well as an ability to anticipate future developments. Old kinds of information were needed more quickly (that is, oil price movements); new kinds of information had to be obtained.

2. Develop policy alternatives to pass up to top political leaders.

3. Convey these central government priorities and preferences to the economy and society as a whole, and especially to key energy actors in the public and private sectors. Also, to establish appropriate channels of communication and participation

with nongovernmental groups for purposes of legitimacy and information gathering.

4. Establish state priorities for government-owned corporations through government participation on their boards of directors, through administrative instructions and personnel appointments. These are often the most important energy agencies in the country.

5. Coordinate key decisions between energy subsectors.

6. Coordinate sectoral policies with macroeconomic priorities.

7. Coordinate national policy with subnational level governments, which often jealously guard their authority over critical areas like power plant siting.

8. Manage relations with international actors, bilateral and multilateral.

These eight can be reduced to two core activities—information gathering and coordination—that proved especially problematic. Traditionally policy was organized along subsectoral lines and information tended to stay within those boundaries. Closely coordinating coal or oil or nuclear plans wasn't important given cheap prices and sure supplies and the information to do so was rarely collected in detail or widely distributed. Given sure supply and low prices governments devolved responsibilities on private or semiprivate companies, and when things went well they could get by with limited information and separate subsectoral policies. These activities, thin on the supply side, were almost entirely lacking on the demand side. Data on energy demand such as it was was also industry specific.

This situation did vary by the kind of country. The LDC governments had the poorest information and the least coordination, with the United States next down the line. It was mainly in other industrialized countries with strong interventionist traditions, like Japan and France, where there was more effort to coordinate subsectoral investment or pricing priorities and to collect the information necessary to set them. Still, as we have argued throughout, the oil shocks forced much greater attention to improved intersectoral coordination and improved information management.

Institutional Form

The ultimate institutional form governments selected after 1973 to perform these activities typically followed one of several patterns. Most countries possessed multi-portfolio ministries when the first oil shock occurred, that is, ministries responsible for energy as well as other economic or resource duties. Most countries retained this form after the oil shock, although with several notable exceptions that included the United States and the United Kingdom. These two opted for the second major form of energy administration by creating a single portfolio ministry responsible solely for energy issues although the United States retained considerable energy responsibilities in the Department of Interior.

Within the multiportfolio ministry arrangement one can further identify two types: There is one kind that typically regroups energy, natural resources, and mining functions. Typically these are countries with some domestic oil production, such as Canada, Brazil, and Norway. Other countries which lack significant domestic oil production are more likely to rely on multiportfolio ministries that are essentially economic in focus to also handle energy policy. Thus the ministries for industry, trade, or commerce will handle energy policy, and responsibilities of energy pricing, imports, fuel switching, and R&D.

One cannot assume that countries with single portfolio ministries have a more effective and coordinated energy policy, or that the single portfolio ministries are necessarily more powerful than multiportfolio ministries. Few could accuse the Delegation Générale à l'Énergie in France of being weak or ineffective because it is located in the Ministry of Industries. Nor would anyone accuse the U.S. Department of Energy of being powerful. On the other hand, the British Energy Department tends to be both effective and powerful. The performance of energy administration probably has more to do with the traditions of business-government relations than with a particular form.

Multiportfolio Ministries: Economics and Trade

There are several benefits to retaining a multiportfolio ministry during a period of crisis and thereafter. When energy officials are housed with officials responsible for industry or commerce they can be in contact with the overseers of the major energy consumers in the country on a regular basis. This may help reduce the problem of policy coordination described above. Second, the larger ministry may have more clout in the economy precisely because it includes a variety of powerful subunits. In this way, for example, the Japanese energy agency may benefit from the reputation and political influence of the super-

ministry MITI (Ministry of International Trade and Industry).
Third, in a period of rapid change, hiving off a separate energy
ministry from an existing one (or bits and pieces from several,
as is more likely) may create inefficiencies at precisely the time
when one most needs greater efficiency. Thus retaining the old
multiportfolio form encourages continuity in difficult times, a
boon both for intragovernmental operations and for private
sector actors seeking consistent signals from public officials.

Within most multiportfolio bodies there were special separate
subdivisions responsible for energy policy. These were usually
retained, and sometimes beefed up with additional staff and
budgets; they also underwent some administrative reorganizations
within the energy sections. Agencies were most powerful where
governments had real control over prices; otherwise there was
little for them to do.

The executive energy agencies in France had for years
been under the tutelage of the powerful Industry Ministry. It
has long had a number of "directions" or bureaus responsible
for specific subsectors and the relevant subsectoral operating
companies that produce and distribute a specific fuel (see Table
11).

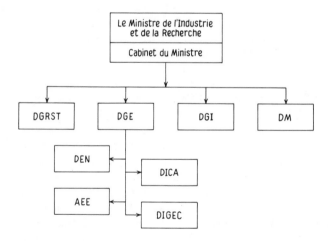

FIGURE 7.1 A part of the organization structure of the Ministère
de l'Industrie et de la Recherche. DGRST: Délégation Générale
à la Recherche Scientifique et Technique; DGE: Délégation
Générale à l'Energie; DGI: Délégation Générale de l'Industrie;
DM: Direction des Mines; DEN: Délégation aux Energies Nouvelles;
DICA: Direction des Carburants; AEE: Agence pour les Economies
d'Energie; DIGEC: Direction du Gaz, de l'Electricité et du Char-
bon.

In 1963 a specialized secretariat was formed directly under the minister himself and above the separate directions to coordinate their work and to act as a kind of mini-ministry for energy within government councils, and this partly explains why the government did not feel the need to create a separate ministry.

Conservation and Renewables

Two of the most interesting administrative changes that have occurred in the oil-importing countries in single and multi-portfolio countries is the addition of offices responsible for energy conservation, and those responsible for new sources of energy.

In France, the Agence pour les Économies d'Énergie was set up after the oil shock with the usual sentiments that it was a good thing to do in a resource-poor country, but that perhaps one couldn't expect too much by way of money saving hard results. But under the aggressive leadership of its first director it launched a nationwide public education program that did help reduce French oil use (which is not to deny the importance of prices). Not only externally but inside the rather opaque French government's energy system the AEE was also rather effective. According to N. J. D. Lucas, its director convinced other government officials that state money invested in conservation had an equal or larger pay-off than the same money spent to expand supply. This argument apparently fell on fertile ground in the Finance Ministry which had felt for some time that the accelerated French nuclear program was wasteful and too expensive. This was a time of course when demand management was still getting short shrift, but AEE was able to make headway with the key Finance Ministry, and to keep up its budgetary allocations. "Little by little, forecasts of future demand began to drop; the estimated contribution from nuclear energy began to fall and that of oil began to rise again. The Agency became the main channel for reasoned opposition to the size of the nuclear programme" (Lucas 1979, p. 153). This is one interesting example among many of energy agencies jockeying for influence within their government.

While the case of the AEE is not the only example, it is a striking one. The other principal institutional change within the Ministry was the 1975 addition of the Délégation aux Énergies Nouvelles (DEN) to the cluster of energy offices under the Délégué Générale de l'Énergie. Like the AEE, it has primarily a promotional role, to acquaint businessmen and government and the public about the issues of renewable energy. It is especially active in solar energy through coordination with the Commissariat a l'Énergie Solaire and the Centre National de la Recherche Scientifique.

While these offices represent important organizational additions, the 1973 crisis dramatically increased official ministerial attention to the major strategic fuels like oil and nuclear power. The latter was under the general supervision of the DGE, but more directly the responsibility of the semiindependent Commissariat a l'Énergie Atomique which conducts research and oversees the sector. Also involved is Cogemax (fuel cycle processes) and the nuclear construction company Framatome.

Japan demonstrates similar changes and continuities in its energy administration. Also lacking a separate ministry, energy tasks thrive under a similarly powerful ministry—the Ministry of International Trade and Industry. This ministry was the guiding inspiration for postwar reconstruction and supported the subsequent economic miracle, and its role in energy was not insignificant. Separate divisions for coal, petroleum, and public utilities were grouped under the Agency for Natural Resources and Energy by the Basic Petroleum Law of 1962. This occurred as Japan became more aggressive in shaping its own energy policy after the heavy U.S. tutelage of the postwar years. ANRE became the premier energy planning, implementing, and review body for the sector as a whole, analogous to the French Délégué Générale a l'Énergie.

Like MITI, as a whole, the energy agency's power was exercised through indirect persuasion backed by subsidies and administrative muscle. There was also public-private consensus on the broad lines that energy policy should take; this did not include direct government ownership of most of the sector as occurs in France or Britain.

Advisory Councils

This form of cooperation was given a strong institutional expression in Japan, as in some other countries, through a number of consultative advisory councils with mixed public-private membership. Most importer countries relied on such councils as a means of both gaining expert advice from industry and consumers but also as a political arena in which parties with different perspectives could try to thrash out a common approach. Some, like Brazil or Zambia, created a single large national advisory council. Others, like Japan, created a series of smaller and more fuel-specific ones.

In Japan, for example, these advisory committees included
the Committee for Energy Policy Promotion, formed in 1973 by
73 of the major energy producers, consumers and trading companies in the country. Perhaps the major advisory group is
the Council on Overall Energy Policy, which encompasses most
of the key governmental energy actors in Japan, as well as
some well-respected outside members in the energy field.

There have been a few post-1973 administrative reorganizations in Japan within the public sector. For example, the New
Energy Development Organization was set up in October 1980;
it parallels the U.S. Synthetic Fuels Corporation. On the whole,
however, new projects and policies were initiated and implemented
within administrative units that predated the first oil shock.

Multiportfolio Ministries: Energy, Resources and Mining

Some countries placed their energy units not under economic or trade ministries, but under ministries with responsibility
for energy and resource related matters. Canada, for example,
with its vast resources of oil, gas shale, and hydropower
assigns energy policy and administrative oversight to a Department of Energy, Mines and Resources. Brazil, South Korea,
and Norway also follow this general pattern.

Canada, also an oil and gas producer, after 1973 decided
to retain formal responsibility in its two main agencies of the
National Energy Board and the Department of Energy Mines and
Resources, but the balance between them tilted. This continued
a more activist policy of the Ministry begun in the early 1970s.
This was also affected by the government's proposal to set up
three new bodies: Petro-Canada, a national oil company described
elsewhere; an Energy Supplies Allocation Board to allocate supplies in a national emergency; and a new Energy Conservation
office within the Ministry, given a $500,000 budget the first
year to do research, supply advice to government, and to
publicize the need for energy conservation (Hunter 1975, pp.
15-16). The Department of Energy, Mines and Resources had
responsibility mainly over Canadian offshore mineral rights,
located for the most part off the east coast. Broader, multi-
subsectoral coordination and authority was exercised by the
National Energy Board, created as an advisory and regulatory
agency in 1959 to be relatively free of political intervention,
but still under the formal aegis of Energy, Mines and Resources.
The N.E.B.'s principal responsibilities were in electric power

TABLE 7.4

The Energy Establishment

MINISTRY OF INTERNATIONAL TRADE AND INDUSTRY

Agency of Natural Resources and Energy

Director General's Secretariat Divisions	Petroleum Dept. Divisions	Coal Mining Dept. Divisions
General Coordination	Planning	Planning
Ocean Development	Petroleum Refining	Administration
Geothermal Policy Planning	Petroleum Distribution	Development
International Division	Petroleum Reserve	Mine Damage
Mining Division	Development Division	
Nuclear Energy Industry		

Other Bureaus and Agencies*

Public Utilities Dept.
Divisions

Planning
Electric Power Administration
Electric Power Development
Electric Power Technology
Hydro-Electric Power
Thermal Electric Power
Nuclear Power General
Nuclear Power Safety Examination
Nuclear Power Administration
Gas Industry Division
Gas Safety Division

* 1. Minister's Secretariat
  2. International Trade & Policy Bureau
  3. International Trade Administration Bureau
  4. Industrial Policy Bureau
  5. Industrial Location & Environmental Protection Bureau
  6. Basic Industries Bureau
  7. Machinery and Information Industries Bureau
  8. Consumer Goods Industries Bureau
  9. Patent Office
  10. Small and Medium Enterprise Agency
  11. Agency of Industrial Science & Technology

241

and the hydrocarbon industries where they were expected to perform four functions:

1. To provide the federal government with information and advise on energy issues.
2. To operate the 1960 National Oil Policy which divided the country into two separate markets (a self-sufficient Western market with high prices, and the import-dependent Eastern market with access to cheaper Middle East and American supplies.
3. To control and license natural gas, power, and (after 1973) oil imports and exports; and
4. To approve or disapprove pipe line construction. (Hunter 1975.)

Single Portfolio Ministries

There are also benefits to a single-portfolio ministry of the kind found in Great Britain, the United States, and Denmark. It provides a high level advocate of a coordinated energy policy and resource development. This is especially the case in federal and/or decentralized systems where government activities are already fragmented, when responsibilities overlap and coordination may be poor, and where the history of government intervention in the economy may be less than in other countries.

New federal energy departments were created in the United States and the United Kingdom after the onset of the oil shock in 1973, which in both countries simply accelerated a trend toward administrative consolidation of energy and resource programs already underway. Existing subunits were transferred and reorganized and new units were created to form one department responsible for energy. This occurred in 1974 in Britain and 1977 in the United States.

In the early 1970s both countries were facing unparalleled problems of resource management and policy choices. In the United States this came about because of the simultaneous upsurge in oil imports along with what appeared to be a decline in oil and gas production in 1970 and 1971. In Britain, the development of the North Sea fields was coming to fruition after a number of years of exploration and drilling. Thus production level changes prompted reorganizations: decline in one, expansion in the other. Both concerns challenged the subministerial levels of experts and managers and percolated up to the cabinets and to the chief executives of both countries.

In Britain, a series of policy miscalculations and blunders in the years before 1973 led to public and parliamentary demands for more effective steering of a national energy policy. One important consequence was the creation of BNOC in 1975.

In the United States the resource management problem was the unanticipated upsurge in crude oil imports which by 1973 had reached one-third of national supply. This came as a shock to policymakers long raised on a diet of self-sufficiency. This concern began to bubble up through the bureaucracy, helped along by outside experts warning of an impending crunch.

In the United States these converging pressures led President Nixon in 1973 to create a Federal Energy Office within the White House, modeled somewhat on the Office of Emergency Preparedness which had previously had some emergency energy authority. The FEO's first director was Colorado Governor John Love, leader of a state rich in the shale and coal resources needed to achieve Nixon's goal of "energy independence."

President Nixon had earlier, before the oil shock, submitted legislation to Congress to create a Department of Natural Resources with the Interior Department at its core, but that proposal, submitted in 1971 and again in early 1973, died on the legislative vine.

Then in 1974 Congress passed legislation to create a rather weak Federal Energy Administration within the executive branch which brought over several Interior Department offices to the old FEO. Simultaneously the Atomic Energy Commission and several other research programs from Interior, the Environmental Protection Agency, and the National Science Foundation were united to form the Energy Research and Development Administration (E.R.D.A.).

Finally, based on a similar idea submitted in the last days of the Ford administration, President Carter proposed a new Cabinet-level department which consolidated many oil, gas pipelines, coal, nuclear, and power activities under one roof. It is interesting to note however that the single largest budgetary and personnel basis for the Department was Atomic Energy from ERDA, which would have provided 46 percent of the new department's employees (with 25% from Interior, 20% from FEA, 7% from the Federal Power Commission, and 2% from elsewhere, for a total of almost 20,000 employees). The programs under DOE were scheduled to be funded at $10.6 billion under the Carter plan. But the retention of leasing authority under Interior left a split system with two departments doing different pieces of energy.

Both the U.S. Senate and the House agreed with Carter's proposals but with large reservations. In finest U.S. political tradition both houses rejected key provisions which empowered the secretary of the new department to set prices for oil and natural gas. They felt it gave this secretary too much discretionary power. Again, in a typically regulatory response a compromise measure set up an independent five-member commission to set price levels except in national emergencies when the president could step in. The Federal Energy Regulatory Commission (or FERC) was an updated replacement for the Federal Power Commission.

It is generally agreed that the DOE and its predecessors performed rather abysmally as an uncoordinated octopus. This contributed to the poor emergency allocation system (especially in auto-saturated California) and to Reagan's campaign promise to eliminate the department if elected. He attempted to do so but met opposition from too many quarters including some private firms.

The 1974 transition from Department of Trade and Industry to Department of Energy, in Britain, was much more direct. First, the debate over the role of government in energy affairs had already been conducted and largely settled 20 years earlier in the 1940s (although it came up again under Thatcher). Second, as a practical matter, the existing bureaus neatly "hived off" and were given their own minister. Unlike the United States, there were already ample numbers of expert governmental personnel in each area.

There are naturally other institutions that have played increasingly significant roles in the conception and conduct of energy policy in oil-importing countries during this decade as part of the Energy Policy Explosion. These include legislatures, especially in the United States, regulatory agencies, and courts.

Legislatures

The U.S. Congress has an important role in initiating, approving, and often blocking national energy policies. In the post-1974 period the congressional energy policy role has been equal to that of the executive in final decision-making power. Congress framed the 1975 oil price control system, blocked major parts of Carter's 1977 energy plan, rejected Reagan's 1981 plan to dismantle the DOE, and has been the main actor on gas deregulation throughout. This congressional power, inherent in the U.S. system, has often been considered a detriment to

systematic U.S. policy making in energy, but in reality, because
of the wide swings in policy planning at the White House and
DOE since 1974, the Congress has acted more as a brake on
rash lurches to and fro in policy, assuring what actions are
taken such as the oil price decontrol, linked to a windfall tax,
are based on a clear, broad political consensus.

Courts and Regulatory Agencies

The legal side of energy policy has grown up strongly in
the last ten years as part of the policy explosion as more regulations, controls, projects, and actors have become involved.
Most industrial countries have developed a set of regulatory
agencies separate from line ministries to handle more technical,
legalistic energy questions. Most frequent are price-setting
agencies such as FERC in the United States. Also several countries have agencies to regulate nuclear safety, and to control
foreign investment in domestic energy exploitation. These
agencies are not meant to be political but they often fill a
political function, deciding crucial policy questions. Frequently
the boards act on narrow legal bases and the key factor is the
underlying political opinions of board members. Frequently
interest groups have preferred to keep semiindependent boards
in charge of regulation affairs, attempting to keep out direct
government policy influence.
The energy policy explosion has also increased judicial
activity especially in two areas: (1) deciphering and adjudicating
energy price disputes and claims; and settling environmental
complaints about large energy projects, especially nuclear plants.
In the United States the load of cases arising from the
confused oil price regulations system overburdened the federal
court system forcing the creation of a special appeals court
solely for energy price cases. On the environmental side,
where the problem was exhaustive use of appeals by protest
groups the solution was to seek legislative and regulatory
changes to cut down the scope for appeals. Needless to say,
the legal explosion in energy also created a large new group of
lawyers specializing in energy matters.

Federal-State Relations

Another area of governmental relations that has been
buffeted during the energy policy explosion is federal-state or

federal-provincial relations. Several policies, especially resource exploitation, siting of large projects, transportation,
pricing, and emergency allocation schemes all provide grist
for political fights between state and regional authorities and
central governments. In several countries such as Canada,
West Germany, and Australia the local authorities have wide
power over oil, gas, and coal leasing, and the national government must deal with them almost as an equal to get a coherent
national policy. In the United States, state governments have
almost no direct authority on oil leasing except for small parcels
of state-owned lands but states with extensive federal oil leasing
such as California and Alaska have played major roles in legal
and regulatory battles in Washington.

On the demand-control side central governments have
normally staged major efforts to get state and local officials to
support national energy savings plans with varying success.
Local officials, on the other hand, are generally most worried
about their allocation rights in energy crisis periods. In both
cases national and local interests can easily clash, rupturing
the normal policy flow and giving the public the unsettling
spectacle of authorities squabbling over emergency policy.

CONCLUSION

This chapter recapitulates our major themes: the multiple
impacts of disintegrating and volatile world oil markets on the
conduct and content of national energy policy in oil-importing
states. Public attitudes and political behavior responded directly
to major events in world markets—the Three Mile Island incident
of 1979, the fall of the Shah in 1978, the original oil shock in
1973. These international events, filtered through national
structures, led to demonstrations in the streets, new referenda,
novel coalitions and even new political parties. We are now in
a period of relative calm but continuing uncertainty in world
energy markets. Nuclear markets have collapsed, costing
investors billions of dollars. In oil, OPEC has for the moment
slowed the free fall from the peak of $40 per barrel in some
markets down to a general low of around $28.

Will these conditions continue? Can we expect the unexpected and anticipate crisis-free energy markets? Most forecasts
see stable supply and demand through the end of the 1980s.
We are less optimistic. It should be clear by now that governments are very good at planning today for yesterday's crisis.
It is true that new agencies and programs are in place in many

countries. However, so long as energy remains a precious commodity in world trade, as long as groups vie for political and commercial advantage, and while so much oil comes from the world's most unstable regions, there is little room for complacency. The Energy Policy Explosion was a kind of consumers revolution that answered successfully in many ways the antecedent OPEC revolution. Still, no revolution is ever fully complete, and there are always reactions. As oil scarcity grows and demand increases, we anticipate further volatility of markets, confronting energy-importing governments with serious policy challenges into the next decade and beyond.

BIBLIOGRAPHY

BOOKS

Adelman, M. A., 1972. The World Petroleum Market. Baltimore: The Johns Hopkins University Press.

Blair, John M., 1976. The Control of Oil. New York: Vintage Books.

Bohi, Douglas R., and Russell, Milton, 1978. Limiting Oil Imports: An Economic History and Analysis. Baltimore: The Johns Hopkins University Press.

Bupp, Irvin C., and Derian, Jean-Claude, 1978. Light Water: How the Nuclear Dream Dissolved. New York: Basic Books, Inc.

Carmoy, Guy de, 1977. Energy for Europe: Economic and Political Implications. Washington, D.C.: American Enterprise Institute for Public Policy Research.

Conant, Melvin, 1982. The Oil Factor in U.S. Foreign Policy. Lexington, Kentucky: Lexington Books.

Congressional Quarterly, 1979. Energy Policy. Washington, D.C.: Congressional Quarterly.

Cook, P. Lesley and Surrey, A. J., 1977. Energy Policy: Strategies for Uncertainty. London: Martin Robinson, p. 96.

Court, Thijs de la; Pick, Deborah; and Nordquist, Daniel, 1982. The Nuclear Fix: A Guide to Nuclear Activities in the Third World. Amsterdam: WISE Publications.

Crabbe, David and McBride, Richard, 1978. The World Energy Book. Cambridge, Massachusetts: The MIT Press.

Danielson, Albert L., 1982. The Evolution of OPEC. New York: Harcourt Brace Jovanovich.

Darmstadter, Joel, Dunkerley, Joy, and Alterman, Jack, 1977. How Industrial Societies Use Energy. Baltimore: The Johns Hopkins University Press.

Davis, David Howard, 1978. Energy Politics, 2nd ed., New York: St. Martin's Press.

Deese, David A., and Nye, Joseph S., 1981. Energy and Security. Cambridge, Massachusetts: Ballinger.

Doran, Charles F., 1977. Myth, Oil, and Politics. New York: The Free Press.

Dunkerley, Joy; Ramsay, William; Gordon, Lincoln; and Cecelski, Elizabeth, 1981. Energy Strategies for Developing Nations. Baltimore, Maryland: The Johns Hopkins University Press.

Eden, Richard, 1981. Energy Economics. New York: Cambridge University Press.

Evans, Douglas, 1979. Western Energy Policy: The Case for Competition. New York: St. Martin's Press.

Ford Foundation, 1979. Energy: The Next Twenty Years. Cambridge, Massachusetts: Ballinger.

Ford Foundation, 1974. Exploring Energy Choices. Washington, D.C.: The Ford Foundation.

Goodman, Gordon T.; Kristoferson, Lars A.; and Hollander, Jack M. (eds.), 1981. The European Transition from Oil: Societal Impacts and Constraints on Energy Policy. New York: Academic Press.

Goodwin, Craufurd D. (ed.), 1981. Energy Policy in Perspective: Today's Problems, Yesterday's Solutions. Washington, D.C.: The Brookings Institution.

Greenberger, Martin, 1983. Caught Unawares: The Energy Decade in Retrospect. Cambridge, Massachusetts: Ballinger Publishing Company.

Hunter, Lawson A. W., 1975. Energy Policies of the World: Canada. Newark, Delaware: Center for the Study of Marine Policy.

Itteilag, Richard L., 1983. Government and Energy Policy. Boulder, Colorado: Westview Press.

Kash, Don E., and Rycroft, Robert W., 1984. U.S. Energy Policy Crisis and Complacency. Norman, Oklahoma: University of Oklahoma Press.

Kohl, Wilfrid L., 1982. After the Second Oil Crisis. Lexington, Massachusetts: Lexington Books.

Krapels, Edward N., 1980. Oil Crisis Management: Strategic Stockpiling for International Security. Baltimore, Maryland: The Johns Hopkins University Press.

Landsberg, Hans, ed., 1979. Energy: The Next Twenty Years. Cambridge, Massachusetts, Ballinger.

Lawrence, Robert M., and Heister, Martin O., 1980. International Energy Policy. Lexington, Massachusetts: Lexington Books.

Lindberg, Leon N., 1977. The Energy Syndrome. Lexington, Massachusetts: Lexington Books.

Lucas, N. J., 1979. Energy in France. London, England: Europa Publications Ltd.

McGraw-Hill, 1980. International Petroleum Review. Washington, D.C.: McGraw-Hill.

Mendershausen, Horst, 1976. Coping with the Oil Crisis: French and German Experiences. Baltimore, Maryland: The Johns Hopkins University Press.

Moran, Theodore H., 1978. Oil Prices and the Future of OPEC. Washington, D.C.: Resources for the Future.

Nash, Hugh (ed.), 1979. The Energy Controversy: Soft Path Questions and Answers. San Francisco: Friends of the Earth.

Nelkin, Dorothy, and Pollack, Michael, 1981. The Atom Besieged. Cambridge, Massachusetts: The MIT Press.

Noreng, Oystein, 1978. Oil Politics in the 1980's: Patterns of International Cooperation. New York: McGraw-Hill.

Nuclear Energy Policy Study Group, 1977. Nuclear Power Issues and Choices. Cambridge, Massachusetts: Ballinger.

Quandt, William B., 1981. Saudi Arabia in the 1980's: Foreign Policy, Security, and Oil. Washington, D.C.: The Brookings Institution.

Quester, George H., 1981. Nuclear Proliferation: Breaking the Chain. Madison, Wisconsin: University of Wisconsin Press.

Rosenbaum, Walter A., 1981. Energy, Politics and Public Policy. Washington, D.C.: Congressional Quarterly, Inc.

Sampson, Anthony, 1975. The Seven Sisters: The Great Oil Companies and the World They Shaped. New York: Bantam.

Schneider, Steven A., 1983. The Oil Price Revolution. Baltimore, Maryland: The Johns Hopkins University Press.

Smith, Peter S., 1976. Oil and Politics in Modern Brazil. Toronto, Ontario, Canada: Macmillan.

Stobaugh, Robert, and Yergin, Daniel (eds.), 1979. Energy Future: Report of the Energy Project at the Harvard Business School. New York: Random House.

Stunkel, Kenneth R., 1981. National Energy Profiles. New York: Praeger.

Tanzer, Michael, 1969. The Political Economy of International Oil and the Underdeveloped Countries. Boston: Beacon Press.

Taylor, June H., and Yokell, Michael D., 1979. Yellowcake: The International Uranium Cartel and Its Aftermath. New York: Pergamon Press, Inc.

Taylor, Robert P., 1981. Rural Energy Development in China. Washington, D.C.: Resources for the Future.

Verleger, Philip K., 1982. Oil Markets in Turmoil: An Economic Analysis. Cambridge, Massachusetts: Ballinger.

Vernon, Raymond, 1976. The Oil Crisis. New York: W. W. Norton.

Willrich, Mason, 1975. Energy and World Politics. New York: The Free Press.

Wilson, Carroll, 1980. Coal: Bridge to the Future. Cambridge: Ballinger, p. 230.

Yanarella, Ernest J., and Yanarella, Ann-Marie, 1982. Energy and the Social Sciences: A Bibliographic Guide to the Literature. Boulder, Colorado: Westview.

Yergin, Daniel and Hillenbrand, Martin, 1982. Global Insecurity: A Strategy for Energy and Economic Renewal. Boston, Massachusetts: Houghton Mifflin.

ARTICLES

al-Chalabi, Fadhil, 1980. "Oil Prices, Costs, Taxes." In World Energy: Issues and Policies. Robert Mabro (ed.). Oxford, England: Oxford University Press, pp. 143-156.

Amuzegar, Jahangir, 1982. "Oil Wealth: A Very Mixed Blessing." Foreign Policy, Spring, pp. 814-835.

Cook, James, 1982. "The Great Oil Swindle." Forbes, March 15, pp. 99-108.

Der Spiegel, June 22, 1981.

Energy Resources and Technology, Vol. 8, 32, August 8, 1980.

Erickson, Kenneth Paul, 1980. "The Political Economy of Energy Consumption in Industrial Societies in Industrial Societies." In International Energy Policy, Robert M. Lawrence and Martin O. Heisler (eds.). Lexington, Massachusetts: Lexington Books.

Finance and Development, March 1983.

Ghader, Fariborz, 1982. Petroleum Investment in Developing Countries. Special Report No. 132. London, England: The Economist Intelligence Unit Limited.

Goldstein, Walter, 1979. "U.S. Energy Policy—The Continuing Failure." Energy Policy, December, pp. 275-306.

Kemezis, Paul, 1979. "Sharing and Stockpiling: Will the Latest Oil Crisis Bring Economic Disaster and/or a Real Energy Policy?" Europe, March-April, pp. 3-10.

_____, 1979(b). "'Petrol' versus 'Gas': Europe and America View Gasoline Policy, Price, and Tax Differently." Europe, November-December, pp. 19-22.

_____, 1980. "The Permanent Crisis: Changes in the World Oil System." Orbis 23,4. Winter 1980, pp. 761-784.

_____, 1981. "The New Oil Era: State-backed European Companies Challenge Majors." Europe, Jan.-Feb., pp. 43-47.

Krapels, Edward N., 1982. "Methods of Controlling Oil Prices." Petroleum Economist, December, pp. 494-497.

Levy, Brian, 1982. "World Oil Marketing in Transition." International Organization 36, 1, Winter, pp. 113-133.

Lichtblau, John, "What Factors Influence Oil Prices." Oil & Gas Journal, Nov. 9, 1981.

Mabro, Robert, 1981. "In Glut or Scarcity, Energy Problems Will Remain." Petroleum Intelligence Weekly, Special Supplement, September 28, pp. 1-4.

Makins, C. J., "The Atlantic Alliance," in Setting National Priorities: An Agenda for the 1980s. Washington, D.C.: Brookings Institution, 1980, edited by Joseph Pechman.

Mohnfeld, Jochen H., 1980. "Changing Patterns of Trade," Petroleum Economist, August, pp. 329-332.

Moran, Theodore H., 1981. "Modelling OPEC Behavior: Economic and Political Alternatives." International Organization, Boston, Massachusetts: Massachusetts Institute of Technology.

Neff, Thomas L., 1981. "The Changing World Oil Market." In Energy and Security, edited by David A. Deese and Joseph S. Nye, pp. 23-46. Cambridge, Massachusetts: Ballinger.

Nelkin, Dorothy, and Fallows, Susan, 1978. The Evolution of the Nuclear Debate: The Role of Public Participation. Annual Review of Energy.

Nelkin, Dorothy and Fallows, Susan, 1978. "The Evolution of the Nuclear Debate: The Role of Public Participation." In Jack Hollander, Melvin K. Simmons and David O. Wood, eds., Annual Review of Energy. Volume 3. Palo Alto: Annual Reviews, Inc., 1978, pp. 275-312.

The OECD Observer, July 1981.

"OPEC Pricing Policies in 1983." 1982. Bankers Trust Company Energy Viewpoint.

Petroleum Economist, various issues.

Petroleum Intelligence Weekly, various issues.

Platt's Oilgram News, various issues: September 28, 1978, March 21, 1979, April 19, 1979, September 10.

Sankar, T. L., 1977. "Alternative Development Strategies with a Low Energy Profile for a Low GNP/Capita Energy-Poor Country: The Case of India." In The Energy Syndrome, edited by Leon N. Lindberg, pp. 205-254. Lexington, Massachusetts: Lexington Books.

Schipper, Lee, and Lichtenberg, Allan J., 1976. "Efficient Energy Use and Well-Being: The Swedish Example." Science, December, pp. 1001-1013.

Sivard, Ruth Leger, 1979. World Energy Survey. New York: Rockefeller Foundation.

Tussing, Arlon R., "An OPEC Obituary." Public Interest, Winter, 1983, pp. 3-21.

Underwood, David C., 1982. "West African Oil: Will It Make a Difference?" Ph.D. Thesis, Naval Postgraduate School.

Wilson, Ernest J., 1983. "The Politicization of World Oil Markets: 1970-1982." Ann Arbor: University of Michigan.

____, 1982. "Africa, the Energy Crisis, and the Triangular Relationship," in Interdependence in a World of Unequals. Dunstan Wai, ed. Boulder, Colorado: Westview Press.

____, 1982(a). "The 'Oil Crisis' and African Economies," with Willard Johnson. Daedalus. Spring 1982, pp. 211-242.

Wilson, Ernest J., 1981. "Nigeria." In National Energy Profiles. Kenneth Stunkel, ed., pp. 315-358. New York: Praeger.

DOCUMENTS, REPORTS AND UNPUBLISHED MATERIALS

Broadman, Harry, 1983. Determinants of Oil Exploration and Development in Non-OPEC Developing Countries. Washington, D.C.: Resources for the Future.

Central Intelligence Agency National Foreign Assessment Center, 1979. The World Oil Market in the Years Ahead. Washington, D.C.: Government Printing Office.

Commission of the European Communities, 1978. The European Community and the Energy Problem. Luxembourg: Office for Official Publications of the European Countries.

Conant, Melvin, 1981. "Oil and Gas Logistics, Erosion of Commercial Control." Conference Paper.

Deagle, Edwin A., 1983. "The Future of the International Oil Market." New York: Group of Thirty.

Deagle, Edwin A.; Mossaver-Rahmani, Bijan; and Huff, Richard, 1981. "Energy in the 1980's: An Analysis of Recent Studies." Occasional Paper 4. New York: Group of Thirty.

Desai, Ashok V., 1981. "Interfuel Substitution in the Indian Economy." Discussion Paper, Center for Energy Policy Research.

Dunkerley, Joy; Knapp, Gunnar; with Glatt, Sandra, 1981. "Factors Affecting the Composition of Energy Use in Developing Countries." Discussion Paper, Center for Energy Policy Research.

Exxon Corporation, 1980. "World Energy Outlook." New York: Exxon Corporation.

International Energy Agency, 1978-1982. Energy Policies and Programmes of IEA Countries: Annual Reviews. Paris: Organisation for Economic Co-operation and Development.

Jankowski, John E., 1981. "Industrial Energy Demand and Conservation in Developing Countries." Discussion Paper, Center for Energy Policy Research.

Landsberg, Hans H., 1980. "Let's All Play Energy Policy!" Washington, D.C.: Resources for the Future.

Mitchell, Edward J., 1977. Energy and Ideology. Washington, D.C.: American Enterprise Institute.

National Foreign Assessment Center, 1979. The World Oil Market in the Years Ahead. Washington, D.C.: Government Printing Office.

The OECD Nuclear Energy Agency, 1982. NEA Activities in 1981. Paris: The OECD Nuclear Energy Agency.

Office of International Energy Development Programs and Energy and Environmental Systems Division, 1981. Republic of Korea/United States Cooperative Energy Assessment. Argonne, Illinois: Argonne National Laboratory.

Russell, Milton, 1983. "Energy: The International Dimension." Washington, D.C.: Resources for the Future.

Samuels, Richard J., 1982. "Public Energy Corporations and Public Policy in Japan." Discussion Paper, Sloan School of Management.

Schipper, Lee; Hollander, Jack; Milukas, Matthew; Alcomo, Joseph; Meyers, Stephen; with Noll, Scott A.; Dunkerley, Joy; and Jankowski, John E., 1982. "Energy Conservation in Kenya's Modern Sector: Progress, Potential and Problems." Discussion Paper, Center for Energy Policy Research.

U.S. Congress, Senate Committee on Energy and Natural Resources, 1980. Hearings Before 96th Congress, 2nd session Geopolitics of Oil. Washington, D.C.: Government Printing Office.

____, Committee on Energy and Natural Resources, 1980. The Geopolitics of Oil, Staff Report. Washington, D.C.: Government Printing Office.

____, 1981. Energy Industries Abroad. DOE/IA-0012. Washington, D.C.: Government Printing Office.

_____, 1980. Energy Programs/Energy Markets Overview. DOE/EIA-0201/16. Washington, D.C.: Government Printing Office.

_____, 1978. International Petroleum Annual 1978. Washington, D.C.: Government Printing Office.

_____, 1977. The Role of Foreign Governments in the Energy Industries. Washington, D.C.: Government Printing Office.

U.S. Comptroller General, 1980. The Potential for Diversifying Oil Imports by Accelerating Worldwide Oil Exploration and Production. Washington, D.C.: Government Printing Office.

World Bank, August 1979. Energy Options and Policy Issues in Developing Countries. Washington, D.C.: The World Bank.

World Bank, July 1981. Energy Prices, Substitution, and Optimal Borrowing in the Short Run. Working Paper No. 466. Washington, D.C.: The World Bank.

World Bank, August 1981(a). Global Energy Prospects. Working Paper No. 489, Washington, D.C.: The World Bank.

World Bank, October 1980. The Newly-Industrializing Developing Countries After the Oil Crisis. Working Paper No. 437. Washington, D.C.: The World Bank.

World Bank, 1979-1983. World Development Report, annually. New York: Oxford University Press.

World Bank, 1983(a). The Energy Transition in Developing Countries. Washington, D.C.: The World Bank.

INDEX

INDEX

V

Veba, 91, 99, 109
Venezuela, 57, 103
Vietnam, 162

W

Watt, James, 143, 153
Westinghouse, 9
Windfall profits, 33, 146, 147,
    162, 196; U.S. & German
    tax, 19; (see also, Taxa-
    tion of crude oil)
Wood fuel, 55-56
World bank, 57, 113, 120, 157

Y

YAP, 140, 144
Yugoslavia, 162

Z

Zaire, 56
Zambia, 103
Zimbabwe, 122

ABOUT THE AUTHORS

PAUL KEMEZIS, Bureau Chief for McGraw-Hill World News in Paris, reporting for Platt's Oilgram News, has also covered energy policy in Bonn, Brussels, and Washington, D.C. He is the author of several articles on international and comparative energy policy appearing in European Communities, Orbis, The New York Times, and the London Economist. Kemezis was educated at Georgetown and the University of Missouri.

ERNEST J. WILSON III teaches in the Political Science Department of the University of Michigan, and has written widely on energy policy in developing countries. He has lectured in Europe and Latin America on world oil market changes, and held several national energy-related fellowships. Dr. Wilson has also served as an energy consultant for the World Bank, the U.S. Departments of State and Interior, and a number of private clients. Born in Washington, D.C., he was educated at Harvard and Berkeley.